ON BEING BUDDHA

SUNY Series, Toward a Comparative Philosophy of Religions
Frank E. Reynolds and David Tracy, editors

ON BEING BUDDHA

The Classical Doctrine of Buddhahood

Paul J. Griffiths

State University of New York Press

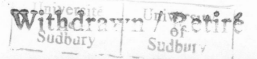

Published by
State University of New York Press, Albany

Printed in the United States of America

For information, address the State University of New York Press,
90 State Street, Suite 700, Albany, NY 12207

Production by Marilyn P. Semerad
Marketing by Nancy Farrell

Library of Congress Cataloging-in-Publication Data

Griffiths, Paul J.
On being Buddha : the classical doctrine of Buddhahood / by Paul J. Griffiths.
p. cm.—(SUNY series, toward a comparative philosophy of religions)
Includes bibliographical references and index.
ISBN 0-7914-2127-9(acid-free paper). — ISBN 0-7914-2128-7
1. Buddha (The concept). 2. Buddhahood. I. Title. II. Series.
BQ4180.G75 1994
294.3'63—dc20 93-45500
CIP

10 9 8 7 6 5 4 3 2

This book is for my children, Amy and John

"Le Buddha n'a jamais promis à ses disciples une assistance eternelle"

—*Étienne Lamotte*

"jig rten ji srid pa dang nam mkha' ji srid pa de srid du sangs rgyas rnams tshul 'dis sems can gyi don kho na mdzad cing rnam par bzhags so"

—*Madhyamakāvatārabhāṣya*

"buddha iti buddhatvaṃ sarvākārajñatety arthaḥ"

—*Aṣṭasāhasrikāprajñāpāramitāpañjikā*

"tathāgato yat svabhāvas tad svabhāvam idaṃ jagat"

—*Mūlamadhyamakakārikā*

"yat kiñcin maitreya subhāṣitaṃ sarvaṃ tad buddhabhāṣitam"

—*Śikṣāsamuccaya*

"ad Dei naturam neque intellectum, neque voluntatem pertinere"

—*Spinoza, Ethics*

Contents

Chapter One:
The Doctrinal Study of Doctrine

Chapter Two:
Buddhist Doctrine

Chapter Three: Buddhalogical Doctrine

Chapter Four: Buddha in the World

Chapter Five: Buddha in Heaven

Chapter Six: Buddha in Eternity

Chapter Seven: Doctrinal Criticism

Foreword

Frank E. Reynolds

"Scholasticism" and "doctrine" would seem to be self-evidently central categories for any discipline devoted to the comparative philosophy of religion(s). Yet attempts to formulate, in a comparative context, theories of these two quintessentially religious and closely related phenomena have been very few and far between. Serious studies of particular scholastic and doctrinal traditions, based on such theories and carried forward with theoretically sophisticated methods, have been virtually non-existent.

José Cabezón, in Volume VI of our *Toward a Comparative Philosophy of Religions Series* entitled *Buddhism and Language: A Study of Indo-Tibetan Scholasticism* has formulated the notion of "scholasticism" as a comparative category; and he has gone on to provide—as an illustrative example of its use—a superb study of Buddhist scholasticism in Tibet. Now, in Volume VIII, Paul Griffiths takes up the closely associated task of developing the notion of "doctrine" as a comparative category; and he demonstrates the usefulness of the category by providing a fascinating study of a central Buddhist doctrine that was formulated in India during the period from the 3rd to the 9th centuries C.E.

In *On Being Buddha* Griffiths, like Cabezón before him, engages the comparative task at a variety of levels. He formulates and carefully hones a very sophisticated theory of doctrine; he proposes a closely correlated method for implementing what he calls a "doctrinal study of doctrine;" and he goes on to employ this method to carry through an in-depth study of what he calls in his subtitle *The Classical Doctrine of Buddhahood.*

In the specifically buddhalogical segment of Griffiths' study (Griffiths uses the terms "buddhalogy" and "buddhalogical" in ways that directly parallel the uses of the terms "christology" and "christological" in the Christian tradition), he organizes his very rich and far-reaching discussion around a particular theme that he identifies as fundamental. He derives this primary theme from Immanuel Kant's broadly generalized notion that "human beings need an idea of highest perfection in order to have a standard to apply in making determinations of an axiological kind." Griffiths appropriates and utilizes Kant's suggestion for his own purposes by organizing his study around the notion that classical buddhalogical doctrine may usefully be thought of as "a systematic attempt to define and list those properties that something must have, within the constraints of Buddhist metaphysics, to be maximally great," and as "the basis for, and fullest representation of, Buddhist axiological commitments" (p. 58).

Philosophers of religion who are interested primarily in theoretical and methodological issues may be tempted to focus their attention on Chapter One ("The Doctrinal Study of Doctrine"), and to pass over the subsequent buddhalogical chapters rather quickly. Area specialists, on the other hand, may be tempted to skim through Chapter One, and to focus their primary attention on Chapters Two through Six—chapters which provide by far the most complete and insightful description and analysis of the classical doctrine of Buddhahood available in any western language.

It is, however, important for all readers to recognize from the outset that the theoretical fomulations and the illustrative discussion of the Buddhist materials are integrally related and mutually illuminating. And it is also important to recognize that only those who have attended carefully to both the theoretical formulations on the one hand, and the substantive

Buddhalogical discussions on the other, will be prepared to fully appreciate the final and culminating chapter if the book.

In his brilliantly executed conclusion Griffiths moves—under the rubric of "Doctrinal Criticism"—to the level of normative evaluation. And he does so by providing powerfully marshalled (and necessarily controversial) arguments in which he makes and defends judgements concerning a variety of doctrinal issues that involve the notion of maximal greatness—doctrinal issues that are, as he explicitly points out, central not only to the Buddhist tradition, but to the Christian tradition and to other religious traditions as well.

David Tracy and I are delighted that we have been able to publish Paul Griffiths' book as Volume VIII in the *Toward a Comparative Philosophy of Religions Series.* Most of all, we are delighted because of the quality and intrinsic interest of the book itself. But, in addition, we are delighted because the book will provide those interested in the Series with a fuller introduction to Griffiths who, along with Laurie Patton, will—at the moment that this manuscript goes to press—succeed us as co-editors of the Series.

In the late 1980s, when David Tracy and I took on the task of initiating and editing the *Toward a Comparative Study of Religions Series,* we did so in order to assure the publication, in a common setting, of books that were being generated and refined in the context of a series of international conferences on the comparative philosophy of religions sponsored by the Institute for the Advanced Study of Religion at the Divinity School of the University of Chicago. During the past four years eight volumes have been published in the Series, including seven that were directly associated with conference presentations and discussions. These include—in addition to the previously mentioned books by Cabezón and Griffiths—three collections of conference-generated essays edited by Tracy and Reynolds (*Myth and Philosophy,* SUNY 1990; *Discourse and Practice,* SUNY 1992; and *Religion and Practical Reasons,* SUNY 1994). The Series has also provided a home for three other single-authored volumes—Lee Yearley's *Mencius and*

Aquinas, SUNY 1990; Francis X. Clooney's *Theology After Vedanta,* SUNY 1993; and Ben-Ami Scharfstein's *Ineffability,* SUNY 1993.

Each of the new co-editors has worked very closely with all aspects of the *Toward a Comparative Philosophy of Religions* project ever since its inception in 1986. Paul Griffiths, presently an Associate Professor of the Philosophy of Religions at the Divinity School of the University of Chicago, has contributed an important essay on "Denaturalizing Discourse" to the very first *Myth and Philosophy* collection, as well as the present single-authored volume. Laurie Patton, presently Assistant Professor of the History of Religions at Bard College, has written three of the "conference summaries" published in Francisca Cho Bantly, *Deconstructing/Reconstructing the Philosophy of Religions* (Divinity School, University of Chicago, 1990); she has contributed an essay on "Hymn to Vāc" in the *Myth and Philosophy* volume; and she has also contributed an essay entitled "Dis-solving a Debate: Toward a Practical Theory of Myth" in *Religion and Practical Reason.*

This particular transition from one generation of editors to the next should ensure both the continuity of the Series and an infusion of new vitality. David Tracy and I have enjoyed the challenge of guiding the Series through its early years. And we now look forward with great expectations to observing and profiting from the new directions that Paul Griffiths and Laurie Patton will surely initiate and pursue.

Frank Reynolds
University of Chicago
April 3, 1994

Preface

In this study I am concerned at the level of theory with the nature of doctrine and its uses by religious communities, as well as with the heuristic value of the concept 'doctrine' for cross-cultural studies in the philosophy of religion.

In chapter one I state a formal definition of doctrine; this definition is intended to serve my substantive and exegetical interest in Buddhist doctrine. More precisely, I am concerned to lay bare the structure and meaning of classical Indian Buddhist doctrine about Buddha, and to do so by applying to it the theoretical framework given in chapter one. My goal here is to show that this framework may profitably be used in a particular case, and so also to suggest by example that the category 'doctrine' may have significant heuristic and analytical value for the cross-cultural study of one important aspect of the lives of religious communities.

In chapter two I consider in what ways and to what extent the category 'doctrine' can be applied to the texts of Indian Buddhism, and make some suggestions as to those terms in the technical discourse of Indian Buddhists that cover some of the semantic ground embraced by the English word 'doctrine.'

In chapter three I offer an overview of the particular doctrinal discourse developed by Indian Buddhists that is the central focus of this book. This is a discourse concerned with the properties of Buddha, with those qualities that must, according to the tradition, be predicated of every Buddha. It is a discourse analogous in important ways to that which Christians call 'christology.' I shall, following David Snellgrove and to avoid confusion with 'buddhology' (which labels all discourse about Buddhism, not just that about Buddha), call this discourse 'buddhalogy.'[1]

In chapters four through six I explore this buddhalogical discourse in some detail, dividing my analysis according to the location (spatial or metaphysical) in which Buddha functions. Chapter four deals with Buddha in the world; chapter five, with Buddha in heaven; and chapter six, with Buddha in eternity. My intention throughout is to isolate and explore the doctrinal dimensions of Buddhist discourse about these matters, and by so doing to arrive at a synthetic view of buddhalogical orthodoxy among medieval Indian Buddhist intellectuals.

Even though the interests of this study are not primarily either historical or textual, some words about its historical and textual basis are necessary. I use as my sources mostly the philosophical (or, better, doctrinal) digests that became important for Buddhist intellectuals in Gupta and immediately post-Gupta India (that is, from roughly the fourth to the eighth centuries C.E.). These digests were intended and used mostly as teaching tools written by monks for the training of other monks. While they do have have scholastic affiliation—that is, according to traditional Buddhist doxography and its western counterparts some are called Yogācāra texts, some Mādhyamika texts, and so forth—I shall not be much interested in these putative affiliations, nor in the differences among the schools. This is partly because such matters are not of central imortance so far as the questions that concern this study go; but it is also because the scholastic affiliation of many of the texts is problematic in any case, and our perceptions of it are often unduly and improperly influenced by the categorizations developed and applied by later Tibetan and Chinese scholiasts.

I think that a reasonably accurate synthetic view of orthodox medieval Indian buddhalogy can be obtained by detailed study of the major doctrinal digests of the period, together with judicious use of the extensive commentarial literature that accrued to such texts. This is an enormous body of literature; I shall therefore necessarily be extremely selective in my use of it. The notes and bibliography will indicate the works that have been of most importance for this study.

Finally, in chapter seven I offer an example of the kind of doctrinal criticism and analysis that the theory of doctrine offered in chapter one is intended to make possible.

A note on usage. In this book I use the term 'Buddha' in the singular and without a definite article to refer to the category most often designated in Sanskrit by the abstract noun *buddhatva* or *buddhatā* ('Buddhahood'). 'Buddha' thus includes all particular Buddhas and embraces all properties held in common by them. When, as sometimes happens, the exigencies of the English language require the use of a pronoun in place of 'Buddha' I use 'it' rather than a gender-specific pronoun. This sometimes produces odd stylistic effects, but it seems to me the best possible solution. Buddha is not constitutively male or female. Naturally, when referring to a particular Buddha (usually by name, as in 'Gautama Śākyamuni' or 'Vipaśvin') who is constitutively male, I use masculine pronouns.

Acknowledgments

I gratefully acknowledge the assistance of the following organizations and individuals: the American Academy of Religion, for a research assistance grant in 1986–87, which enabled me to purchase a microfiche copy of the Cone Tanjur and so to read more easily the Tibetan versions of some of the works used in this study; the National Endowment for the Humanities, for a summer stipend in 1990, which gave me time to draft the first two chapters of this book; the Luce Foundation and the Institute for the Advanced Study of Religion in the University of Chicago's Divinity School, for a research fellowship in the first half of 1991, which enabled me to get the work more than half done; to the graduate students at the University of Chicago, who suffered with me through drafts of some of this material in the winter of 1991 (I owe special thanks here to Anne Blackburn); to the Luce Foundation and the Booth-Ferris Foundation for funding the gathering of a group of scholars (Aziz al-Azmeh, Fran Bantly, José Cabezón, Frank Clooney, Steven Collins, M. David Eckel, Charles Hallisey, Laurie Patton, Sheldon Pollock, Fitz John Porter Poole, Philip Quinn, Frank Reynolds, Lee Yearley) in May 1991 to discuss this work at the stage it had then reached; to my research assistant, Nick Collier, for giving me invaluable help in the winter and spring of 1992 and for preparing the index in 1994; to Steven Collins and Charles Hallisey, without whose critical friendship and (still more critical) comments this book would be worse than it is; to Frank Reynolds, who made it possible by helping persuade me back to Chicago; to all my colleagues in the Divinity School and the Department of South Asian Languages and Civilizations at the University of Chicago; and to Judith Heyhoe, without whom not.

Ancestors of various parts of this book have appeared elsewhere, often in considerably different form. A version of much of chapter one was published in the *Proceedings* of the American Catholic Philosophical Association (1992), © ACPA; parts of chapter six have appeared in the *Journal of Religion* (1989), © University of Chicago, in the *Indo-Iranian Journal* (1990), © Kluwer Academic Publishers, and in Robert K. C. Forman, ed., *The Problem of Pure Consciousness* (New York: Oxford University Press, 1990), © Robert K. C. Forman; a version of a small part of chapter seven appeared in *Philosophy East & West* (1989), © University of Hawaii Press. I am grateful to the copyright-holders of these pieces for permission to reuse them in revised form here.

Chapter 1

The Doctrinal Study of Doctrine

1.0 Prolegomena

It seems obvious that religious doctrine is both worth studying in its own right and very important to religion. Both claims have been axiomatic for most scholars thinking and writing about religion in the academies of the west for the past century or so; as a result many properly doctrinal studies of doctrine were produced, studies concerned with the history and meaning of particular instances of doctrinal thought and expression considered as phenomena of intrinsic interest. But such studies are no longer in the ascendant. They have been called into question in theory, even if not yet abandoned in practice, by the view that instances of doctrinal thought and expression should be treated only in terms of their relations to the nondoctrinal phenomena that constitute the setting in which they occur. So analyses of doctrinal phenomena in terms of their institutional location, their social setting, their deployment as instruments of oppression, and their political uses (among many other things) increase, while doctrinal studies of doctrine correspondingly decrease.

There are still historians doing good doctrinal studies of doctrine.[1] But such studies are fewer than they were. And although there are some encouraging signs of a recent growth of interest in the theory of doctrine among some Christian theologians (for instance in George Lindbeck's work and the extensive response it has prompted,[2] as well as among those with purer theoretical interests, such as William A. Christian, Sr.[3]), on the whole it still seems true to say that doctrinal studies of doctrine have lost the privileged place they once held in the academic study of religion. In addition, as is entirely to be expected, interest in matters doctrinal among historians of religion and practitioners of religious studies is, as far as I can tell, close to zero.

I offer here, by way of corrective, a theory of doctrine intended to make possible the properly doctrinal study of doctrine. The theory is a formal and systematic one: it picks out a discursive practice and its artifacts, provides an outline of questions of concern to those engaged in this practice, and discusses the properties of the artifacts produced by the practice. I shall state the theory in formal and abstract terms, very largely without supportive examples. But I hope and intend, nonetheless, that it will be consonant with (though not adequate to) the ways in which Christians have used the term 'doctrine' (*didachē, didaskalia, doctrina,* and so forth). I want to avoid both descriptive and explanatory reductionism, the former at all costs and the latter unless there are pressing theoretical reasons to adopt it. One of the more striking aspects of current theories of doctrine is a tendency toward a too-rapid explanatory reduction and a concomitant weakening of the theory as a heuristically valuable tool.

The theory will act in this book as a heuristic device. I shall be studying a particular complex of Buddhist doctrines, and the theory offered here will guide my work, providing me with questions I want to ask and have answered. Its utility must in the end be judged by its results, and since it is a theory intended primarily as a first step in grounding and making possible the constructive and critical study of doctrine considered as such, and not in terms of other phenomena, to criticize it by saying that it pays insufficient attention to nondoctrinal phenomena will be to miss its point.

The enterprise sketched by the theory may reasonably be called formalist in the sense that it is concerned almost exclusively with conceptual relations among ordered sets of sentences, and is therefore concerned as little as possible with the nonformal conditions of production of those sentences. It manipulates concepts, patterns of argument, and structures of systems, without paying attention to the material (social, political, institutional, financial) conditions of production of those sentences. In this it does not assume, as do some kinds of legal formalism debated by jurists during the past thirty years or so, that there is a "deductive or quasi-deductive method capable of giving determinate solutions to particular . . . problems"[4] once the proper rules have been stated; this I take to be a thesis much stronger than any needed for the doctrinal study of doctrine as I understand it.[5] The formalism in play here, then, goes only so far as to require the possibility of studying doctrine formalistically and to suggest that there may be some benefits in so doing; it does not assume that formalism will provide a method by which all properly doctrinal problems can be resolved, much less that there are no doctrinally illuminating connections between doctrinal and nondoctrinal phenomena.

The enterprise is also objectivist in the pejorative sense given to that term by Pierre Bourdieu,[6] and about this I have no apologies to make. The doctrinal study of doctrine as I understand it does privilege, by paying exclusive attention to, a synchronic study of logic, relations, and constructed linguistic items as objects in their own right, without adverting much to their history, their practical uses, or their nondoctrinal functions. Bourdieu, of course, judges this strategy to be undesirable and indefensible, but I do not find his fulminations against it at all convincing, for reasons that will become apparent.

I claim also that attention to the formal properties of doctrinal systems—to the argument-patterns evident in them, to the rules that govern their construction and development, to both what is taken to be good evidence for the claims made by them and what actually is so—is essential even to nondoctrinal histories and explanations of doctrine. Without such attention, understanding of the discursive practices that produce doctrine will languish; without it we will have, as Ronald Dworkin has put it in arguing against social-theoretic jurisprudence as the dominant model for understanding law, theories that "grow steadily more programmatic and less substantive, more radical in theory and less critical in practice."[7] Dworkin claims, rightly, that to give an account of law exclusively in terms of its social functions, its economic effects, or its "ideological force and witness,"[8] necessarily misses its distinctive properties as a discursive practice. To explain law as an instrument of oppression used by one race against another, one class against another, or one sex against the other, may very well say true and interesting things about it, but can say nothing about law in itself. Such explanations assimilate law to all those other phenomena with such oppressive functions, and they are legion. If, then, we want to be anything more than programmatic and totalizing in our analysis of distinctive discursive practices such as the legal or the doctrinal, we must pay attention to the formal properties that individuate them; we must not obscure their distinctiveness by appealing only to incidental instrumental properties they share with many other phenomena. Northrop Frye, with his customary elegance, long ago made a similar point about the study of literature.[9]

To put this in another way: I am centrally concerned in this work with the doctrinal study of doctrine, with the analysis of doctrine-expressing sentences considered as expressive of doctrine, not as epiphenomena of social settings or institutional arrangements of any kind. I shall, in the body of this study, attempt to analyze, understand, and assess the buddhalogical doctrines evident in some Buddhist discursive practices entirely in doctrinal terms: as substantive claims and injunctions governing the intellectual lives of the virtuosos who engaged in such practices, and in what these claims and injunctions state or imply about the ontology, metaphysics, anthropology, and soteriology of those who assert them. In imitation of Michael Frede's approach to the study of ancient philosophy, my explanations and analyses of these claims and injunctions will themselves be doctrinal in the sense that I shall adopt as a procedural principle the rule of not appealing to social or institutional facts except where doctrinal explanations and analyses fail.[10]

The following assumptions and stipulations will govern what is to come. First, I assume that doctrines are artifacts located in communities, and that religious doctrines are possessed and used by religious communities. Second, I stipulate that, while a religious community's doctrines may be expressed in many ways (sententially, liturgically, architecturally, iconographically, and so on), I shall be concerned here only with the sentential expression of doctrine, and, to delimit the investigation still further, only with collections of such sentential expressions in written texts. Third, I assume (and shall show in the case of Indian Buddhism) that religious communities typically have virtuoso intellectuals among their members, and that one of the functions of such intellectuals is to engage in discursive practices that express, organize, and defend the community's doctrines. These discursive practices issue in the production of the texts that are the primary objects of a properly doctrinal analysis of doctrine.

Religious communities usually have few virtuoso intellectuals among their members. This means that only a small minority of religious people engage in the discursive practices that produce doctrine. Rather more, perhaps, know something of the doctrinal discourse of their community; and still more have their doxastic practices, affective states, and religious lives formed by that discourse. The relations between the doctrines of a community's virtuoso members and what the nonvirtuoso members of that community believe, say, and do are complex, and I shall not be much interested in them in this study. I shall, nonetheless, speak of doctrines as belonging to religious communities without intending any particular view as to the relations between the discursive practices of that community's virtuoso intellectual representatives and the broader religious life of the community. So, speaking of 'the community's doctrines' and the like will often be a kind of shorthand for 'sentences of the relevant kind found in the textual artifacts produced by the community's virtuoso intellectuals'; and 'community' will often mean simply a community of virtuoso intellectuals whose existence is evidenced, for the purposes of this study, solely by its texts.

It follows from all this that what I offer here is not a complete theory of doctrine (I doubt the existence of any such, and certainly the desirability of seeking it), but a doctrinal theory of doctrine.

1.1 Primary Doctrines

William Christian calls a religious community's primary doctrines those sentences it uses to describe the setting of human life and to recommend as desirable or attribute value to certain patterns of conducting that life.[11] Sentences of the first kind will typically be declarative, attributing to some existent or existents some property or properties (for example, the claim *Buddha is omniscient*). Sentences of the second kind will typically be injunctions or recommendations, framed in the optative or imperative moods (for example, *one should give to monks* or *do not take sentient life*). But not all sentences of these kinds set forth in the authoritative texts of religious communities express doctrines for them. Suppose we call a sentence whose status as expressive of doctrine for some community is unclear a 'doctrine-candidate' for that community. In order for it to be proper to classify some doctrine-candidate as expressive of doctrine for some community, I suggest that it should possess the following properties:

1. Being taken by its community to possess to a greater degree than any of its known competitors whatever property or properties the community thinks of as making doctrine-candidates acceptable in their spheres of relevance—or, if the property controlling acceptability does not, for some community, admit of degrees (as may be the case for truth), then the doctrine-candidate must have it in the eyes of the community, and its known competitors must lack it.

2. Being taken by its community to be of significance for its religious life.

3. Being taken by its community to be binding upon its members.

Each of these properties is indexed to a community's perceptions of its artifacts. These conditions are therefore properties of communities; they may also be properties of sentences, but they need not be.

I take each of these properties to be necessary in order that a particular doctrine-candidate may properly be acknowledged to express doctrine for some community. But I do not take them to be jointly sufficient. That is, there will be doctrine-candidates that meet all these requirements for some community and yet do not express doctrine for it. It is not possible, I think, to specify a set of necessary and sufficient conditions in this connection. This is because each religious community will have criteria peculiar to itself that control which sentences can be said to express its doctrines, and no theory of doctrine applicable across several different communities can or should take account of all these. So it is important to remember that a doctrine-candidate may meet all these conditions for some community and yet not express doctrine for it.

There is also an important terminological ambiguity here concerning the word 'doctrine.' This word has been used by Christian thinkers to refer both to collections of sentences and to what is expressed by those sentences. This is not usually confusing, but in this context it may be since doctrines can be expressed otherwise than sententially, and the customary extension of the term to cover both the instrument of expression and what is expressed tends not to occur when the instrument is something other than a sentence. I shall usually restrict my usage of the term to refer to what is expressed by some artifact, and shall refer to these artifacts as 'doctrine-expressing Xs'—usually sentences. But the demands of euphonious English will sometimes lead me to give the term its customary extension.

I turn now to a closer examination of the first property that doctrine-candidates must possess in order properly to be regarded as expressive of doctrine for some community. This property has to do with the acceptability of a sentence for some community in comparison with the acceptability of other sentences of which the community is aware as competitors to it. To be expressive of doctrine for the community, the doctrine-candidate must be more acceptable to it than all known competitors. If the community's criterion for acceptability in some sphere of relevance does not allow degrees—if, that is, all doctrine-candidates are thought either to have it or to lack it—then this definition should be modified to say that, for such a community and such a sphere of relevance, all doctrine-candidates must possess the acceptability-creating property and all known competitors must lack it. More briefly, the point of this condition is to ensure that a doctrine-candidate has more acceptability for some community than all its competitors known to that community in some sphere of relevance. Only then is it possible to judge it to express doctrine for that community.

Some observations on what it is for one sentence to compete with another will be of use here. I shall take it that some sentence—call it S—is a competitor to a doctrine-expressing sentence—call it D—of some community if that community takes assent to S to be incompatible with assent to D. Again, incompatibility as here used is a property of communities (or, more properly, of their attitudes toward assenting to sentences), not primarily of the sentences themselves. Incompatibility, in this sense, may take the strong form of apparent outright contradiction. Consider the sentence *Jesus Christ is God's only-begotten son*, affirmed as expressive of doctrine by some Christian communities, and the Islamic doctrine-expressing sentence *God does not beget*. If, as the surface grammar of these sentences suggests, each is intended as an attribution of some property to God (in the first case, that of having begotten just one son; in the second, that of having begotten nothing), then it is clear that God cannot possess both properties, and that the competition between these two sentences may be taken by their communities to be intense—so intense, perhaps, that it may be thought impossible to hold to both and preserve sanity.

It may of course be that the surface grammar of these sentences is deceptive, and that when they are set in a broader context it will turn out that the competition between them is less intense than it seems, or even that it is nonexistent. Perhaps one community (or both) has a theory about the referential capacities of language that makes such competition impossible; or there may be some theory about what it means to predicate properties of God that makes competition among such predications impossible. But, absent such theories, the strong competition suggested by the surface grammar of these sentences may sometimes occur (and was taken to occur by some Muslim and Christian communities).

Competition may be less intense than outright contradiction. A community may, for example, take some sentence to be a competitor to one of its doctrine-expressing sentences because of a perceived lack of consonance between the two. Such might be the case, for example, for those Christians who would take the sentence *scripture alone is sufficient for salvation* to express doctrine, and those who would so take the sentence *the body and blood of Christ received at the Eucharist is the primary means of sanctification for Christians.* These two sentences are not obviously contradictory, but neither are they obviously consonant, and it is perfectly comprehensible that some community for which the former is a doctrine-expressing sentence might take the latter to be a competitor just because of such a lack of consonance. And there may also be other modalities of competition that, like this perceived lack of consonance, fall short of perceived contradiction in intensity.

This condition has been stated in an entirely formal way: the property that makes sentences acceptable to some community in the spheres of relevance covered by its doctrine-expressing sentences might theoretically be anything at all. This formal way of putting things seems to me preferable to that used by William Christian, who specifies acceptability-creating properties in terms of truth for sentences describing the setting of human life, or rightness, for sentences attributing value to some pattern of human conduct.[12] While it is true that these are very likely to be found as acceptability-creating properties among religious communities, there seems no reason to suppose them the only ones, nor to suppose that truth need be the acceptability-creating property always linked to sentences describing the setting of human life, nor rightness that always linked to sentences attributing value to some pattern of human conduct. One might imagine, for example, some religious community for which the only acceptability-creating property is neither truth nor rightness but salvific efficacy, or one for which it is *being seventeen syllables long*. For these reasons it seems preferable to keep the definition at the formal level.

In looking at the textual artifacts produced by virtuoso intellectuals it will usually be abundantly clear which sentences fulfill this first condition: they will be those sentences for the acceptability of which the text(s) in question argue. They will be the discursive practice's tenets, what a Buddhist theorist would call its *siddhānta*s and what a Christian theorist would call its doctrines. But some texts will do no more than state or list the relevant sentences, without arguing for them or against their competitors, as in a Christian catechesis or a Buddhist *mātṛka*. In such cases the student will have little idea of what the acceptability-creating properties are, or what competitors the community was aware of when it set them forth. In other cases—say, a Christian conciliar document or a Buddhist *śāstra*—arguments are offered, competitors are canvassed, and acceptability-creating criteria are manifest. In either case, it will be the texts' tenets that meet this first criterion.

The next condition to be fulfilled so that some doctrine-candidate might be thought of as a doctrine-expressing sentence for some religious community is that it must be regarded by that community as being significant for its religious life. This condition is intended to rule out the possibility of judging some doctrine-candidates thought of by all members of some religious community as true (or as more acceptable than all known competitors in some sphere of relevance) to be expressive of doctrine for it when they are of no significance for or relevance to the religious life of that community. For example, the substantive claim that *the United States began active hostilities against Iraq in January 1991* would presumably be acknowledged as true by most members of most religious communities. Yet few would wish to regard it as expressive of doctrine for them—except, perhaps, for those with idiosyncratic eschatological views about the significance of events in the Middle East.

Finally, in order for a doctrine-candidate properly to be regarded as a doctrine-expressing sentence for some religious community, it must not only be thought of as acceptable to and significant for the religious life of that community (conditions one and two), but also as in some way authoritative for or binding upon it (condition three). This, I suspect, will be the most difficult condition for which to provide anything close to precise specification. It can be cashed out in institutional terms for those communities that have centralized and hierarchical institutional structures: here, 'being binding' might mean that if public assent to some doctrine is refused membership in the community is relinquished. But not all communities possess such structures, so I suggest, schematically, that a sentence should be thought binding upon a community if that community feels obligated (1) to teach it to its members; (2) to defend it against perceived competitors; (3) to explain why it is to be preferred to those competitors. The first of these is catechesis; the second is negative apologetics; and the third is positive apologetics, categories I have discussed in more detail elsewhere.[13] All these motivations will often be present in the discursive practices that produce doctrine-expressing sentences, and there might be added to them a fourth: system-building, which is the attempt by the community to integrate a particular doctrine-expressing sentence into a coherently ordered system of such.

Finally, any particular doctrine-expressing sentence will always be embedded in cognitive and epistemic systems that extend far beyond its own range of relevance; this has been effectively argued by Roberto Unger in the sphere of jurisprudence. It will, that is, have extensive entailments and truth-conditions that may not have been articulated by the community for which it is a doctrine. So, for example, the sentence expressive of doctrine for some Buddhist communities, *everyone should practice mindfulness ceaselessly*, has among its truth-conditions an entire and complex metaphysic that includes both an ontology and a systematic and imaginative axiology. Even if no one in this community has ever articulated some aspects of this ontology and axiology, all of it should still be said to be part of the community's doctrine. For whenever a community formulates and uses a primary doctrine, it also commits itself by necessity to all its truth-conditions and entailments as doctrinal (assuming, of course, that the sentences expressing these truth-conditions and entailments meet the conditions stated above). I am not suggesting, though, that it will ever be possible to elucidate all these truth-conditions, for they are infinitely many for any given case.

1.2 *Secondary Doctrines*

Secondary doctrines are also sentences expressive of doctrine for some community, but the object of these sentences is neither the setting nor the conduct of human life, but rather other doctrine-expressing sentences of that community. Such doctrines are generally intended to state rules governing how the community's primary doctrines are to be ordered, derived, recognized, interpreted, and used. A category such as this has long been used by theorists working on legal doctrine;[14] William Christian was the first to make systematic use of it in the analysis of religious doctrine.[15] Not all religious communities will possess such secondary doctrines since not all will have felt the need for them; but all communities with a long history of doctrinal reflection prompted by internal crises, divisions, or disagreements, or by contact with alien communities will have secondary doctrines of these kinds.

1.2.1 Rules of Recognition and Patterns of Derivation

These secondary doctrines are formulated by religious communities to provide the community with criteria for use in answering questions of this form: Is this doctrine-candidate expressive of doctrine for the community? Such questions will often be answered in terms of the origins of the doctrine-candidate. For example, a Buddhist community might have a rule of recognition of the following form: *a doctrine-candidate is expressive of doctrine for this community if and only if it was uttered by Buddha*. This is a strong rule of recognition, one that specifies both necessary and sufficient conditions. (It is not, I think, a rule of recognition espoused by any actual Buddhist community.) Others may be weaker, specifying only necessary or only sufficient conditions. And, of course, a community's rules of recognition need have nothing to do with the origins of a doctrine-candidate; they might instead refer to some property of the doctrine-candidate that is neutral as to its origin—perhaps *being in the* śikhariṇī *meter in Sanskrit* or *being shorter than the Gettysburg Address* or the like. But I suspect that most rules of recognition operative in religious communities (as also in law-governed ones) will have to do with the origins of doctrine-candidates, so I now offer a schematic outline of what seem to me the main options here.

A rule of recognition will often say that to be expressive of doctrine for the community a doctrine-candidate must have its origin in some authoritative text or collection of such; perhaps by being contained in it, entailed by what is contained in it, consonant with what is contained in it, or the like. To put this another way: rules of recognition will often be couched in terms of allowed patterns of derivation from an authoritative source. These need to be looked at more closely, beginning with authoritative texts.

Suppose we understand 'text' broadly to mean any articulated system of communicative signs. The category would then include written artifacts (books and the like), oral artifacts (speeches, sermons, discourses), ritual acts (liturgical celebrations), icons (visual images of all kinds), musical performances (sacred sound), and no doubt much else.

Every religious community necessarily possesses especially authoritative texts, texts that carry and communicate to the community's members in special ways whatever it is that the community takes to be of religious value. Some of these texts will contain natural-language sentences (as, for example, do sacred books of all kinds and almost all liturgical acts; many musical performances; and some buildings and other three-dimensional artifacts); but some will not (as, for example, most icons and some musical performances). But all authoritative texts can, I suggest, become sources of doctrine for religious communities, and can therefore be appealed to in the construction of rules of recognition.

I do not intend to be very specific as to the types of authority that texts may possess. A broad spectrum of positions is possible, and much will depend upon the institutional structure of a particular community. At one extreme, perhaps, are those texts explicitly regarded by some community as possessing supreme religious authority: they may, for instance, be thought of by the community as the sole source of its doctrines. Some Christians think in this way (or say they do) about the written text of the Bible. Even more extreme would be a community that regarded some text not only as the sole source of its doctrines, but also as coextensive with those doctrines; from such a position it will usually follow that the commmunity's doctrines are doctrines for it just because of their presence in such an authoritative text, and not because of any other property they might possess. It is difficult to think of an instance of such an extreme position being held. Not even conservative Islamic views on the nature and authority of the Qur'ān come close.

Paralleling this broad range of positions on a text's authoritativeness is an equally broad range of patterns by which doctrine-expressing sentences may be derived from authoritative texts. Suppose we consider first texts that contain natural-language sentences, such as the Bible or the ritual performance of baptism. First, there is derivation by simple identity. That is, a sentence found in the authoritative text may be simply appropriated by the community as expressive of doctrine for it. This pattern is evident for a good many Christian communities in the case of many sentences found in the Bible, as well as for those uttered during the baptismal liturgy: they are to be taken as expressive of doctrine for the community, and their status as such is traceable to their occurrence in the authoritative text.

Second, some sentences may become expressive of doctrine for some community in virtue of their entailment by sentences found in an authoritative text. Some Christians might want to make the (implausible) claim, for example, that the doctrine-expressing sentence *the Son and the Father are consubstantial* is derived by entailment from sentences found in the biblical text—such, for example, as "I and the Father are one" (John x.30), or "Before Abraham was, I am" (John viii.58). Others have made the claim (more plausibly) that doctrine-expressing sentences about the subjection of infants to the world, the flesh, and the devil because of original sin are entailed by sentences uttered in the authoritative texts of the baptismal liturgy.

Third, and perhaps most common, the doctrine-expressing sentences of a community may be related to those of its authoritative texts that contain sentences neither by simple identity nor by entailment, but by consonance. That is, it may often be taken by a community to be a necessary condition for some doctrine-candidate to become a doctrine-expressing sentence that it be consonant with what the community takes its authoritative texts to say. Consider, for example, the importance of narratives, stories told in authoritative texts, for many communities. A strong case can be made for the claim that narrative—whether written in the biblical text or reenacted by the community in the text of a liturgical act—is the single most important source of Christian doctrine-expressing sentences: that Christian doctrine is largely the result of the community's meditation upon its foundational narrative.[16] If this or something like it is the case, then the community's doctrine-expressing sentences will naturally have to be consonant with this narrative: they must appear to the community to give expression to the narrative's structure and implications, to make explicit in a faithful manner what the story implies. Alister McGrath puts this well: "Doctrinal formulations are the result of the early church's correct perception that the mere reiteration of the scriptural narrative was not enough; it was necessary to interact with other modes of discourse."[17] It may then be asked by the community whether, for example, some doctrine-expressing sentence is consonant with or legitimately generated by the narrative that it purports to explain.

Rules of recognition can be formulated in terms of all these patterns of derivation. One example will suffice, based on the pattern of derivation by entailment: a community may have a rule of recognition of the form *a doctrine-candidate is expressive of doctrine for this community if the community takes it to be entailed by what the community takes its authoritative texts to say*. Notice that this rule of recognition, like the properties of primary doctrines discussed above, is indexed to the community's perceptions of the entailments of its authoritative texts; this must be the point of first refuge in a descriptive analysis of a community's rules of recognition. Variants of the rule of recognition cited above in terms of identity or consonance can easily be formulated.[18]

Religious communities also possess authoritative texts that contain no sentences—some buildings and other three-dimensional objects; music; and some kinds of ritual. Ritual observances that do as a whole contain sentences may also have sentence-free parts. Consider, for example, the complex of gestures used by Christian priests during the consecration of the elements at a celebration of the Eucharist. Such wordless authoritative texts may also act as sources of doctrine-expressing sentences, though when they do the process of derivation will typically be harder to trace than in the case of derivation from some sentence-possessing authoritative text.

In such cases it is difficult to see, for example, that there can be a relation of strict entailment between a wordless authoritative text and some doctrine-expressing sentence. For strictly speaking entailments flow only from one verbal formulation to another. But there can certainly be relations of consonance and contiguity between nonverbal authoritative texts and doctrine-expressing sentences. Liturgical acts, as Geoffrey Wainwright puts it, often have doctrinal incidence.[19] Perhaps they always do. But such incidence will often be extraordinarily hard to trace in detail or with precision. What, for example, is one to say about the doctrinal incidence of church architecture or the arrangement of ecclesiastical furniture inside a church building? Such things are certainly authoritative texts for the community whose buildings and furniture they are; this follows from the fact that they are articulated systems of communicative signs. But the exact nature of this doctrinal incidence is difficult to determine.

A sentence-free authoritative text will usually underdetermine the doctrine-expressing sentence or sentences for which it acts as a source. For example, there will usually be many doctrine-expressing sentences that can be seen by the community as consonant with some wordless ritual act, and the choice of which among these is to be adopted will rest upon factors additional to the ritual act in question.

Rules of recognition may, of course, be formulated in terms of authoritative texts that possess no sentences with roughly the same range of possibilities (ruling out entailment) evident in rules appealing to sentence-possessing texts.

Rules of recognition may also be formulated in terms of authoritative experience, for it is possible that a community might judge its doctrine-expressing sentences to be causally related to the occurrence of such experiences (and that they might be so).

Most—perhaps all—religious communities think of certain experiences as having doctrinal incidence. This is most obvious when one considers the techniques aimed at producing valued experiences so commonly developed and preserved by religious communities. The entire tradition of Christian ascetical theology, to take one of the more baroque examples of intellectual theorizing about such techniques, is an example of a practice that orders, relates, describes, and recommends methods designed to be efficacious in producing such authoritative experience. More broadly still, all of a community's ritual practice may be seen as an instrument for producing in its participants some desired and thus authoritative experiences, experiences that are at once cognitive, affective, and conative.

Suppose, then, we consider a religious community's authoritative experiences to be those it collectively values, regards as significant for its religious life, and develops techniques to inculcate and preserve. Naturally, such experiences will be had by individuals (though perhaps most often in a communal setting), and will be related to the doctrine-expressing sentences understood and assented to by those individuals in various and complex ways. Some comments on the nature of these relations are in order here.

Perhaps the most widespread and influential position on this issue in the west since the seventeenth century, among both theologians and historians of religion, has been the view that religiously authoritative experience is always in some sense prior to the formation of doctrine-expressing sentences, and that the central function of the latter is to express (or describe, or symbolize) the former. George Lindbeck has given this position the clumsy but accurate name "experiential expressivism,"[20] and Friedrich Schleiermacher is often taken as a classical and influential exponent of this view. He defines Christian doctrines (*Glaubenssütze*), for example, in the title to the fifteenth paragraph of the *Christliche Glaube*, as "accounts of the Christian religious affections set forth in speech" (*Auffassungen der christlich frommen Gemützustände in der Rede dargestellt*), and though his position is in the end considerably more nuanced than this bold statement makes it sound, he does, in spite of careful qualifications, appear to give affect logical and temporal priority over doctrine. A case can be made that a similar judgment has informed, often at the axiomatic level, much theorizing in the field ever since.[21] This position is also often combined with the claim that there are core religious experiences, recognizable as such cross-culturally.[22] I shall not discuss this latter claim here since it is tangential to my interests in this study; but it is worth noting that if the observations made in the next several paragraphs are well grounded, then this claim too—at least in its more naive forms—will turn out to be false.

If experiential expressivism were correct, authoritative experience would be the single most important source of a community's doctrine-expressing sentences. The view, however, always rests upon an attempt to separate the religious individual's life from her or his theoretical commitments, and to postulate a one-way causal connection between the former and the latter. This is not successfully defensible. Conceptually complex theory-laden claims such as those found in most doctrine-expressing sentences simply do not flow straightforwardly from preconceptual or prelinguistic experience (even if it is allowed that there is any such thing); rather, there is an exceedingly complex symbiotic and reciprocal relationship between religious experience and doctrine-expressing sentences. Each conditions the other, but if there is a dominant direction of influence it is from doctrine to experience and not vice-versa. Assent to a given set of doctrine-expressing sentences (with all that usually accompanies such experience) makes possible the occurrence of certain kinds of experience, and may at times act as both necessary and sufficient condition for the occurrence of some apparently doctrinally unsullied moment of consciousness, as Wayne Proudfoot puts it.[23]

In order that someone can judge some experience to be religiously authoritative, that person must be able to identify the experience under some description that gives it such a status. And the metaphysical commitments and causal claims operative in the category-systems that govern and make possible such descriptive identifications are not given in the experience itself; they are, rather, part of the cognitive equipment of the person doing the judging, and as such are produced by a long process of formation and acculturation.[24] Neither the occurrence of religiously authoritative experiences, nor their identification as such by those who have them can be separated from the highly ramified[25] and strictly doctrinal claims that are symbiotically intertwined with them. Doctrine-expressing sentences can, therefore, never be said to be straightforwardly derived from pre- or nondoctrinal experience. God cannot address or be heard by the experiencing subject unless that subject already knows how to hear God and how to identify what is heard as God's voice. Schleiermacher should be stood on his head: the engagement of the religious affections is possible only when there already exists an appropriately developed doctrinal context.

The same claims should be made in cases in which a religious community's paradigmatic experiences are neither theistic nor dualistic. Even if it should turn out to be the case that there are, as Robert Forman has recently argued,[26] "pure consciousness events," states of consciousness without content or phenomenal properties, and even if such (non)-experiences are identified by some religious communities as religiously significant, such an identification can only be made in an already highly ramified doctrinal context.

None of this is to say that religious experiences are doctrinally insignificant. Without them—whether occasional and dramatic or quotidian and unexciting—religious communities could not long endure. And the members of such communities will often appeal to the occurrence of such experiences as evidence for the truth of their doctrine-expressing sentences, and will frame rules of recognition at least partly in terms of them.

1.2.2. Rules of Interpretation and Combination

These secondary doctrines, unlike rules of recognition, are used by religious communities to provide guidelines for interpreting and understanding doctrine-expressing sentences already acknowledged as such by application of the proper rules of recognition. They will often be akin to what the academic community would call hermeneutical principles, second-order descriptions of how to deal with first-order artifacts.

The need for such secondary doctrines will arise when the set of sentences that the community agrees, by the application of its rules of recognition, to call doctrine-expressing sentences, yields prima facie contradictions or inconsistencies; or when interpretations of this set of doctrine-expressing sentences (or some subset of it) by one group within the community differ in significant measure from those offered by another (or others). One or both scenarios will usually obtain in any community with a long history, or with a complex set of authoritative texts and rules of recognition.

Rules of interpretation will usually be framed by creating a hierarchy within the set of doctrine-expressing sentences, and requiring that those lower down the hierarchical order be interpreted in terms of those higher up. For example, such a rule might say *all doctrine-expressing sentences of this community are to be interpreted so that they are consonant with a particular subset of them.* The rule of interpretation used by some Buddhist communities, that Sūtras whose meaning is definitive (*nītārtha*) are to be used as guides for the interpretation of those whose meaning requires interpretation (*neyārtha*), is of just this kind. Sūtras are, for Buddhists, collections of *buddhavacana*, Buddha's word, and as such are by definition collections of sentences expressive of doctrine for the community. But the assumption that all these sentences are of equal weight leads to problems, since there are many prima facie contradictions among them. Hence the specification of some subset of them as more authoritative: the prima facie meaning of these is to govern the interpretation given the rest.

The creation of hierarchy, or the establishment of a subset of especially authoritative doctrine-expressing sentences, will be a common feature of rules of interpretation and combination. A good example of this kind of move is the "post-Tridentine baroque concept of dogma"[27] developed by Roman Catholic theologians since the First Vatican Council, most especially in response to the modernist controversy at the beginning of this century. It sets apart a subset of the community's doctrines, calls them dogmas, and gives them a controlling interpretive power over the members of the larger set.[28] Therefore rules of interpretation can also be called rules of combination: they specify how doctrine-expressing sentences are to be ordered and related one to another. The goals of such ordering and relation will always include the creation of a coherent system: this is one of the most pressing goals informing doctrinal discourse.

1.3 The Doctrinal Uses of Primary Doctrines

Primary doctrines have many uses for the communities whose doctrines they are. Prominent among these is the demarcation of the community, the marking-out of boundaries to separate those inside from those outside. Significant also is the pedagogical use of doctrines to make nonmembers of the community into members: the conceptual and practical links between doctrine and catechesis in the Christian west go very deep. But I take these uses of doctrine—and many others like them—to be nondoctrinal uses, concerned as they are to have effects upon nondoctrinal states of affairs such as community membership. Therefore, although an understanding of them would be essential to a complete theory of doctrine, and although these are among the most important functions of doctrine (and conceivably, for some communities, the only uses to which doctrines are put), they are only marginally relevant to a strictly doctrinal study of doctrine.

Among the strictly doctrinal uses of doctrine, then, I distinguish first the descriptive use. Many doctrine-expressing sentences appear to make descriptive claims about the setting of human life and the properties of the existents that constitute that setting.[29] If we follow the surface grammar of these sentences it seems perfectly natural to assume that religious communities at least sometimes use their doctrines to describe the world, to describe human persons, and to describe whatever is taken by the community to be of salvific value.

Notice that my claim here is not that all religious communities use at least some of their doctrine-expressing sentences in this way (although I suspect this to be the case). Whether this is so I take to be an empirical issue rather than a theoretical one that can be decided without paying attention to cases. Neither is my claim even that all doctrine-expressing sentences whose surface grammar might lead one to believe that they are being used descriptively are in fact being so used. Surface grammar can be deceptive, and further investigation of context may very well lead to the conclusion that what looks like a descriptive claim is in fact being used in another way by its community.

My suggestion at this point is only that if some doctrine-expressing sentence's surface grammar does indeed give the impression that it is being used as a description by its community, this possibility should not be ruled out a priori unless there are very good theoretical reasons for doing so. Some theorists think that there are such reasons, and therefore that the surface grammar of such sentences is always deceptive,[30] but I see no convincing arguments for this as an a priori judgment, and much interesting a posteriori work can be done if such a judgment is eschewed. Indeed, one of the chief interests that doctrinal studies has lies here: religious communities typically use their doctrines to make complex and interesting claims of metaphysical, ontological, ethical, and epistemological interest. Deciding in advance that no claims of these kinds are what they seem rules out much important work, as well as being at least interpretively reductionist.

The second important function that doctrine-expressing sentences have is that of recommendation. This is simple, obvious, and uncontroversial. I shall dismiss it quickly. Religious communities frequently use their doctrine-expressing sentences to recommend courses of action or attitudes to their members—and sometimes also to those outside the community. In my analysis of doctrine-expressing sentences I suggested that they will typically either describe or recommend; this second properly doctrinal use of doctrine-expressing sentences will naturally use sentences of the second kind. Religious communities use their doctrine-expressing sentences to commend many things, including ethical behavior, ritual action, doxastic practice, and personal piety. It might be possible to reduce this function of doctrine-expressing sentences to that of description by claiming that all injunctive or commendatory sentences presuppose and are based upon some descriptive sentences. But it seems preferable for heuristic purposes to keep the function of recommending separate from that of describing.

1.4 Applying the Theory

What can be done with a heuristic device such as this? Why would anyone consider it important? I expect the following benefits. First, the theory is intended to identify an intellectual practice at a sufficiently high level of abstraction that it can be used as a tool for directly comparative analysis. The first level of such analysis would be classificatory: the theory could be used to develop schemata of the kinds of secondary doctrines (rules of recognition, interpretation, and combination) that actual religious communities use to recognize, sort, and order their doctrines, as well as of the patterns of argument employed in such activities. Such classificatory schemata could then in turn be used to order religious communities into types according to their doctrinal practices. I would expect such an ordering to correlate with nondoctrinal variables.

The second level of analysis would be substantive, and would have to do with religious communities' primary doctrines. I envisage here the possibility of criticizing such doctrines in two ways. First, they could be criticized in terms of the rules of recognition and interpretation operative within the community; one could ask, for example, whether a given doctrine-expressing sentence, recognized by the community as authentic, should be so recognized given the rules of recognition stated and used by that same community.

Second, and more controversially, a community's primary doctrines might be criticized in terms of the criteria governing their acceptability in their sphere of relevance for some community. Suppose, for example, that some Buddhist community claims the sentence *abstention from taking sentient life is desirable* to be expressive of doctrine for it because it, more than any of its known competitors in its sphere of relevance, meets the community's acceptability-governing criterion in that sphere—which might here be *being conducive to the attainment of Nirvana*. A critical analysis might want to argue that this is not so (or that it is). Or, imagine a Christian community claiming that the sentence *God the Holy Spirit proceeds from God the Father and God the Son* is expressive of doctrine for it because this claim, more than any of its known competitors in its sphere of relevance, meets the community's acceptability-governing criterion in that sphere—which might here be *being accurately descriptive of the Trinitarian economy*. Again, a critical analysis might want to argue that this is not so (or that it is). In either case, the negative form of such criticism will usually go on by suggesting a new doctrine-candidate that the critic takes to possess more of the acceptability-creating criteria in the proper sphere of relevance than the doctrine-expressing sentence under criticism. This kind of analysis, like that which criticizes a community's primary doctrines in terms of how well they comport with that same community's rules of recognition and interpretation, is intrasystematic: no criteria foreign to the system being analyzed are introduced.

Finally, and most controversially, one might want to claim that the acceptability-governing criteria used by some communities are undesirable, ethically or epistemically. That is, a critical analysis might claim that a particular community's doctrines are authentically doctrinal for it in terms of its own rules of recognition, that the meaning attributed to these sentences by the community is consistent with its own rules of interpretation, that the sentences do possess the proper acceptability-governing properties in the proper degree—but that no community should have sentences that possess all these properties as doctrines, either because having them will lead to ethically inappropriate behavior, or because it will lead to improper doxastic practice.

This is a truly radical kind of extrasystematic criticism. It introduces normative criteria that are extrinsic to the system being criticized. This does not make it illegitimate; it simply requires a high degree of methodological self-consciousness and ethical sensitivity on the part of the critic.

These are the heuristic benefits of the theory. I intend to attempt all these kinds of analysis in the case of the buddhalogical doctrines that form the subject-matter of this book.

Chapter 2

Buddhist Doctrine

2.0 Prolegomena

In chapter one I constructed an abstract and formal heuristic device, an ideal-typical category to which I gave the label 'doctrine.' Doctrines, I there claimed, are expressed by natural-language sentences, and I called these sentences 'doctrine-expressing sentences.' I suggested also that the doctrine-expressing sentences of a religious community will, ideal-typically, be regarded by that community—or by its representative intellectuals, who are usually the only ones interested in such matters—as more acceptable to the community than their known competitors in their sphere of relevance; as significant for the religious life of the community; and as authoritative for and binding upon the community. It now remains to ask whether this heuristic device can be used to pick out and learn something about some Buddhist phenomena. Are there sentences that express doctrines in Buddhist texts, and if there are what do Buddhists say about them, how are they derived, and how are they used?

2.1 The Doctrinal Digests

I shall not ask these questions of the whole range of phenomena that might be called Buddhist. I shall ask it instead of a specific body of Buddhist literature produced by virtuoso monastic intellectuals in medieval India. None of the texts important to this study was composed earlier than the third century, and none later than the ninth. But the nature of the relations between text and commentary in this period makes questions of date and provenance almost irrelevant to the kind of study pursued here. All these texts, whatever their differences on substantive matters (and these are many and of considerable interest), are recognizably products of the same intellectual practice. They use the same methods, presuppose the same technical vocabulary, and do their work, for the most part, in an intellectual universe constituted entirely inter- and intratextually.

This literature is entirely scholastic. That is to say, its goal, necessarily approached asymptotically, is the construction of a complete system; its method is essentially exegetical; and its style, shared with all medieval Sanskrit treatises, Buddhist and non-Buddhist, is elliptical, abstract, and thoroughly denaturalized.[1] In calling the style of this literature 'denaturalized' I am following W.V.O. Quine's distinction between a naturalized epistemology and a denaturalized one.[2] The former, he says, makes epistemology a branch of psychology, and so turns it into an essentially descriptive and local discipline: its focus is upon how specific groups or individuals get what they call knowledge. The latter is, by contrast, an essentially normative enterprise whose scope is universal. It wants to show what knowledge really is and how anyone who wants to get it should go about doing so. Works that exhibit a denaturalized style try to minimize the evidence of their rooting in a specific sociocultural context, and to abstract themselves from the messy ambiguity of everyday talk in natural languages. They almost always do this by developing their own artificially disambiguated lexicon of technical terms, a lexicon intended to communicate with a precision not available to the users of natural languages. Such abstraction, precision, and disambiguation can never be completely realized, but the style of the texts with which I shall be dealing shows a high degree of interest in getting as close to it as possible.[3]

More specifically, I shall use as my sources some of what I take to be the more important corpora of Buddhist scholastic literature, corpora composed usually of a root- or core-text, sometimes in verse and sometimes in prose, surrounded by concentric layers of prose commentary, subcommentary, and subsubcommentary. The root-text is usually relatively short, and is essentially a mnemotechnical aid for the student, to be learned by heart as a first step in coming to grips with a particular corpus; the layers of commentary then provide exegesis and systematization, as well as extended discussion of controversial questions. Each corpus forms an organic whole, or at least was taken to do so by its users; the historical-critical questions so dear to the hearts of western scholars are hardly ever mentioned in these Indic texts, and they will also be almost entirely eschewed in this study. The fact that a particular root-text may have been composed five hundred years earlier than one of its commentaries and as many miles away will be of no interest to me. I shall take the texts as they present themselves: as of transhistorical systematic doctrinal interest, not as historically or institutionally located artifacts (although they are of course that too).[4]

These corpora are *śāstras*, technical treatises composed by virtuoso intellectuals for the formation and regulation of the religious lives of those communities who took their authority seriously. *Śāstra* is a Sanskrit word used by Indian intellectuals to refer to much more than Buddhist technical treatises. In fact, in what Buddhists say about their *śāstras* it is easy to see a variant of a much more broadly based Indic intellectual practice, as Sheldon Pollock, in his recent studies of śāstric discourse in non-Buddhist India has pointed out.[5] Pollock sees *śāstras* as an attempt to provide a complete classification of cultural practices in every possible sphere of human activity, from sexual intercourse to elephant-raising to politics. These classifications have normative force: they are prescriptive rather than simply descriptive, and the theoretical classifications contained in them are presented as prior to and controlling of the cultural practices that are their notional object. The *Kāmasūtra*, for example, claims that sexual practice is both caused and preceded by śāstric knowledge about it; and Rāmānuja, a non-Buddhist theorist, claims that knowledge produced by *śāstra* is a necessary condition for the attainment of liberation. Pollock concludes that śāstric discourse gives priority to codified theory over practice; that it presents its theory as primordial and changeless (often attributing it to nonhuman authors, or making it part of the fabric of the cosmos); and that change in either theory or practice thus becomes theoretically impossible, since these things are "frozen for all time in a given set of texts."[6] So, finally, Pollock presents śāstric ideology as a discourse of power in which the codified rules of the activity being treated are reified, given an ahistorical status, and asserted as the transcendent nature of things.

For Pollock, *śāstra*s are primarily codifications of rules, and only secondarily bodies of descriptive claims about the nature of things. With this outline in mind I now turn to the question of Buddhist *śāstra*. As a preliminary statement, following Pollock and the theoretical analysis of doctrine given in chapter one, I would say that a Buddhist *śāstra* is typically an ordered set of descriptive and injunctive sentences, together with arguments to ground and defend them, taken to give systematic and authoritative expression to Buddhist doctrine, either as a whole or within some specified area of human inquiry. Its functions are both pedagogical and soteriological: that is, it teaches those who need teaching;[7] provides religious training for those who need that;[8] and guards, guides, and protects those who study it.[9] It does all this through the medium of natural-language sentences.[10]

My generic term for corpora of texts of this kind is 'doctrinal digests.' This is in part a genre-label. These texts are 'digests' (often called *saṅgraha*, *samuccaya*, and the like—terms covering much of the same ground as 'summary' and 'digest' in English) in so far as they attempt to provide, in relatively brief compass, a systematic conspectus of what the intellectual tradition they represent claims about their subject-matter. They do this largely to meet the needs of their communities: neophyte monks need to be trained in the tradition, to be formed intellectually; and systematic doctrinal digests are ideal tools for such a purpose.

One explanation of these indigenous genre-terms found in the digests is that a *saṅgraha*, or digest, gathers together doctrines (*tattva*, more literally 'realities'); the first result of this is their easy comprehension (*avabodha*) or apprehension (*udgraha*, a term that perhaps also includes the idea of learning by heart).[11] Such definitions suggest that it is prima facie proper to call these texts doctrinal in the sense introduced by my formal definition in chapter one. That is, they contain natural-language sentences that appear to meet the criteria set forth in that definition. The exact sense in which this is true will become apparent only after the material in this and subsequent chapters has been studied. The body of this work will provide a detailed analysis of the claims and injunctions that constitute one specific area of Buddhist doctrine, namely, the buddhalogical. But some comments need to be offered first, given the theoretical considerations in chapter one, on the terms and concepts used by these doctrinal digests when they become self-conscious about their own content, and especially about the authority of their own discourse.

First, some general considerations. For Buddhist theorists, the most basic terms used to denote the kinds of authoritative natural-language sentences that concern me in this study all indicate the origin of such sentences in what Buddha said. So, most commonly, we find *buddhavacana*, 'Buddha's word'; *buddhaśāsana*, 'Buddha's teaching'; *buddhadeśanā*, 'Buddha's instruction'; and *buddhadharma*, 'Buddha's doctrine'. All these terms are predicated upon the idea of Buddha as teacher (*śāstṛ*), the final source of all those descriptions and injunctions that govern the intellectual and religious lives of Buddhists. The parallels with *didachē* and *doctrina* in Christian discourse are strong and clear: just as those terms are used by Christians to denote both what the community teaches and the community's act of teaching it, so also the terms mentioned above can denote both the act and the content of Buddha's teaching. Verbal forms of *vacana*, *deśanā*, and *śāsana* are commonplace, and are used to label the act that produces Buddhist doctrine.

There are other terms used by Buddhists to denote sentences expressive of doctrine. Among these perhaps the most important is *siddhānta*, literally 'established conclusion' but better translated 'tenet.' This term has no direct reference to any act of Buddha, denoting instead an established conclusion of some school preserved and presented in some text.[12] But since, as I shall show, the texts in which these tenets are presented always assimilate their tenets to *buddhavacana* in order to give them the necessary weight, it will not be misleading to focus attention on this and associated categories.

It is possible that some Buddhists have taken terms such as 'Buddha's word' to denote only those things actually said by the historical individual whom the tradition calls Gautama Śākyamuni, and have thus limited the community's doctrine-expressing sentences to members of that set. But this has never been the only view, not even among Theravāda Buddhists, who have generally been more conservative than Mahāyānists in controlling and limiting the range of what such terms may properly be taken to refer to. Instead, Buddhist communities have typically adopted two principal strategies to extend the range of the sentences denoted by these terms. The first strategy involves developing some rules of recognition by the application of which the status of some doctrine-candidate (or, more often, of a collection of such in a text) which does not claim to be a word of Buddha in any directly historical sense, can be ascertained; such criteria always extend the meaning of *buddhavacana* and the like beyond the literal historical reference—that is their purpose. The second strategy involves extending the meaning of the term 'Buddha' so that it no longer refers only (nor even primarily) to the historical individual Śākyamuni. If there are, at any given time, many Buddhas teaching in many world-realms, and if access can be had to their teachings through the use of various visionary or meditational methods, then clearly it will be possible to extend the range of what is designated by *buddhaśāsana* and the like.

Exploring the second of these two strategies will require an excursion into buddhalogy proper, and I shall defer this to chapter three. But some further words about the first strategy will be useful here, since it has been of importance in most Buddhist communities, and is operative in the textual corpora that concern me in this work. I shall begin, then, by asking how these texts think about their own authority, content, subject-matter, and goals.

2.2 *The Authority of the Doctrinal Digests*

It was integral to my definition of doctrine that a community's doctrine-expressing sentences must somehow be authoritative for or binding upon it. I have already suggested that, for Buddhist intellectuals in India, the single most important property that could be predicated of a sentence in order to give it authority was to say that it was an instance of Buddha's word or Buddha's doctrine. And yet none of the doctrinal digests that form the basis of this study presents itself as Buddha's word in any direct and obvious sense. Not one of them, for instance, says that it is what the historical person Gautama Śākyamuni said. How, then, do they account for the authority that they and their communities take them to have?

It is traditional for one or more of the commentaries or subcommentaries in a corpus belonging to this genre to begin with a statement of the corpus's *sambandha,* its origin or provenance. By doing this the corpus's authority is established; such authority is often designated by the term *gaurava,* literally 'weight' but perhaps best translated 'significance' in such contexts. If something has *gaurava* it is worthy of reverence, and this makes it authoritative for its community (the term *guru* is derived from the same root). A corpus's significance is often (though not always) established by making appeal to the status, authority, or importance of the authors of the individual works that constitute it. It will be useful to look at some examples of how this works.

One of the digests, the *Madhyāntavibhāga*-corpus, is especially clear and interesting in its treatment of this matter. This corpus—its name means, roughly, 'discrimination between middle and extremes'—consists of a root-text in verse, divided into five chapters; this is the *Madhyāntavibhāga* proper. The first layer of commentary upon these verses is a short and relatively simple prose exposition (*bhāṣya*); and the second is a much more extensive prose subcommentary (*ṭīkā*) commenting upon both verses and initial commentary. The verses are traditionally ascribed to Maitreya, the first commentary to Vasubandhu, and the subcommentary to Sthiramati.

The first commentary, Vasubandhu's *bhāṣya*, begins with an exordium, a dedicatory verse (*prastāvanā*) in which the author explains his relationship to the verses of the root-text upon which he is about to comment:

> śāstrasyāsya praṇetāram abhyarhya sugatātmajam/
> vaktāraṃ cāsmadādibhyo yatiṣye 'rthavivecane/[13]

> After paying homage to the promulgator of this
> treatise, the offspring of Buddha,
> And also to the one who has spoken it for people like
> me, I shall strive to elucidate its meaning.

The subcommentary explains that one purpose of composing verses like this is to amass merit for their authors, and that another is to make evident the significance or weight of the words of both the promulgator (*praṇetṛ*) and speaker (*vaktṛ*) of the root-text.[14] It may seem odd that a single work (the verses of the *Madhyāntavibhāga*) can be said to have both a promulgator and a speaker; I shall return to this in a moment. It is important to notice first that the verses of the *Madhyāntavibhāga*, which in the commentary's exordium were called a treatise (*śāstra*), are in the subcommentary called a sacred text (*sūtra*), a term traditionally reserved for works that purport to preserve the direct speech of Buddha (*buddhavacana*). The subcommentary at once goes on to explain why:

> tatra praṇetrā vaktum upadiṣṭāt sūtre gauravam utpadyate/ yasmād asya kārikāśāstrasyāryamaitreyaḥ praṇetā/ sa caikajātipratibaddhāt sarvabodhisattvābhijñādhāraṇīpratisamvitsamādhīndriya-kṣāntivimokṣaiḥ paramaṃ paraṃgataḥ sarvāsu bodhisattvabhūmiṣu niḥśeṣam api prahīṇāvaraṇaḥ/[15]

> The sacred text has its significance because it is spoken by its promulgator; and the noble Maitreya is the promulgator of this treatise in verse. He is separated [from becoming

> Buddha] by only one birth, and so he has realized the supreme perfection of all the bodhisattva's supernatural knowledges, magical formulas, specific understandings, concentrations, powers, steadfastnesses, and liberations; and having abandoned the obstructions, he has gone through all the stages of the bodhisattva's path.

This is high praise. The qualities attributed to Maitreya here are all also attributed to Buddha, and it seems as though the subcommentary is here giving Maitreya status as Buddha; this explains its use of the term 'sacred text' to denote the verses of the *Madhyāntavibhāga*. In the exordium to the commentary, translated above, Maitreya is called "offspring of Buddha," and in commenting upon this epithet the subcommentary explains the difference between Maitreya and Buddha in these terms:

> tasmāt tasmin vā jātaḥ sugatātmajaḥ/ atha vā sugatātmanā jāta iti sugatātmajaḥ/ yathoktaṃ sūtrāntare jāto bhavati tathāgatavaṃse tadātmakavastu pratilābhād iti/ evaṃ sati bodhisattvasya daśamabhūmau pratiṣṭhitasya sarvākāraṃ jñeyaṃ vastu karatalastham ivāmalakiphalāṃśukāvacchaditalocanasyevābhāsam āyāti/ bhagavataḥ punar apanītalocanāvaraṇasyevety ayaṃ viśeṣaḥ/[16]

> "Offspring of Buddha" means 'born from' or 'born in' that [Buddha]. Alternatively, "offspring of Buddha" means 'born with Buddha's own nature.' For another sacred text says: "He is born of the Tathāgata's lineage because he has obtained his nature." Since this is so, for a bodhisattva [like Maitreya] established on the tenth stage [of the path], all objects of awareness appear as clearly as a dried fruit on the palm of someone's hand when that person's eyes are covered with fine filaments of cloth. The difference for Buddha is just that the eye-covering has been removed.

Maitreya is clearly almost Buddha. He has Buddha's own nature and is very nearly omniscient. The only difference between Maitreya's omniscience and Buddha's is that the former's vision is still very slightly obstructed, as though by fine filaments of cloth, while Buddha's vision is not obstructed at all.

But the difference is minor: Maitreya can see everything just as well as an ordinary person can see a dried fruit on the palm of her hand with nothing more than some fine filaments of cloth in front of her eyes—and this is meant to convey the impression that Maitreya sees very well indeed. Maitreya's cognition is thus effectively the same as Buddha's, and so his words carry virtually the same weight as do Buddha's; the verses of the *Madhyāntavibhāga* are thus called 'sacred text,' which means that they function as Buddha's word for the community.

Maitreya's function in producing the *Madhyāntavibhāga* is said in the dedicatory verse to be that of *praṇetṛ* or "promulgator." This term is explained in the subcommentary to mean "creator" or "maker" (*kartṛ*).[17] This means that it will not be misleading to think of Maitreya as the author of these verses. This function is distinguished from that of "speaker" (*vaktṛ*). The subcommentary identifies the speaker as the one who makes the text known, and further says that he is Asaṅga. Also:

> tasya hīdaṃ śāstram abhivyaktam ākhyātaṃ
> cāryamaitreyādhiṣṭhānād dharmasrotasā/[18]

> This treatise has been made manifest and declared to him [i.e., to Asaṅga] through the grace of the noble Maitreya by the [concentration called] 'stream of doctrine.'

The "[concentration called] 'stream of doctrine' " is a state of ecstatic trance wherein bodhisattvas obtain doctrinal instruction direct from Buddha or from some functional analogue thereof such as Maitreya.[19] Both the source and the method are taken to guarantee the efficacy and accuracy of the instruction obtained, and that it is mentioned here points to the strong emphasis placed by this corpus upon the authoritativeness and accuracy of its own words. The words of the verses are thus *buddhavacana* because they are formed, made, and communicated by Maitreya, one who functions like Buddha, to Asaṅga, their human speaker, and because the latter's utterance of them reproduces Buddha's speech.

So much for the status of the verses of the *Madhyānta-vibhāga*. I turn now to the status and authority of the commentary and subcommentary that together make up the remainder of the corpus. Recall that the exordium in the commentary translated above is written in the first person: "I shall strive to elucidate its meaning" and so forth. The subcommentary identifies the subject of these utterances as Vasubandhu, and says:

> tasmāc chrutvācāryabhadantavasubandhus tadbhāṣyam akarot/ tāv apy uttamaprajñavato 'bhrāntipratives dhadhāraṇopadeśasāmārthyād atra sūtrārtho 'bhrāntam upadiṣṭa iti vṛttyāṃ gauravam utpadyate/ evaṃ ye pudgalaṃ pramāṇīkurvanti teṣāṃ sūtravṛttigauravotpattiḥ/ ye ca dharmānusāriṇas teṣāṃ sūtravṛttyoḥ śubhārthe 'vabodhaḥ/ jāte ca niścaye iyaṃ praṇetur vaktuś ca pratītya prabhāvanā na tu tarkāgamamātreṇa prabhāvaneti praṇetṛvaktṛgauravotpattiḥ/[20]
>
> Upon hearing it [i.e., the verses of the *Madhyāntavibhāga*] from him [i.e., Asaṅga], the venerable master Vasubandhu composed a commentary upon it. These two had supreme discernment; as a result of their capacity to retain and teach their understanding without error, they taught the meaning of the sacred text [i.e., the verses of the *Madhyāntavibhāga*] also without error. This sets forth the significance of [Vasubandhu's] commentary. The sacred text and its commentary acquire significance in this way for those who make persons their authorities; and for those who follow doctrine, these texts acquire significance in the realization that the meaning of the sacred text and its commentary is pleasing—and when a definite judgment [of this kind] is made, its power comes from its dependence upon the promulgator and speaker, and not just from scripture or reasoning. In this way the significance of the promulgator and of the speaker are set forth.

This passage states first that Asaṅga and Vasubandhu had supreme insight, and that therefore their words, as contained in these texts, can be relied upon as bearing unimpeachable authority in matters of doctrine. These teachers make no errors; Vasubandhu's words, as contained in the commentary, are therefore given equal weight to that possessed by Maitreya's words as communicated to Asaṅga. The passage also says why it is important that these texts should have been composed by weighty individuals such as Asaṅga and Vasubandhu, and in doing so it refers to two types of individual: "those who make persons their authorities" and "those who follow doctrine." With these phrases the subcommentary makes passing reference to two of the 'four points of refuge' (*pratiśaraṇa*), a set of rules of interpretation employed in the digests to which I shall return later in this chapter.

For "those who make persons their authorities" the sentences of the corpus are significant—have doctrinal force—just because of their composition by significant individuals; and even for "those who follow doctrine," those who are capable of making a judgment about the texts' meaning independently of claims about the authority of their authors, the veridicality of such judgments is finally underscored by the status of these authors.

The authority of the *Madhyāntavibhāga*-corpus therefore, in its own eyes and in those of the communities for which it is a significant text, stands very high. The corpus is without doctrinal error, and so, functionally, Buddha's word. What has been said about this corpus applies also to other corpora. So, for example, the *Mahāyānasūtrālaṅkāra*-corpus also came, at least in Tibet, to have its root-text attributed to Maitreya and its layers of commentary given the same significance as those of the *Madhyāntavibhāga*-corpus.[21]

Another case is that of the *Abhidharmakośa*-corpus. This also consists of a root-text in verse, a prose commentary by Vasubandhu, to whom the verses are also attributed, and a large number of sub- and subsubcommentaries. Vasubandhu opens the root-text with an exordium, a verse of homage to Buddha "the teacher of truth" (*yathārthaśāstṛ*), and then, in the prose commentary, proclaims his intention of promulgating (*praṇi-*) or announcing (*pravad-*) a treatise of his own.[22] He is not without humility about the importance, accuracy, and authority of his work. Although Yaśomitra, the author of one of the subcommentaries, says that Vasubandhu is of supreme intelligence and like a second Buddha,[23] Vasubandhu himself says at the end of his work that his intention has only been to explain

Buddhist metaphysics (*abhidharma*) according to the system of the Vaibhāṣikas of Kashmir, and that whatever has been poorly understood by him is his own fault. Only Buddhas and sons of Buddhas, he adds, are proper authorities for the interpretation of the true doctrine.[24] Yaśomitra's subcommentary here mentions Śāriputra, one of the historical Buddha's chief disciples, as a member of the class-category 'sons of Buddhas,'[25] and this suggests that any noble disciple of Buddha can act as a proper authority for the interpretation of Buddha's word. But if this is so then one would expect Vasubandhu, the author of the *Abhidharmakośa* and its first commentary, to be a member of that class, and so to produce teaching (*śāsana, deśanā*) or systematic metaphysics that can be relied upon as authoritative and accurate. The tradition has certainly taken it that way: not only does Yaśomitra say that Vasubandhu is like a second Buddha, but, as I have shown, the subcommentary to the *Madhyāntavibhāga* makes similar judgments as to his importance. We meet here a common theme: a status and authority are claimed for the author of a digest that the author himself is not willing to assert.[26]

Yaśomitra too, in his subcommentary upon the *Abhidharmakośa,* makes humble reference to the efforts of his predecessors in the work of commentary, and says that his purpose is to follow them in whatever they have said that is proper, while rejecting whatever is not proper, whatever departs from the *siddhānta,* the tenets of the school. Rather less humbly, he concludes his exordium by saying that his intellect is not capable of being deceived by false interpretations of the doctrine's meaning.[27] It seems clear, then, that Yaśomitra intends his subcommentary to be an authoritative restatement of what Vasubandhu, the one who is like a second Buddha, had already said in the verses of the *Abhidharmakośa* and its first commentary.

The authority of these texts in their own eyes is thus very great. The corpora as a whole contain an authoritative statement of Buddhist doctrine, one that has *gaurava* or *pramāṇikatva,* an authority guaranteed by the level of spiritual attainment reached by their authors. This exalted level at times inspires the authors of and commentators upon these texts to designate the objects of their commentary not just as treatises or systematic works, but also as sacred texts, the express words of Buddha (though not the utterance of Gautama Śākyamuni). These corpora are therefore authoritative texts in the sense I gave to that term in chapter one; their content is regarded by their communities as itself doctrinal, and is used as an instrument both to justify and to derive further doctrine-expressing sentences.

This location of textual authority either in something akin to revelation (in the case of texts communicated by Maitreya to Asaṅga), or in the transmission of the insights of an authoritative human teacher through a line of reliable preservers and transmitters of those insights (through a *guruparamparā*) is not peculiarly Buddhist. It is, rather, pan-Indian, a feature of śāstric discourse generally. Its presence in the doctrinal digests is another indication of the extent to which Buddhist theorizing had, by the third or fourth century, entered the mainstream of Indian virtuoso intellectual life, though some caveats will have to be entered below, since there are also some significant differences between the Buddhist view of theory and the broader pan-Indian one.

Some of the terminology used to describe the authoritativeness of these texts—their teaching is *abhrānta,* without error; their composers have *uttamaprajñā,* supreme discernment, or are like a second Buddha—sounds, indeed, as though one should assimilate the kind of authority given these texts to that given the text of the Bible by some Christian fundamentalists, or to that given the text of the Qur'ān by some Muslims. This would not be correct, but to see why would involve an analysis of the hermeneutical strategies employed by Buddhists in interpreting the sentences of these texts; and that will be deferred to a later point in this chapter.

The material surveyed in this section suggests that these corpora are authoritative just because of their authorship by weighty figures (Maitreya, Asaṅga, Vasubandhu, and so forth); and it is certainly true that, when the question of authority is explicitly raised as a matter for debate, or as a matter of which some account needs to be given, such an appeal is always made.

It may seem, then, that the authority of these corpora always reduces to the authority of the individuals to whom their composition is attributed. But to conclude this would also be wrong—or at least too simple—since, as I shall show, there are explicit warnings against it contained in some Buddhist hermeneutical theories. And it is also the case that the theories about Buddha's word contained in these very corpora go beyond locating it in the utterance of authoritative persons. Nonetheless, it is important, given the emphasis placed by many Buddhist theorists and more western interpreters, upon perception (*pratyakṣa*) and inferential reasoning (*anumāna*) as the only valid means of gaining knowledge (*pramāṇa*), to stress, as a corrective, the importance given here to authoritative persons as the guarantors of textually transmitted doctrinal knowledge.

2.3 The Content and Subject-Matter of the Doctrinal Digests

The doctrinal digests contain natural-language sentences whose goal is to communicate to those who read or hear them. This sounds almost too obvious to need saying, but since the digests themselves almost always find it necessary to say it when they come to define their own genre, it seems worth saying it here also: doctrine cannot be communicated, for these texts, without reliance upon doctrine-expressing sentences.

Consider the following, in answer to an objection that only sentences (*vākya*) can possess meaning, and that it is therefore not permissible to claim that a treatise (*śāstra*) as a whole has subject-matter (*abhidheya*), since having subject-matter requires being able to express meaning:

> naitad asti/ yady api vākyasamūhātmakaṃ śāstraṃ tathāpi tāni vākyāni parasparavyapekṣa-sambandhāvasthitāni anyathonmattādivākyasamūhavad asaṅgatārtham eva syāt/ tataś ca paraspara-sambaddhānekaśabdasamūhātmakatvāt tadanyavākyavad vākyam eva śāstram/ na hi padair eva vākyam ārabhyate 'pi vākyair api/ ato mahāvākyatvād abhidheyavad eva śāstram ity acodyam/[28]

> This [objection] does not hold. For even though a treatise is a collection of sentences, these sentences are coherently collected together and interrelated. If this were not so, the treatise would simply be incoherent, like a crazy collection of sentences. So, because this treatise consists of a variety of utterances that are coherently interrelated, it is precisely a sentence comprising other sentences; for a sentence need not be made up only of words, it can also be made up of sentences. So one should not be surprised that a treatise can have subject-matter: it can because it is a single great sentence.

This idea, that a *śāstra* as a whole is capable of communicating meaning and having a specifiable subject-matter in virtue of the interconnected and coherent nature of its parts, is an important one. To say that entire text—or even an entire corpus—is a single great sentence is to suggest that it is an ordered system, each part of which relates to every other part in order to communicate a single (if complex) meaning. A doctrinal digest, then, is a sentence-possessing artifact whose goals are irreducibly systematic, though this says nothing about the understanding present in these texts of how sentences communicate meaning, nor of the rules of interpretation to be applied to them in order to extract that meaning. I shall return to these matters below. For the moment the formal point will have to suffice.

What, then, is the subject matter (*abhidheya*) of these works? What are they about? Various answers are given, including: dependent co-origination (*pratītyasamutpāda*);[29] the doctrine of emptiness (*śūnyatā*);[30] metaphysics (*abhidharma*) aimed at the discernment and accurate classification of existents;[31] and complete statements of ontology and soteriology.[32]

The differences among these statements about the subject-matter of particular doctrinal digests are partly to be explained by differences in scholastic affiliation. Mādhyamika texts naturally claim to be concerned with key Mādhyamika doctrines, while Abhidharma texts say that they are concerned to set forth the main themes of Buddhist metaphysics. Exploration of these differences would require a discussion of what separates and what unites these different schools doctrinally, and that is not my concern here. I am interested instead in what unites the subject-matter of these texts at the formal level, and this is their concern to provide a systematic and authoritative statement of the doctrinal claims of their school, and to do so in a way that makes the statement usable for pedagogical purposes, as well as for the spiritual training of the user. This may be done through the organizing principle of the seven stations of religious training (*śikṣāsthāna*), as in the *Mahāyānasūtrālaṅkāra*-corpus; through the stages of the path (*bhūmi*), as in the *Madhyamakāvatāra*-corpus; or through the systematic classification of existents and their properties and relations, as in the *Abhidharmakośa*-corpus, the *Abhidharmasamuccaya*-corpus, and the *Mahāyānasaṅgraha*-corpus. But the goal is always the same: systematic completeness.

The urge toward systematic completeness is also evident in and served by the style in which these works are written. It is a severe, precise, and abstract style, a style, as Louis Renou has put it, which is "un instrument monotone mais puissant de raisonnement, d'interpretation, de dialectique, approprié à servir d'expression doctrinale à tous les types de problemes et de disciplines."[33] A style of this kind is, I suspect, one of the hallmarks of scholasticism in all cultural spheres, and certainly places Buddhist *śāstras* firmly within the mainstream of the practice of theory in India.

It should be sufficiently obvious that the subject-matter of these digests requires them (at least in terms of the surface grammar of their sentences) to make substantive claims and to issue recommendations as to appropriate courses of action. That is, these texts use doctrine-expressing sentences both for description and for recommendation, and so they fall precisely within the scope of a properly doctrinal study of doctrine.

2.4 *The Goals of the Doctrinal Digests*

The proximate goals of these corpora are pedagogical and explanatory: they aim to elucidate the doctrinal system with clarity, precision, and persuasive force, and by so doing to produce understanding and conviction on the part of those who use the texts. The remote goal is always soteriological: proper use of these texts is claimed to be directly productive of the transcendence of suffering and the attainment of Buddhahood. Further, there is a direct causal link between these proximate and remote goals. To attain a clear and systematic understanding of Buddhist doctrine—the proximate goal—is taken to be productive of awakening—the remote goal.

The digests distinguish two defining characteristics of a *śāstra* in this connection. The first is that such texts are a form of tutelage or instruction (*upadeśa*) whose content, after repeated cultivation, becomes clear to the student; this leads to the abandonment of all defilements and their effects. The second is that they are a form of tutelage that protects from bad rebirths. A verse on the nature of *śāstra* is quoted at several places in the digests:

> yac chāsti ca kleśāripun aśeṣān santrayate durgatito bhāvāc ca/
> tac chāsanāt trānaguṇāc ca śāstram etad dvayaṃ cānyamateṣu nāsti//[34]

> That which controls all our enemies, the afflictions, and which protects us from continued existence and bad rebirths,
> Is a treatise because it controls and protects. These two [advantages] are not found in other systems.

There is a quasi-etymological play with words here. The term *śāstra* is related first to the root *śās-*, 'to control,' and then to the root *trā-*, 'to protect'; the passions are what is to be controlled, and bad rebirths are those things from which one is to be protected. Both functions make the soteriological purposes of the digests abundantly clear.[35]

Similar themes are repeated throughout the digests. The *Abhidharmakośa*-corpus, for example, says of itself that it is an abhidharma treatise, which is to say a treatise "aimed at the attainment of undefiled discernment" (*anāsravaprajñā*), a treatise with goals that the tradition takes to be salvifically significant. The text is intended by its author to be an aid in the development of proper doxastic practices, and so also in the attainment of accurate knowledge. The attainment of such knowledge and the development of such practices are, in turn, a necessary condition for gaining liberation from Samsara.[36] Similar claims as to the salvific effect of proper doxastic practices, and as to the efficacy of the digests in bringing such practices into being, are found throughout these works.[37]

The proximate goal of the doctrinal digests is therefore pedagogical: the creation of understanding of some set of doctrinal claims on the part of their users. The ultimate soteriological goal is causally dependent upon the attainment of this proximate goal: only when intellectual comprehension has been realized is it possible to advance further toward Nirvana. This strong link between what it is that one understands and assents to and one's potential for attaining awakening is an entirely standard Buddhist theme. Bad doxastic habits and wrong cognitive commitments are among the most effective hindrances to progress on the path, and while their correction will not guarantee advancement along that path, it is a necessary condition for it.

One of the digests puts this point thus: "Cognitive error is the root-cause of all affliction; its absence causes the attainment of happiness and ultimate felicity, which is what brings well-being to the world."[38] The digests usually give a list of four cognitive errors. They are: (1) taking that which is impermanent to be permanent; (2) taking that which is unsatisfactory to be satisfactory; (3) taking that which is impure to be pure; and (4) taking that which is not a self to be one.[39] Such errors are misjudgments, misapprehensions as to the nature of things, and are themselves based upon still more basic cognitive mistakes about the nature of the self.

It should be evident that one of the uses to which the doctrinal digests put their doctrine-expressing sentences is cognitive formation. These sentences are meant to shape, form, and control the doxastic practices and cognitive habits of their users, to provide them with the terms within which their intellectual lives are lived, and to constrain those intellectual lives within the boundaries of the doctrinal systems presupposed by and expressed in the one great sentence that each of these corpora takes itself to be.

The emphasis here on the priority and importance of codified theory is also entirely in accord with Pollock's findings. Just as one cannot engage in sexual practice properly without śāstric knowledge, so also one cannot pursue awakening and dispose of the obstacles (*āvaraṇa*) to that awakening without study of the doctrinal digests.

2.5 Theories of Doctrine in the Doctrinal Digests

The digests are self-conscious about more than their own status, content, subject-matter, and goals; since they are the product of a highly sophisticated and self-reflective intellectual practice, they also engage in explicit theorizing about the nature, origins, and proper uses of the doctrine-expressing sentences they employ. In the course of this they make use of some traditional terminology and conceptual schemata, and to the more important among these I now turn.

2.5.1 Rules of Recognition

Rules of recognition, as I described them in chapter one, are those rules by the application of which communities make decisions as to whether doctrine-candidates should become doctrine-expressing sentences. They state criteria whose application is meant to distinguish the members of the set of those sentences that do express doctrine from the members of the (usually much larger) set of those sentences that do not.

There was a special need for rules of recognition during the period when the doctrinal digests were being compiled. From about the third century onward, Mahāyāna Buddhist theorists were faced with the necessity of explaining how the traditional terms used by Buddhist theorists to label doctrine-expressing sentences—*buddhavacana* and the rest—could be applied to their own discourse when it seemed that the traditional rules of recognition might rule it out as expressive of Buddhist doctrine.[40]

As to these traditional rules of recognition:[41] the most influential traditional formulation refers to the "four great appeals to authority" (*caturmahāpadeśa*).[42] It claims that there are four and only four sources from which *buddhavacana* may be derived: the mouth of Buddha; a community (*sangha*) of elders; a group of learned (*bahuśruta*) monks who are specialists in doctrine, monastic discipline, and mnemonic formulas (*mātṛkā*) used to order Buddhist metaphysical systems; and a single learned monk with the same capabilities. But teachings (*śāsana*) or doctrinal claims of any kind derived from these sources are not thereby guaranteed status as doctrine-expressing sentences, as *buddhavacana*. They must then be subjected to further tests, and in the doctrinal digests these tests are most often formulated thus: Does it—the doctrine-candidate in question—appear in the sacred texts, the Sūtras? Is it apparent in the Vinaya, the texts in which the disciplinary regulations governing the life of the community are found? And does it cohere with reality?[43] There are some oddities about this set of tests. First, it is at least not obvious why some teaching derived directly from Buddha's lips should require further tests to determine whether it is worthy of being judged to have doctrinal force. And, second, it is far from clear to what extent the terms 'Sūtra' and 'Vinaya' were intended to refer to well-defined collections of texts with canonical weight. The earliest form of this fourfold formula is found as part of Gautama Śākyamuni's final instructions to his followers before his apparent death, and it seems unlikely that well-defined canonical collections existed then. But these are historical problems that cannot be pursued here; I am satisfied that in the doctrinal digests collections of texts are meant: for them 'Sūtra' means *sūtrapiṭaka*, the collection of sacred texts called 'Sūtra'; and likewise 'Vinaya' means *vinayapiṭaka*, as suggested, for example, in the *Mahāyānasūtrālaṅkāra*-corpus.[44]

The third of the authenticity-questions—that of conformity with reality—was not mentioned in earlier formulations. In those it was thought sufficient to test a doctrine-candidate by seeing whether it was consonant with what was said in Sūtra or Vinaya. That an extra criterion came to be thought necessary is surely indicative of the conceptual problems raised for Mahāyāna theorists by these earlier formulations. It became important for them to extend the meaning of *buddhavacana* beyond what Gautama Śākyamuni actually said, and also beyond any simple appeal to conformity with text or tradition, a tendency taken still further in the fourfold rule of recognition to be discussed below.

It appears from the treatment given these three questions in the digests that in order for a doctrine-candidate to be classified as Buddha's word, it must meet all three of these criteria. A great deal of trouble is taken to show that the claims of the Mahāyāna do meet all three, and this would hardly have been done were one or two sufficient. The first two criteria seek legitimation by reference to some agreed body of authoritative texts: Sūtra and Vinaya. It is necessary (though not sufficient) in order for some utterance or claim to be considered Buddha's word that it appear or be found in an authoritative text of this kind.[45]

What kind of presence is required here? Is the demand for direct quotation, verbatim reproduction of what is said in some such text, or for something weaker? One example discussed in the digests is the assertion of the existence of *skandha*s, *āyatana*s, and *dhātu*s as real, an assertion made, it is said by those Buddhists who are not followers of the Mahāyāna on the ground that such a claim is also found in the discourses. From this perspective, the Mahāyāna claim that all existents are without essence (*niḥsvabhāva*)—which entails the conclusion that all *skandha*s, *āyatana*s, and *dhātu*s cannot exist in the way that non-Mahāyānists say they do—must be rejected, not because it is not explicitly said in the Sūtras, but rather because it is not in accord with what is said in them. The same argument is repeated, though with different particulars, in the case of what is and what is not present, what does and what does not cohere or accord with what is present in the Vinaya.[46]

The real disagreement between Mahāyānists and non-Mahāyānists over these first two criteria is actually both more simple and less tractable than a disagreement about rules of recognition. It is more simple because it reduces to a basic disagreement about which texts should be counted as authoritative; and it is less tractable because the scope for discussion and theoretical subtlety here is much less than in the case of complex hermeneutical questions. Brute disagreement about whether words attributed to Buddha in some text that calls itself a Sūtra should or should not be accepted as such (because the Sūtra is taken by one party to be a genuine token of the type and by another not to be) cannot easily be resolved without appeal to criteria other than the genre of texts or the surface credentials of utterances. Without such criteria disagreement often reduces to name-calling, and this is what sometimes occurs in the digests.[47]

The third criterion—that a doctrine-candidate must not contradict reality (*dharmatā*) in order to be characterized as Buddha's word—is of a different kind. Unlike the first two, it makes no reference to the etiology of the candidate; it refers instead to its relationship with something outside itself, to reality, or to the way in which reality is understood by the participants in the debate. And here too, of course, there are deep differences, differences that in the end can only be resolved by resolving properly metaphysical questions, not by appealing to the status or genre of texts.

All this suggests the following: first, that the application of the term *buddhavacana* to some sentence (or text) is sufficient to make that sentence (or text) authoritative for the community; second, that the sentence (or text) in question is, in virtue of being Buddha's word, taken by the community not to misrepresent reality; and third, that the community expects those sentences called 'Buddha's word' to cohere with what is said (or what is implied by what is said) in the texts that directly represent themselves as being what Buddha said. *Buddhavacana*, therefore, has considerable overlap with the category 'doctrine' as I outlined it in chapter one. That to which both refer is sets of sentences with the properties analyzed in that chapter.

To say of some sentence that it is worthy to receive the ancient formula of approbation *idaṃ śāstuḥ śāsanam* ("this is the teacher's teaching") is just to say that it is *buddhavacana*, and it is noteworthy that, just as 'doctrine' may apply to sets of sentences as well as to single sentences, so also this formula is often applied to single sentences.[48] This suggests an even stronger homology between the category 'doctrine-expressing sentence' as developed in chapter one, and the category *buddhavacana* as analyzed and defended by the digests.

The rules of recognition offered in the digests are clearly moving away from concern with etiology, with questions about the origins of doctrine-expressing sentences in the utterance of authoritative persons or texts, and toward a concern for questions about the truth-value and effects of such doctrine-candidates. This tendency goes as far as it can with yet another formula, cited in two of the digests:

> api tu maitreya caturbhiḥ kāraṇaiḥ pratibhānaṃ sarvabuddhabhāṣitam/ katamaiś caturbhiḥ/ iha maitreya pratibhānaṃ satyopasamhitaṃ bhavati nāsatyopasamhitam/ dharmopasamhitaṃ bhavati nādharmopasamhitam/ kleśahāyakaṃ bhavati na kleśavivardhakam/ nirvāṇaguṇānuśamsasandarśakaṃ bhavati na saṃsāraguṇānuśamsasandarśakam/ ebhiś caturbhiḥ . . . yasya kasyācin maitreya ebhiś caturbhiḥ kāraṇaiḥ pratibhānaṃ pratibhāti pratibhāsyati vā tatra śraddhaiḥ kulaputraiḥ kuladuhitṛbhir vā buddhasaṃjñotpādayitavyā śāstṛsaṃjñāṃ kṛtvā/ sa dharmaḥ śrotavyaḥ/ tat kasya hetoḥ/ yat kiñcin maitreya subhāṣitaṃ sarvaṃ tad buddhabhāṣitam/[49]

> Maitreya, all the eloquent discourse spoken by Buddha can be recognized in four ways. Which four? Maitreya, the four are: (1) [Buddha's] eloquent discourse is useful and not useless; (2) it conforms to doctrine, not to its opposite; (3) it destroys the passions rather than increasing them; and (4) it shows the good qualities and advantages of Nirvana rather than those of Samsara. Whoever, Maitreya, discourses eloquently in these four ways, or will so discourse in the future, will be thought of as Buddha by faithful men and women. Considering such a person as teacher, they will listen to his doctrine. Why? Because, Maitreya, everything that is well spoken is spoken by Buddha.

That which is "well spoken" is *buddhavacana*. It is "eloquent discourse" (*pratibhāna*), a term that connotes pleasingness, inspirational efficacy, accuracy, and completeness all at once.[50] One can recognize what is well and eloquently spoken mostly by its effects upon its hearers: it is useful and salvifically efficacious. This complex rule of recognition comes close to identifying *buddhavacana* with the ordered sets of sentences that comprise the doctrinal digests themselves. For we have already seen that these are precisely the properties attributed by the digests to themselves. A doctrine-candidate is expressive of doctrine for these texts, has the proper significance (*gaurava*) and authority (*pramāṇikatva*), if it conforms to the way things are and is salvifically efficacious, and if it has not yet been refuted or placed in question by the known existence of some undefeated objection.

Here there are some strategic differences between Buddhist śāstric discourse and the non-Buddhist variety. If, following Pollock, we say that non-Buddhist śāstric discourse primordially inscribes the structure of the cosmos, and is authoritative just because it does so, then we should say that Buddhist śāstric discourse is supremely efficacious in bringing about certain desired results (paradigmatically the attainment of awakening), and is authoritative just because it is capable of doing so. The contrast is between authority issuing primarily from descriptive accuracy, on the one hand, and authority issuing primarily from performative efficacy, on the other. This is a difference of emphasis only. Both kinds of authority are inevitably present in both kinds of śāstric discourse. But it does seem true that, in direct accord with basic Buddhist axiological and metaphysical assumptions, the development of rules of recognition in Buddhism exhibits a major interest in the effect of doctrines so recognized: "well-spokenness" (*subhāṣitatvam*) is, on the whole, cashed out in terms of efficacy.

2.5.2 Rules of Interpretation

Rules of interpretation, as defined in chapter one, are secondary doctrines used by religious communities to provide guidelines for interpreting and understanding doctrine-expressing sentences already acknowledged to be such by application of the proper rules of recognition. The classical formulation of the rules of interpretation operative in the digests is:

> catvāri imāni bhikṣavaḥ pratiśaraṇāni/ katamāni catvāri/ dharmaḥ pratiśaraṇaṃ na pudgalaḥ/ arthaḥ pratiśaraṇaṃ na vyañjanam[51]/ nītārthasūtraṃ pratiśaraṇaṃ na neyārtham/ jñānaṃ pratiśaraṇaṃ na vijñānam iti/[52]
>
> There are four points of refuge. What are the four? (1) The doctrine is one's point of refuge, not a person. (2) The meaning is one's point of refuge, not the letter. (3) The sacred texts whose meaning is defined are one's point of refuge, not those whose meaning needs definition. (4) Direct awareness is one's point of refuge, not discursive awareness.

The first rule of interpretation urges reliance upon doctrine rather than upon the person who teaches it. This effectively reemphasizes and restates the point that no authoritative source can guarantee either the doctrinal status or the truth of any sentence or collection of such. The hermeneutical result of this is that primary attention should be paid, when interpreting some sentence, not to its origin or its speaker, but to its content, to what it claims.

Understanding what a sentence claims, though, is no simple matter, and the second point of refuge—the injunction to rely upon a sentence's meaning or referent (*artha*) rather than upon the lexical items (*vyañjana*) used to convey that meaning or referent—points to the initial difficulty: How is one to know what some doctrine-candidate's meaning is (if it is always the case that it has only one)? Most generally, some distinction such as this between form and content, mode of expression and meaning, is necessary if one is to make conceptual sense of the possibility of translating the doctrine from one natural language into another. And since Buddhist theorists appear from the beginning to have set their faces firmly and decisively against the idea that preaching the doctrine in any one particular natural language (or, indeed, in any particular artificial language, if Pali is classified as such) is better than preaching it in any other, and so has actively encouraged the use of various vernaculars, there is no doubt some connection here.

But there is more at stake than this. Buddhist theorists felt it necessary to open up the possibility that some sentences' real meanings are not merely to be differentiated from the words used to express them, but are actually radically at variance with what those words appear to say. The central issue in this second point of refuge, then, is the partial separation of meaning from the words used to express it. The distinction made in chapter one, between what is expressed in a doctrine-expressing sentence and the sentence itself, is thus entirely consonant with Buddhist doctrinal discourse. Doctrine is never identified with natural-language sentences in this discourse, although it may of course be expressed by them.

The third point of refuge is that one should have recourse to those sacred texts whose meaning (*artha*) has been drawn out (*nīta*), made explicit, stated with precision, and not to those whose meaning stands in need of such operations. The general point here is that some sacred texts mean just what they seem to say: their sentences are clear on their face, and do not need further interpretive work in order to reveal their meaning. The sentences that make up such texts are to be used as a guide in the interpretation of those that make up all other texts. The distinction thus establishes a hierarchy of sacred texts, and so also a hierarchy within *buddhavacana* itself. Some utterances of Buddha do not mean what they seem to say, and as a result need careful interpretive handling; some are prima facie clear (and binding). The latter govern and control the interpretation given to the former, though the former are no less *buddhavacana* than the latter.

This distinction was brought into being partly for polemical purposes, most especially as a conceptual tool by which Mahāyāna Buddhists could hold together an acknowledgment that Sūtras containing claims that contradict Mahāyāna views are nonetheless sacred texts, containing authoritative words of Buddha, with the assertion that the views contained in such texts are not to be taken literally. But it also has deep roots in Buddhist doctrinal discourse, since there is much in basic

Buddhist doctrine that requires such a distinction. Important here is the no-self doctrine, which requires that utterances using personal proper names and personal pronouns be taken as requiring further interpretation: they are *neyārtha*.

This third point of refuge permits (and perhaps requires) almost unlimited interpretive activity, activity constrained only by the surface grammar of the sentences being interpreted. So, for example, it is often said that although Buddha used such terms as 'person' (*pudgala*), 'being' (*sattva*), and 'human being' (*puruṣa*), this language is not to be taken at face value, whereas Buddha's use of terms such as 'emptiness' (*śūnyatā*) is.[53] Purely doctrinal decisions therefore appear prior to and controlling of decisions about which texts are *nītārtha* and which *neyārtha*. If this is right, the rule of interpretation under discussion here may be rephrased thus: all assertions made in authoritative texts or by authoritative persons that do not appear to the community consonant with its doctrinal system are to be interpreted in such a way as to make them so appear. This provides a new perspective upon the rules of recognition discussed above. There, it was said that whatever is well spoken is Buddha's word; here, it is claimed that whenever putative utterances of Buddha appear to some community not to be well said, not to conform to its own doctrinal system, its own tenets, they must be capable of an interpretation that makes them so conform.

Such a rule of interpretation necessitated the development of complex theories about Buddha's intentions in speaking nonliterally, and a battery of technical terms was developed to label these intentions; *abhiprāya* and *abhisandhi* are the most prominent among these.[54] For my purposes here it will suffice to say that the application of this rule will not usually create any difficulty in understanding what it is that some specific community is asserting by means of its doctrine-expressing sentences; it will be of interest primarily for those concerned to see how such a community handles those sentences whose plain meaning it does not wish to assert.

The fourth and final rule of interpretation mentioned in the classical fourfold formula is that one should pay attention finally not to one's discursive understanding of one's doctrine-expressing sentences, but rather to one's direct nondiscursive awareness of what those sentences mean. The digests make play here with a distinction between *vijñāna*, here translated 'discursive understanding,' and *jñāna*, here translated 'direct awareness.' The terms are derived from the same verbal root, but the prefix *vi-* has a distributive sense, and thus connotes a kind of awareness that classifies and categorizes its objects by applying verbal designations to them, and so by sorting them into classes and kinds. This contrasts with *jñāna*, which need employ none of these methods to become aware of its objects, and which is, as I shall show at some length in chapter six, the kind of awareness paradigmatically possessed by Buddha. But taking this fourth rule seriously would require moving altogether outside the sphere in which language operates, and so also outside the sphere of scholarly activity. It is an ancient and standard Buddhist claim that the attainment of true wisdom somehow transcends language, and that the sphere of discursive awareness in which doctrine-expressing sentences necessarily have their being, although essential, is significant primarily because the claims made in that sphere are instrumentally effective in producing nondiscursive awareness (*jñāna*). I shall pay some attention to this and associated claims in chapter six, but I do not consider this fourth rule of interpretation to place what Buddhists do with their doctrine-expressing sentences outside the scope of discursive analysis. It merely points to the fact that communities upon which these rules of interpretation were binding did not think that everything of significance about their doctrines was amenable to such analysis; and this is in itself an interesting claim with doctrinal force.

The emphasis given in these rules of interpretation to the need for and importance of doctrinal activity, to the necessity of drawing out and making explicit implicit meanings, suggests another contrast with non-Buddhist śāstric practice. Pollock's work emphasizes the importance of primordiality and changelessness in that discourse, a stance that reduces (in theory, not of course in practice) the importance of interpretive work on the sentences that constitute it. Buddhist rules of interpretation, by contrast, require such activity, positively validate it, and so also positively validate arrival at new understandings of the doctrine by interpreters. This is not to say that the digests would be happy with the idea that the doctrine itself changes; to the contrary, it has all the predicates of eternality, primordiality, and changelessness that Pollock sees in non-Buddhist śāstric practice. But new ways of handling it are not only allowed but required by the rules of interpretation discussed here.

Pollock connects the emphasis given by non-Buddhists to the primordiality and changelessness of śāstric codifications with the dominance, philosophically speaking, of *satkāryavāda*, the theory that effects are already present in their causes. Similarly, for non-Buddhists, all knowledge in the proper sphere of relevance is already present in the transcendent and primordial *śāstra*. Buddhists, by contrast, are almost never adherents of *satkāryavāda* (although in chapter seven I shall suggest reasons for doubting the universal application of this claim). For them, as a rule, effects are produced by causes by way of real modifications, a classical formulation of which view is given in the *pratītyasamutpāda* formula. In terms of theorizing about *śāstra*, then, it is perhaps not surprising that more scope is allowed by Buddhists than by non-Buddhists for the modification of *śāstra* according to time and circumstance.

In sum, my objects of study are, according to their own self-understandings, authoritative and systematic collections of doctrine-expressing sentences, proper and properly salvific presentations of Buddha's word. These sentences were taken by those who constructed, elaborated, and defended them to be consonant with—indeed, entailed by a proper understanding of—what is said in the sacred texts, and to be consonant with the way things are (though not to exhaustively describe or reflect the way things are; this is not a capacity possessed by language according to these texts). Many of these artifacts have a good deal to say about Buddha, and to that discourse I now turn.

Chapter 3

Buddhalogical Doctrine

3.0 Prolegomena

I have suggested that the formal definition of doctrine-expressing sentences offered in chapter one can profitably be used to pick out some Buddhist phenomena. In chapter two I established, descriptively, that there were in India certain Buddhist discursive practices whose central concern was with the construction, systematization, and defense of just such phenomena: sentences (*vākya*) whose formal properties make it proper to call them doctrine-expressing sentences as defined in chapter one. I further suggested that these discursive practices typically issued in the production of texts of a peculiar and technical kind called *śāstra;* such texts will form the basis of this study.

In this chapter I shall make some preliminary comments about a particular kind of doctrinal discourse found within these texts, a discourse concerned with the properties or attributes (*guṇa, dharma, lakṣaṇa*) of Buddha. I shall call the products of this discourse buddhalogical doctrines. I begin by offering a preliminary and formal analysis of the kind of intellectual enterprise evident in the construction of these doctrines. This analysis will be offered at first without exegetical support, as a guide to understanding the material to be discussed in the remainder of this chapter, and in those following.

Then, I shall offer some observations on the methods used by Buddhist theorists to engage in this doctrinal enterprise, and on what these methods reveal about the kind of enterprise it is.

It is here that, in a preliminary way, the exegetical support for the formal analysis offered at the outset will be found. Finally, I shall say something about the place that buddhalogical doctrine has within the broader context and structure of the doctrinal digests.

3.1 Buddhalogy and Maximal Greatness

Immanuel Kant suggested that human beings need an idea of highest perfection in order to have a standard to apply in making determinations of an axiological kind.[1] Kant appears to have thought that this was a general and universal feature of human reasoning, and that he could show, transcendentally, all determinate judgments about truth or value to be made in terms of such an idea. This may be so. I use the claim here only as a starting-point for the suggestion that buddhalogical doctrine may usefully be thought of as an attempt to construct a notion of something maximally great, a systematic attempt to define and list those properties that something must have in order, within the constraints of Buddhist metaphysics, to be maximally great, and so also as the basis for and fullest representation of, Buddhist axiological commitments. As Kant puts it, the *ens realissimum* would both exclude every deficiency and include all realities.[2]

This is an entirely formal definition. The term 'greatness' has not been given content, and is intended here only to pick out that in virtue of which some community decides to attribute properties to the object of its attempt to limn maximal greatness. Properties that a community decides to predicate of a possessor of maximal greatness will then necessarily be, for that community, great-making properties. A possessor of maximal greatness will possess the largest possible set of these properties, and will possess each member of the set to the greatest degree possible (in the case of those great-making properties that admit of degrees; where gradations are inadmissible the possessor of maximal greatness will simply possess, coherence permitting, the great-making property in question). This definition, like that of doctrine offered in chapter one, is linked to the perceptions and conceptual schemes of communities: it can be given substance only by looking at cases, and I attempt such a look in the rest of this book.

If there are any transcultural universals in the sphere of religious thinking it is probable that among them is the attempt to characterize, delineate, and, if possible, exhaustively define maximal greatness. This tends to be done by listing, developing, refining, and arguing about just which attributes any possessor of maximal greatness must possess in order to be such. Debates within Christian theological circles about whether, for example, God is atemporal often deal with surface issues such as the logical problems created by asserting God's atemporality, or the hermeneutical problems created by denying it. But they actually tend to rest upon deeper intuitions about whether atemporality is a proper attribute for a maximally great being to possess. So also, *mutatis mutandis,* for debates about whether and in what sense it is proper to say that Buddha is omniscient. Such deeper intuitions are deeper not in the sense that they are more profound or more important than the surface logical and hermeneutical issues; they are deeper only in the sense that they operate at a level of the individual's or tradition's psyche that is difficult of access and that almost always appears only in the subtext of those texts that openly debate such questions as God's atemporality or Buddha's omniscience. Philosophers from all cultures tend not to discuss openly whether and why the attribute of atemporality contributes to maximal greatness; it is usually perfectly obvious to those moving within a particular tradition of reasoning that it does (or that it does not). The overt debate then centers upon whether an account of the attribute in question can be given that is both internally coherent and consistent with other claims whose truth the tradition holds dear.

I suggest, in sum, that it will be useful and illuminating to think of the buddhalogical enterprise as an example of thinking motivated by the desire to limn maximal greatness, and that the constraints upon such an enterprise will turn out to be, broadly, those provided by the metaphysic of the system within which particular instances of buddhalogical thinking occur; more narrowly, the constraints will be those provided by the rules of recognition and interpretation operative in the community.

3.2 Titles and Epithets of Buddha

From the beginning Buddhists have honored Buddha with titles of dignity and power, and with epithets showing why Buddha is worthy of these titles. Not least among these is the term 'Buddha' itself, a title meaning simply 'awakened' which, though probably first used as an honorific by non-Buddhists, soon became the most basic and widely used title for all those beings who, like Gautama Śākyamuni in India 2,400 years or so ago, were taken to have penetrated to the reality of things, and so to have gone beyond suffering. Long before the period in which the doctrinal digests were composed, these titles and epithets began to be put together into standardized lists, lists that appear to have been intended by those who used them to make available in summary form the most important properties of Buddha. The condensation of the many titles of Buddha into relatively brief standardized epithet-lists was one of the most important ways in which early buddhalogical thought developed; and while it is not central to the buddhalogy of the doctrinal digests, it will be useful to pass the most important of these lists in brief review here, since it shows very clearly the thrust toward maximal greatness, as well as giving some hint of what, substantively, counted as great-making properties for Buddhist theorists.

The list I have in mind runs like this. Buddha is (1) thus-gone (*tathāgata*); (2) worthy (*arhat*); (3) fully and completely awakened (*samyaksambuddha*); (4) accomplished in knowledge and virtuous conduct (*vidyācaraṇasampanna*); (5) well-gone (*sugata*); (6) knower of worlds (*lokavid*); (7) unsurpassed guide for those who need restraint (*anuttaraḥ puruṣadamyasārathiḥ*); (8) teacher of gods and humans (*śāstā devamanuṣyānām*); (9) awakened (*buddha*); and (10) blessed (*bhagavat*).[3]

The first epithet in this list, *tathāgata* or 'thus-gone,' is difficult to translate for two reasons. The first is the ambiguity of the Sanskrit word. It can be analyzed to mean 'thus gone' (*tathā*

+ *gata*), 'thus-come' (*tathā* + *āgata*), or 'thus-not-gone' (*tathā* + *agata*), and all of these interpretations are found in Buddhist texts. In addition to this ambiguity, which is an occasion for rich and creative gloss and comment, there is the difficulty of deciding just what *tathā*—'thus,' 'in such-and-such a way'—means in this context. The most common glosses on this part of the word suggest that it connotes accuracy or precision, in which case *tathāgata* would mean 'gone (or: come) in just the right way.'[4]

Tathāgata, like Buddha and unlike *bhagavat*, is a title given only to fully awakened ones: only Buddha is called *tathāgata*, and only *tathāgata* is called Buddha. The term occurs, on the whole, with much less frequency than either Buddha or *bhagavat* in the doctrinal digests; generally, in so far as it has semantic content—that is, in so far as it is used as an epithet and not just as a title whose sole function is to pick out Buddha—it is understood to describe something that has changed its location, and so also its status, condition, and salvific meaning, in some maximally significant way.

If taken to mean 'thus-gone,' *tathāgata* denotes one who has followed the salvific path to its end and as a result has gone beyond suffering and arrived at Nirvana. If taken to mean 'thus-come,' it denotes one who has come from some heavenly realm in order to teach and engage in other actions for the benefit of living beings. And if taken to mean 'thus-not-gone,' it denotes one who has, although having gone beyond suffering and entered Nirvana, not left the world behind, not gone to a place that would make it unavailable to the world and those who suffer within it. In all cases, the title suggests its holders' maximal attainments and maximal salvific significance for others. The fifth epithet in the tenfold list, *sugata*, 'well-gone,' may be assimilated to *tathāgata*, since this too uses the metaphor of going, and *su-*, like *tathā*, is a generalized term of approbation. To have gone 'well' is to have gone 'just so,' to have gone precisely as one should; and the most common gloss on *su-* in this context is precisely Nirvana.[5]

The second epithet in the list, *arhat* or 'worthy one,' is, like *bhagavat* and unlike Buddha and *tathāgata*, not limited in its application to those who have become completely awakened. In fact, as the Mahāyāna polemics against the so-called Hīnayāna developed in India, it would sometimes be used almost as a term of abuse, and certainly as a term that picks out a class of beings inferior to Buddha in important respects. This is especially evident in the *Lotus Sūtra*.[6] But when it is used as a title for Buddha it is taken by the digests to indicate both Buddha's worthiness to receive the homage (*pūjārhatva*) and offerings of non-Buddhists,[7] and, using a different etymology, Buddha's success in killing (*han-*) the enemies (*ari*) to awakening.[8]

The third and ninth epithets—'fully and completely awakened' (*samyaksambuddha*) and 'awakened' (*buddha*)—may be taken together. In both the concern is with awakening (*bodhi*), the possession of which is what defines Buddha both semantically and etymologically. The reference to full and complete awakening in the fourth epithet is one more example of the thrust toward maximality in the attribution of properties such as this to Buddha. Being awakened (*buddha*) is a great-making property, which is to say that to have it is better than not to have it: if to be awakened is to be made great, then to be fully and perfectly awakened (*samyaksambuddha*) must be to be made maximally great; hence Buddha must be that, too. What then is it that Buddha awakens to? Briefly, awakening consists, according to the digests, in a complete transformation of the cognitive and affective condition of the one who wakes up; sleep-waking imagery runs like a thread through the digests.[9]

The very existence of an epithet like *samyaksambuddha* (which is sometimes coupled with the superlative 'unexcelled,' *anuttara*) suggests, though, that there is more than one kind of Buddha. For if all those to whom the title 'Buddha' was applied were thought to be unexcelled in their awakening, there would have been no need to develop and apply the title *samyaksambuddha*. And it is certainly the case that there is mention in the digests of awakened ones who are not *samyaksambuddha*, most often of *pratyekabuddhas* or 'individual Buddhas,' those who are awakened but who differ from *samyaksambuddhas* in that they do not perform the teaching functions of the latter, and so do not possess the same degree of salvific significance.[10] The epithet *buddha*, then, when not further qualified, will here be understood to mean *samyaksambuddha*. This is also the way in which it is usually taken by the digests.

The fourth epithet in the tenfold list—'accomplished in knowledge and virtuous conduct' (*vidyācaraṇasampanna*)—introduces a new theme. Buddha is here said to have become fulfilled, completed, perfected, or accomplished in certain cognitive and active virtues. *Vidyā*, 'knowledge,' is largely a cognitive term, opposing such undesirable conditions as *avidyā* (ignorance) and *ajñāna* (lack of awareness), and to say that Buddha has become perfected or accomplished in it strongly suggests that Buddha knows everything that should (or can) be known, all possible objects of awareness (*jñeya*). Once again, exactly what it is that Buddha knows will depend upon the metaphysical system in which the claim that Buddha is accomplished in knowledge is made. But the thrust toward showing Buddha to be maximally great is evident here too: to say that Buddha is accomplished in knowledge is just to say that Buddha has a great-making property and has it to the greatest extent possible. The digests differ in identifying what Buddha's *vidyā* consists in: sometimes they say that it is the 'three knowledges,' whose objects are previous lives (*pūrvanivāsa*), death and rebirth (*cyutyupapada*), and the destruction of the defilements (*āsravakṣaya*);[11] and sometimes they say that it is 'perfectly accurate philosophical view' (*samyagdṛṣṭi*), one of the eight limbs of the path to awakening.[12] But whatever specific identification is made, it is clear that the digests intend users of this epithet to understand that Buddha's knowledge is unsurpassably great.

So also with the other part of this fourth epithet: to be 'accomplished in virtuous conduct' (*caraṇasampanna*) is just to have done—or to timelessly be doing; there are, as I shall show, some problems with attributing action in time to Buddha—all those actions the community thinks of as virtuous. Just what these are will be discussed in chapter four; but it should be clear already that most of them will have to do with the liberation of living beings from suffering: Buddha's virtuous conduct is paradigmatically salvific, and just as the digests sometimes identified Buddha's knowledge with one of the eight limbs of the path to awakening, so they also identify Buddha's virtuous conduct with the other seven.[13]

This point is also made with the seventh and eighth epithets—'unsurpassed guide for those who need restraint' (*anuttaraḥ puruṣadamyasārathiḥ*) and 'teacher of gods and humans' (*śāstā devamanuṣyāṇām*). These descriptions of Buddha as teacher and religious guide, while leaving unspecified just what is taught and what kind of religious guidance is provided, make it very clear that Buddha fulfils these functions to a maximal degree.[14] Buddha is unsurpassed (*anuttara*)—an explicit superlative—as guide, which means among other things that Buddha can provide religious discipline (*vinaya*) even for those who are apparently among the most recalcitrant (the notorious Aṅgulimāla, a mass murderer and collector of human fingers—his name means 'garland of fingers'—is often mentioned in this connection); and Buddha teaches not just human persons but also divine ones. This is maximal greatness as teacher and guide.

The sixth epithet, 'knower of worlds' (*lokavid*), like 'accomplished in knowledge,' is an explicitly cognitive epithet, and stresses the extent of Buddha's knowledge: it is limited only by the extent of the cosmos within which it ranges.[15] There are connections with the idea that Buddha has a *kṣetra,* a field of operations,[16] a matter to which I shall return in chapter five.

The list closes with the epithet 'blessed' (*bhagavat*), perhaps the most common and the most devotionally important epithet applied to Buddha. It gives dignity and honor to its possessor, indicating that such a one is worthy of acts of reverential homage (*namaskāra*) and praise. It is often used in the digests together with 'Buddha' to form the single expression 'blessed Buddha,' and when this is done the connection with reverential homage is often made explicit.[17] The etymology of the word *bhagavat* is important for coming to understand what it means as an epithet of Buddha. The digests give two etymologies, one from the root *bhaj-*, meaning 'to share in' or 'to partake of,' and the other from *bhañj-*, meaning 'to rout, shatter, put to flight.'[18] Following the first etymology, *bhagavat* means 'one who possesses a share in,' and is often used in non-Buddhist texts as an epithet of the *yajamāna,* the sponsor of the sacrifice who, in virtue of his sponsorship, 'shares in' or 'partakes of' the merit that comes from performing the sacrifice. As partaker in the sacrifice the *yajamāna* is fortunate, auspicious, meritorious, or, more broadly, blessed. The term is also used as an epithet of various deities, especially of Krishna, and a derived term, which helps to give something of the flavor of *bhagavat*, is *saubhāgya*—welfare, good luck, auspiciousness, beauty. In this last sense *saubhāgya* is often applied to women of great beauty. Buddha, as blessed one, is thus both auspicious and beautiful. If the second etymology is used (it is reflected in the Tibetan translation *bcom ldan 'das*), then Buddha as blessed one has routed or put to flight all obstacles; the meaning of this reading is effectively the same that of *arhat* when derived from *ari* + *han*, meaning 'enemy-killer'.

The digests typically make use of both etymologies in the service of their conclusion that Buddha as blessed one is to be praised because it is completely accomplished or perfected (*sampat*) both in those things that benefit itself, and in those things that benefit others. That is, blessed Buddha has removed or overcome everything that hinders or obstructs its own awakening, and is perfected in its ability to act salvifically toward others—to, as one of the digests picturesquely puts it, "lift the cosmos out of the slime of Samsara" (*saṃsārapaṅkāj jagad ujjahāra*).[19] These facts about Buddha warrant the attribution to it of both the epithet *bhagavat* and the praise and homage that go with it. Buddha considered as the blessed one, the ultimately auspicious one, the one whose good qualities are unparalleled in extent and kind, is also the one who is the most worthy recipient imaginable of praise and homage.

This rapid survey of some of the more important epithets and titles given to Buddha is meant to provide some preliminary textual and exegetical support for my suggestion that buddhalogical discourse can properly be understood as an attempt to sketch the properties that a possessor of maximal greatness should have, and to say that such a possessor has them maximally. It is clear that the epithet-lists can be understood in this way, and it is illuminating to do so, for it suggests a connection between the listing of epithets, at which we have just been looking as the first stage in buddhalogical thinking, and the attempt to provide systematic and ordered lists of Buddha-properties (usually called *buddhaguṇa,* though sometimes also *buddhalakṣaṇa*), which is entirely characteristic of the doctrinal digests. The same motive drives the construction of epithet-lists and property-lists, and the elaboration of some of the Buddha-properties in the doctrinal digests can be seen straightforwardly as an attempt to work out what is implied by the epithets that are so deeply rooted in the tradition.

But the lists of Buddha-properties come from a different world of thought. While the atmosphere of devotion to and reverence for Buddha is just as strong in them as it was in the epithet-lists, and while the property-lists are sometimes presented in a series of verses each of which ends with a reverential vocative of address to their possessor (*namo 'stu te!,* "homage to you!"), there is nonetheless a level of systematic and detailed presentation not found in the impressionistic epithet-lists. We are told not just that Buddha is accomplished in knowledge and virtuous conduct, but also just what Buddha knows and what Buddha does; we are told not just that Buddha is fearless, but what Buddha is fearless about and why; and we are told not just that Buddha is compassionate, but on what Buddha's compassion is based, what its objects are, and what the causes and conditions that govern its operation are. If the epithet-lists limn maximal greatness with the ornamental colors of reverential Sanskrit rhetoric, then the property-lists provide a systematic substructure upon which the epithets can rest secure.

3.3 *Properties of Buddha*

There are many lists of Buddha-properties in the digests. I shall discuss the most common one, found complete in some of them and fragmentarily in others, and shall call this the standard list.[20] This standard list is enumerated and divided differently in different digests. The division, enumeration, and analysis given in the comments that follow do not reproduce exactly those given in any one of the digests, though the broad outline is the same in all of them. Some of the members of this list will be taken up in more detail in subsequent chapters; my purpose here is only to provide a schematic outline, together with the beginnings of an analysis.

I take the sentences claiming that Buddha has these properties to be strictly doctrinal according to the analysis given in chapter one. They are taken by the digests to meet the proper rules of recognition; they describe some (maximally important) features of the setting of human life by predicating properties of a salvifically important aspect of it; and they are binding upon the intellectual life of the community in so far as no properly buddhalogical discourse is undertaken by its representatives without adverting to these sentences.

Here is the list with brief explanatory comments:

1. Buddha has the four immeasurable states (*apramāṇa*) of friendliness (*maitrī*), compassion (*karuṇā*), joy (*muditā*), and equanimity (*upekṣā*), which means that Buddha possesses these desirable attitudes toward all living beings without limit—hence 'immeasurables.'

2. Buddha has mastered the eight liberations (*vimokṣa*), the eight spheres of mastery (*abhibhvāyatana*), and the ten spheres of totality (*kṛtsnāyatana*). These are altered states of consciousness of various kinds, produced by particular meditational techniques.

3. Buddha has noncontentiousness (*araṇā*), which is to say that it does not arouse contentious passions in others with itself as their object; this means that Buddha does nothing to make living beings passionate or deluded about Buddha.

4. Buddha possesses an awareness (*jñāna*) that comes from vows (*praṇidhi*) undertaken in the past.

5. Buddha possesses four kinds of specific understanding (*pratisamvit*): understanding of doctrine (*dharma*), of meaning (*artha*), of grammar and lexical intension (*nirukti*), and of eloquence (*pratibhāna*).

6. Buddha possesses six kinds of supernatural awareness (*abhijñā*), including the ability to see and hear what is happening at a distance; to have direct knowledge of the minds of others; to recollect its own past lives and those of others; and to know that its own defilements are destroyed.

7. Buddha possesses the thirty-two major defining characteristics (*lakṣaṇa*) and the eighty minor marks (*anuvyañjana*) of a great person (*mahāpuruṣa*). These are mostly physical characteristics: marks on, or other physical properties of, Buddha's physical body.

8. Buddha possesses four kinds of purification (*pariśuddhi*): of basis (*āśraya*) or body, which means the ability to appear in, or as, any body whatever; of mental object (*ālambana*), which means the ability to control the kinds of image that may occur in its consciousness; of mind (*citta*), which indicates mastery over any and all meditational techniques; and of discernment (*prajñā*), which comes in the end to mean omniscience.

9. Buddha possesses ten powers (*bala*), which are abilities that issue from various kinds of knowledge or awareness. The ten kinds of awareness mentioned here occur also in some of the other items in the list of Buddha-properties. So, for example, the second kind of awareness in this tenfold list—"the awareness of meditations, liberations, concentrations, and attainments" (*dhyānavimokṣasamādhisamāpattijñāna*)—covers essentially the same ground as that covered in item two above; and the last three kinds of awareness in this tenfold list are identical with those of the six kinds of supernatural awareness mentioned in item six.

10. Buddha has four kinds of fearlessness or confidence (*vaiśāradya*). These confidences have to do with Buddha's own condition as an awakened one, and with its teaching of the path that will lead others to attain a

similar awakening. Thinking that full awakening might not have been reached, or that some error might have been made in teaching, is not possible for Buddha.

11. Buddha is guardless (*arakṣa*) in three ways: that is, its physical, verbal, and mental actions do not need to be consciously monitored or restrained in any way, for there is no possibility that it could ever engage in inappropriate or untoward action.

12. Buddha applies mindfulness or attention (*smṛti*) in three ways: that is, when Buddha teaches and the teachings are received with attention and understanding, Buddha is not enraptured on that account; neither is Buddha depressed when the opposite happens; nor does it have mixed emotions when the teaching's reception is mixed.

13. Buddha's propensities or tendencies (*vāsanā*) toward certain kinds of improper thought, speech, or action have been completely destroyed.

14. Buddha is not confused or deluded (*asaṃmoṣatā*) about what needs to be done for living beings: the right thing is always done at the right time and in the right way.

15. Buddha possesses great compassion (*mahākaruṇā*) for all living beings, compassion that governs all Buddha's actions for their benefit. This compassion is omnipresent and prevenient.

16. Buddha possesses eighteen properties that are exclusive (*āveṇika*) to Buddha. These comprise various perfections of action, attitude, and control; the list as given emphasizes the difference between Buddha's possession of these properties and that of advanced non-Buddhas.

17. Buddha is omniscient, possessed of *sarvajñatva*, *sarvajñāna*, or *sarvākārajñatā*.

18. Buddha has fulfilled the six perfections (*pāramitā*): giving (*dāna*), morality (*śīla*), endurance (*kṣānti*), zeal (*vīrya*), meditation (*dhyāna*), and discernment (*prajñā*).

Each element in this list has deep roots in the Buddhist tradition. Several of them, as is obvious from the brief summary given here, overlap significantly one with another, and there is no attempt within the list itself to structure or order the elements, much less to relate them systematically one to another. The commentarial discussions of the list do make such attempts, using second-order analytical and organizational schemata to sort out the grab-bag of properties mentioned in it, and to the more important among these schemata I shall turn below. Before doing that, however, I shall try to organize the elements of the list using my own scheme.

I suggest that the perfections predicated of Buddha in this list are of five kinds: Buddha has perfections of appearance, action, cognition, attitude, and control. Buddha's perfections of appearance are referred to principally in item seven of the list, in which its thirty-two major defining characteristics and its eighty minor marks are mentioned. I shall say more about these in chapter four. For the moment it must suffice to say that Buddha's physical appearance is here presented as maximally physically pleasing, which is to be expected of a maximally great being. Some of these physical perfections symbolize nonphysical perfections possessed by Buddha; and some are intended simply to engender devotion, confidence, and compassion in those who see them, and so to make religious practice possible.

Buddha, as described in the property-list, also possesses perfections of action. This means that Buddha's action is perfect in both extent and kind; that is, Buddha always does the right thing in the right way and to the right degree. This action is concerned, always and in every particular, with the liberation of living beings from suffering, and it arises from Buddha's great compassion (*mahākaruṇā*), which is treated as one of the most important among the Buddha-properties (items one and fifteen). A typical comment on this explains Buddha's compassion in this way:

thugs rje chen po ni . . . des su ni 'phel su ni 'grib/ su ni yongs su smin par bya ba yin/ su ni rnam par 'grol bar bya ba yin zhes bya ba la sogs par bcom ldan 'das nyin mtshan lan drug 'jig rten la so sor rtog go/ thugs rje chen po de yang 'jig rten thams cad la so sor rtog pa'i las can dang/ phan par bya ba'i bsam pa'i ngo bo nyid do . . . khams gsum pa'i sems can la dmigs pa dang/ sems can thams cad la mtshungs par 'jug pa dang/ de bas ches khyad par du 'phags pa med pa'i phyir ro/[21]

The blessed one, through its great compassion . . . closely examines the cosmos six times day and night [to see] who is making progress and who is backsliding, who is to be matured and who is to be liberated, and so forth. Great compassion is active in closely examining the entire cosmos; it consists essentially in aspiration for the well-being [of living beings] . . . it bears upon all living beings in the triple world, it functions equally for all living beings, and it is unsurpassed.

The phrase "six times day and night" is a periphrasis for 'constantly.' Buddha's compassion is thus that which motivates or permits Buddha to perceive what living beings need: it is the ground or possibility of its salvific action.

Allowing that Buddha's compassion is maximal (notice the "unsurpassed" in the extract translated above), and that it provides the basis for all Buddha's more specific salvific actions, it is important to emphasize that both this compassion and the actions it makes possible are spontaneous, occurring without effort, choice, or deliberation, just as a jewel is choicelessly and spontaneously radiant. This point is made in an enormous number of ways, both in the property-lists (items eleven, thirteen, and sixteen) and throughout the digests; it is significant because it shows that, for those engaged in this discursive practice, freedom and choice are not positive values when it comes to action: spontaneity is. Buddha's action is therefore perfectly spontaneous.

It follows from this that all Buddha's actions—the usual schematic analysis divides them into actions of body, speech, and mind—lack the property of being guarded, which means that they are not subject to the kinds of pragmatic calculation as to the possibility of impropriety or undesired result that usually dominate the actions of non-Buddhas. There is simply no possibility of such impropriety in Buddha's actions, or indeed of anything less than maximal good effect from them. This is mentioned explicitly in items ten and eleven.

So far I have mentioned only the ground for and the abstract attributes of Buddha's action; nothing has been said about the specific things that Buddha does. This is entirely in accord with what the property-lists do: they are concerned primarily with those attributes that all actions undertaken by Buddha must possess just in virtue of being such, and not with specific examples of such action. The digests do, of course, give (or at least mention) such details elsewhere, and I shall discuss them in chapters four and five.

Third, the property-lists represent Buddha as possessing various perfections of cognition. This means that Buddha's cognition is maximally great, which in turn means, as the property-lists explicitly say, that Buddha is strictly omniscient. Buddha is aware of all possible objects of awareness, and is aware of them without error or distortion of any kind. This property of Buddha is labeled *sarvajñāna*, 'awareness of everything,' or, more often in these texts, *sarvākārajñatā*, 'awareness of all modes of appearance' (item seventeen). A full discussion of what is meant by this difficult term will be given in chapter six, when I discuss the essential properties of Buddha as it is in itself. For the moment it will suffice to notice that the standard glosses on omniscience-terms in the digests are very clear in their claims as to the maximal greatness of Buddha's cognition. Being in possession of omniscience is to have attained an unexcelled place or position (*anuttarapada*), a "position of unexcelled awareness."[22] It is also that which makes possible, or grounds, Buddha's salvific actions: on the basis of this exalted cognitive condition Buddha acts for "the well-being of all living being" (*yatrasthaḥ sarvasattvānāṃ hitāya pratipadyate*).[23]

In addition to this emphasis on Buddha as omniscient, a number of items in the list of Buddha-properties describe specific kinds of knowledge or awareness possessed by Buddha. In fact, more items on the list deal with such things than with any other kind of Buddha-property: items four, five, six, parts of nine, fourteen, and part of eighteen all have to do with various aspects of Buddha's cognition. These will be treated in more detail in their proper places.

Fourth, Buddha has various perfections of attitude. By 'attitude' I mean partly affect—Buddha's affective condition is just as it should be (items one, twelve, fifteen, and parts of sixteen and eighteen)—and partly judgment. Under this latter head may be considered especially items ten, eleven, and twelve in the property-list. Buddha, we are told in item ten, is fearless or confident about its own condition and status, as well as about the efficacy of its teachings and instruction. This is clearly in part a matter of affect: Buddha is not troubled by inappropriate emotions, especially the disturbed state of worry about whether it has or has not fully and completely realized awakening. But it is also partly a matter of judgment: Buddha has made the judgment that there is nothing lacking in its status and teaching.

Similarly, item eleven says that Buddha is free from the attitudinal problem of having to guard its thoughts, words, and actions from anything less than maximal salvific effect, and, by implication, from malapropism or any offense against etiquette. This point has connections with the spontaneity of Buddha's action, and is extended by the texts quite explicitly to cover the most minor details of behavior. So, for example, in discussing item sixteen, one of the digests says:

> arhann ekadāraṇye pravaṇe 'nvāhiṇḍan mārgād apanaśya śūnyāgāraṃ praviśya śabdam udīrayati ghoṣam anuśrāvayati mahārutaṃ ravati/ vāsanādoṣaṃ vāgamya kliṣṭaṃ mahāhāsaṃ hasati dantavidarśakaṃ samcagdhitam upadarśati/[24]

> An *arhat,* traveling through the forest groves and losing his way, might enter an empty house and raise his voice, shouting loudly. Or, as a result of the defects of his propensities, he might laugh a great afflicted laugh, openly showing his grinning teeth.

None of this is possible for Buddha. Buddha does not need to guard itself against even relatively small breaches of etiquette.

Fifth, Buddha has perfections of control, perfections that involve the use of power to control and manipulate various mental and physical states. This control has in large part to do with Buddha's own mental and physical condition. So item two explains that Buddha is master of three sets of altered states of consciousness produced by specific kinds of meditational practice. These altered states of consciousness, together with their concomitant meditational practices, are expounded in great and technical detail in the digests. Here it will suffice to say that the eight liberations (*vimokṣa*) are enstatic altered states in which the practitioner progressively reduces the content of consciousness until it ceases altogether; the eight spheres of mastery (*abhibhvāyatana*) are altered states in which the practitioner learns to manipulate perception of physical forms, as also are the ten spheres of totality (*kṛtsnāyatana*). Buddha has complete mastery over all these.

Buddha also controls, through one of the four kinds of purification (*pariśuddhi*) mentioned in item eight, how and when it will appear as a physical body. This involves, as the digests typically put it, control over "taking up, dwelling in, and abandoning bodily supports" (*āśrayopadānasthānaparityāga*),[25] which means in turn that Buddha is born wherever it wishes and lives as long as it wishes, dying as, where, and when it chooses. Similar points are made about Buddha's control over what occurs in its consciousness when it is embodied. The need to assert Buddha's full control over its length of life, and to explain why Gautama Śākyamuni appeared to live only eighty years, were matters that greatly exercised those who composed the early Mahāyāna Sūtras.[26]

This matter of control needs to be understood in the proper context. It is not—even though the digests sometimes make it sound as if it were—principally a matter of decision or volition on Buddha's part. It is not that Buddha decides to exercise its control by entering a particular meditational state at a particular time, or by appearing as a particular body in some specific place. Rather, Buddha's control over these matters is precisely exhibited as its nonvolitional spontaneity in doing these things, a spontaneity that neither does nor can involve conscious decision. Nevertheless, control is a salvific virtue of central importance to the whole of Buddhism: uncontrolled greed, hatred, delusion, conceptual and linguistic proliferation (*prapañca*), and ignorance all have to be brought under control. Any maximally great being will have them perfectly under control; and Buddha is so represented in the property-lists.

I have organized and classified the properties in the property-lists under a fivefold scheme: Buddha is perfect in appearance, action, cognition, attitude, and control. This is not an indigenous classification, though I think it adequately and comprehensively represents what is said in the property-lists, and is more useful than the indigenous classifications for my purposes. But there are also indigenous classifications and analyses of the Buddha-properties, and to these I now turn.

3.4 Analytical and Organizational Schemata

There are two principal schemata used for the analysis and categorization of the Buddha-properties in the doctrinal digests. One is a sixfold set of categories used for the analysis of any concept whatever; the second is a threefold set of categories developed explicitly for the analysis of Buddha and its properties. The point of both sets is to provide a systematic conceptual structure for the analysis of Buddha's properties.

The set of six analytical categories occurs fairly frequently in the digests, and is generally used to give an analytical description of Buddha, or one of the other terms that the digests take to denote whatever is maximally great.[27] Applying the six analytical categories involves asking six questions of the object of analysis—in this case, Buddha. What is its essential nature (*svabhāva*), its cause (*hetu*), its result (*phala*), its activity (*karman*), the properties with which it is endowed (*yoga*), and its function (*vṛtti*)? I shall consider these in turn.

First, what of Buddha's essential nature? Two themes, woven together, are found in the digests' answers to this. The first is purity and the second is mastery. All the texts that make use of these six analytical categories play with variations on these themes when they come to analyze Buddha's essential nature.

Some do it concretely, with images; others do it abstractly, employing the precise technical vocabulary of their schools.

I consider the theme of purity first. One of the digests says that "Buddha's defining characteristic is the purification of the actuality of all things from the two obstacles: those of affliction and those which obstruct objects of awareness" (*kleśajñeyāvaraṇadvayāt sarvadharmatathatāviśuddhilakṣaṇaḥ*).[28] The technical term 'actuality' (*tathatā*) is the key here. It is an abstract noun denoting the way things really are, the true nature of things, and it is frequently used in the digests as a synonym for Buddha or Buddhahood;[29] the most common glosses on the term emphasize its unchangeability, using terms such as 'permanent' (*nitya*), or 'not subject to change' (*avikāra*), though there are also some glosses that emphasize not so much its permanence as its accurate mirroring or reflection of the way things are.[30] But even where actuality's unchangeability is stressed, it would be wrong to identify this unchangeability as a property of a monistic absolute—even though some of the language used about it sounds as though it should be understood in some such sense. Rather, phrases like "the actuality of everything" refer to those properties that all reals (*dharma*), according to Buddhist metaphysics, possess simply in virtue of being real. These are the *sāmānyalakṣaṇāni*, properties such as impermanence (*anityatā*), lack of self (*nirātmatā*), and unsatisfactoriness (*duḥkhatā*). The close connection of *tathatā* with these is evident by the frequent glosses on terms that explicitly mention one or more of them.[31] So to say that Buddha's essential nature is the purification of the actuality of all things is not necessarily to identify Buddha with a changeless monistic principle, but rather to make the first and most basic move in a game whose culmination makes Buddha coextensive with everything. Borrowing Lambert Schmithausen's characterization of actuality as a universal,[32] I should say that Buddha's essential nature when understood as pure actuality is to be the universal of all universals.

Buddha, understood as actuality, is not only the universal of all universals; it is also naturally pure and radiant (*prakṛtiprabhāsvara*),[33] shining like a wish-fulfilling gem (*cintāmaṇi*) that grants all desires immediately in virtue of its spontaneous purity.[34] It is this natural and spontaneous purity that makes possible the perfections of action and cognition described above. Buddha always and spontaneously does the right thing, and is, because of its natural radiance, always and spontaneously aware of everything that can be an object of awareness.

But there is something else implicit in this emphasis on Buddha as pure actuality: this is the idea that it is possible for actuality to be defiled, to stand in need of purification. This is the relevance of the mention of the two obstacles (*āvaraṇa*) in the quotation with which I began this discussion of Buddha's essential nature. The natural purity of actuality may be obstructed, prevented from functioning as it should, by both affective and cognitive obstructions. Affective obstructions can be summarized under the ancient triple division of improper affect as *rāga, dveṣa,* and *moha*—passion, hatred, and delusion. That Buddha, understood as pure actuality, is free from these has already been made clear in the brief comments offered above on Buddha's perfections of attitude. The cognitive obstructions, analyzed at length in all the digests, comprise all improper doxastic habits and false beliefs: to be free of all these is just to have realized the perfections of cognition that Buddha properly possesses. It is, in addition, to be omniscient, in a sense that will be made clear in chapter six.

The removal of obstructions to Buddha's natural purity and radiance is often summarized in the digests by the phrase "the radical reorientation of actuality" (*tathatāśrayaparivṛtti*).[35] Translating this compound is difficult. The English version I give is meant to be neutral as to whether the first two members of the compound (*tathatā* and *āśraya*) should be understood to have a genitive case-relation between them ('the basis of actuality'), or as two nouns in apposition ('the basis that is actuality').[36] Something of metaphysical importance hinges upon this apparently abstruse grammatical point, since if the former option is taken the suggestion is that actuality has a basis that is other than it, whereas if the latter, no such distinction is implied.[37] For my purposes at this stage the main point is that for actuality to be radically reorientated is precisely for the essential nature of Buddha to shine forth as a result of the removal of these obstructions; whether these obstructions were ever really other than this essential nature is an issue that I shall return to in chapter seven.

Coupled with this theme of purity is that of Buddha's mastery or control (*vas-*) over correct cognition. So, for example, we learn that Buddha's essential nature consists in inexhaustible mastery (*vaśitākṣaya*) over awareness (*jñāna*), an awareness that effortlessly conforms itself to its objects and that is free from error.[38] This dimension of Buddha's essential nature comprises all the properties I have classified as perfections of cognition, and some I have classified as perfections of control. Buddha's cognition is effortlessly and naturally radiant and accurate: using the rhetoric of paradox so dear to these texts, we may say that it is perfectly controlled just because it needs no conscious control. It is also universal in scope, a conclusion that springs directly from the identification of Buddha with actuality, which is in turn identical with everything. Some of the digests introduce at this point the image of the mirror (*ādarśa*) to describe Buddha's awareness. Mirror-awareness (*ādarśajñāna*) is one of the four kinds of awareness possessed by Buddha, the kind especially closely connected with Buddha's omniscience. I shall have much more to say about this in chapters six and seven.

So much for Buddha's essential nature. What then of Buddha's cause (*hetu*), which is the next item among the six analytical categories? This can be treated more briefly, since the digests typically refer here simply to the practice of the path as Buddha's cause.[39] It is as a result of hearing, thinking about, and meditating upon what is real that actuality is purified and Buddha is manifest. The digests sometimes connect Buddha understood as cause with another of Buddha's four kinds of awareness, that of 'equality' (*samatājñāna*). Buddha's cause, then, has to do with the methods appropriate to the removal of the obstacles mentioned above. It therefore lies properly outside the purview of this study, since I am concerned here mostly with Buddha's essential properties and functions, not with the means by which these were attained.

Buddha's result (*phala*, the third of the six categories) is the "complete indestructibility of the two provisions for all living beings" (*sarvasattvadvayādhānasarvathākṣayatā*).[40] These two provisions are happiness (*sukha*) and well-being (*hita*). The meaning is clear: Buddha is established as salvifically effective by completing the path. No specific properties or actions are included under this head. This is a simple formal statement of Buddha's maximally salvifically efficacious availability.[41] Naturally enough, many of the images of purity, spontaneity, and radiance already introduced when discussing Buddha's essential nature make their appearance in the digests once again when Buddha's result is analyzed. So we read:

> hrada iva vimalāmbuḥ phullapadmakramaḍhyaḥ
> sakala iva saśaṅko rahuvaktrād vimuktaḥ/
> ravir iva jaladādikleśanirmuktaraśmir.[42]

> [Buddha is] like a lake of pure water that gradually becomes filled with flowering lotuses;
> Like the full moon released from Rahu's jaws;
> Like the sun, whose rays have been released from obscuration by such things as clouds.

The point is that Buddha's essential nature, which it has always possessed, here becomes apparent, manifest, salvifically available. It does so gradually, as the adventitious defilements obstructing it are removed.

Just as Buddha's essential nature and cause were connected with specific kinds of awareness, so too is Buddha considered under the third of the six analytical categories, that of result (*phala*). The awareness in question here is *pratyavekṣaṇakajñāna*, an awareness that differentiates among the various needs of living beings by careful observation of them. This kind of awareness, like the mirror-awareness with which Buddha's essential nature was identified, accurately perceives and cognizes all that can be perceived and cognized; but it does so differently. Unlike mirror-awareness, it is differentiated, apparently being aware of and reacting to specific and conventionally separable and individuatable events.[43] Awareness of this kind is a necessary condition for Buddha's action, since when Buddha acts in the world responses must (apparently) be made to specific events and specific needs: Buddha says one thing to Ānanda and another to Śāriputra, does one thing in Śravasti and another in Kusinagara. So, Buddha thought of under the category of result is Buddha as Buddha is when Buddha's salvific action is ready to begin. The action itself is mentioned under the fourth of the six analytical categories, that of *karman*.

This is typically understood as that which liberates all living beings by showing them the unsatisfactoriness of Samsara, and so producing disgust for it; and by showing them the advantages of Nirvana, and so producing longing for it. Buddha's liberative actions of this type are undertaken with methods ideally appropriate to their recipients, and so are maximally effective.[44] The digests give many examples of these appropriate salvific actions, most of them employing the term *nirmāṇa*, meaning 'magical transformation.' So we are told that Buddha might choose to appear with Indra's or Brahma's body, appearing always in the guise that will be most beneficial to those who see, hear, taste, touch, or smell it. There are also more striking kinds of transformation mentioned: Buddha can transform its voice into that of Brahma, and can fill whole universes with it; it can also transform the voices of others—even of those who do not understand the doctrine—and can cause them to teach the Mahāyāna doctrine; and it can transform nonsentient things, such as the wind, into a voice preaching doctrine.[45]

Buddha's activity, like the first three of the six analytical categories, is also said to correspond to a specific kind of awareness, in this case the awareness that does what has to be done (*kṛtyānuṣṭhānajñāna*). It is this awareness that acts, this awareness that "is active for the benefit of all living beings in all realms, using a variety of inconceivable and immeasurable magical transformations" (*kṛtyānuṣṭhānatājñānaṃ nirmāṇaiḥ sarvadhātuṣu/ citrāprameyācintyaiś ca sarvasattvārthakārakam*).[46] Buddha's activity is thus coextensive with what I have called Buddha's perfections of action.

The fifth of the six analytical categories (*yoga*) concerns those properties that Buddha possesses. In discussing this, the digests simply refer to the property-list already mentioned in this chapter,[47] and so generally add nothing to what has already been said.

The sixth and final category, Buddha's function (*vṛtti*), is interpreted as referring to Buddha's economy, its different modes of operation in different cosmic realms and contexts. It is almost always glossed by reference to the operation of the threefold body of Buddha;[48] this is in some respects an independent set of analytical categories, a set that I shall use to structure my own analysis in chapters four through six. A detailed exposition will be found there; here I will only point to the general meaning of this threefold division. Buddha's first body, the real body or *dharmakāya*, is the basis and support (*āśraya*) of the other two. This body is identical with Buddha's essential nature (it is also called 'essence body' or *svābhāvikakāya*), and so properly possesses all the kinds of purity and mastery mentioned already. The real body is single, and all specific Buddhas are related identically to it: *svābhāvikaḥ sarvabuddhānāṃ samo nirviśiṣṭatayā*.[49] It does not change, is indivisible, and has no beginning or end in time. All this will be explored at length in chapter six.

This single real body can function as a 'body of communal enjoyment' (*sambhogakāya*), and when it does it is, by contrast, multiple. These bodies of communal enjoyment are differentiated by name: for instance, there is one called Amitābha and another called Vairocana. They are active in heavenly realms, usually called 'Buddha-fields' (*buddhakṣetra*), and these realms, too, may be differentiated one from another: some are decorated with precious stones of one kind, some with another; some contain living beings of one kind and some another. Bodies of communal enjoyment are accessible by the practice of visualization to those who do not live in such realms; in these heavenly realms Buddhas manifest some of their perfections of appearance, attitude, action, and control (a fuller exposition of all this is given in chapter five).

Buddha's single real body can also function as a 'body of magical transformation' (*nirmāṇakāya*): this is its third body, and it, like the bodies of communal enjoyment, is multiple. Gautama Śākyamuni is the paradigm for this world-realm and this age. All bodies of magical transformation have essentially the same career: they are born, they renounce the world, they attain awakening, they preach the doctrine, found the monastic community, teach, gather followers, and eventually die. But they differ in their names, their appearance, and the times and places in which they are born, live, and die. In its bodies of magical transformation, too, Buddha exhibits all five kinds of perfection, and it is here more than anywhere else that Buddha's *karman*, its activity, is fully manifest. (A more complete analysis of this will be given in chapter four.)

3.5 *Metaphysical Embeddedness and Systematic Location*

I suggested in chapter one that every particular doctrine-expressing sentence—and, *ex hypothesi,* every set of such—will be embedded in and given sense by a broader metaphysical, ontological, and epistemological context. If that suggestion is correct, this must be true also for buddhalogical doctrine, of which a first sketch has been made in this chapter. I want now to offer some brief comments on what this means in the case of buddhalogy, and to do so principally by showing where the doctrinal digests locate their buddhalogical discourse within the broader edifice of their doctrinal systems.

A preliminary and very general caveat is in order. No complete account of the metaphysical embeddedness of any particular set of buddhalogical doctrines is possible. An attempt at such an account would ramify rapidly into a vain attempt to give an account of everything—not just of the whole of Buddhist doctrine, but of everything in the strict and full sense. For a complete account of the embeddedness of buddhalogical doctrines would require a full account of Buddhist doctrine in general, which would require a full account of all Indic and other Asian thought, which would require . . . Drastic circumscription is necessary. This is all the more true when, as here, the doctrines under consideration claim as their sphere of relevance the actuality (*tathatā*) of everything (*sarvadharma*). Buddhalogical discourse very easily and very rapidly shades into Buddhist metaphysics in general, especially when we are told that among the synonyms for Buddhahood are *śūnyatā, dharmadhātu-viśuddhi, bhūtakoṭi,* and the like. Obviously, no substantive account of all this can be given.

But some useful formal comments are possible. The first is that buddhalogical doctrine in general—at least as presented in systematic form, as it is in the digests—appears in part as an attempt to provide a maximally coherent statement of the truth-conditions of claims that the community's intellectuals have always held as axioms. For example, as far as I can tell, the claim that Gautama Śākyamuni was not the only Buddha, not the only individual to whom the high honorific 'awakened one' should be applied, is very deeply rooted in the Buddhist intellectual tradition; if there was ever a time when it was not axiomatically known there is no longer any clear evidence of it. The same, I think, is true of the implicit understanding of Buddha as maximally great, maximally salvifically significant and efficacious. Recall the comments made above on the early epithet-lists.

Clearly, the truth-conditions of these two claims cry out for some elucidation. Are all Buddhas equally (that is, maximally) great? If so, how are the relations among them to be explained? In what do they differ, and why? If they are not all equally great, how are they to be ranked and ordered? It is not hard to see how attempts to deal with these questions, understood as attempts to deal systematically with the truth-conditions of axioms, could lead quickly to speculative system-building, culminating, among other things, in the three-body theory.

Another example of the same pattern of reasoning is evident in the attempt to provide an explanatory account that makes sense of the following claims: (1) *Buddha is possessed of perfect and complete awareness,* a claim entailed by a fairly straightforward argument from the axiom that having accurate awareness is a property contributing to greatness, and the axiom that Buddha is maximally great; both these axioms are either stated explicitly by the digests, or easily derived from others that are so stated. And (2) *Buddha once had to learn to speak.*

The second formal comment, already suggested above when I introduced the idea of maximal greatness, is that the best way to understand the metaphysical embeddedness of buddhalogical doctrine is to try and understand which properties are taken by a particular community to be great-making and (ideally) why. For if this can be done it will be easier to see why buddhalogical discourse takes the form it does. Some of these properties should already be evident from the sketch given in this chapter: purity, spontaneity, choicelessness, eternality, changelessness, and so forth. It is just at this point, of course, that talk about Buddha becomes generic metaphysical talk, just at this point, to put it buddhalogically, that the analysis of the *buddhaguṇa* becomes analysis of *dharmadhātuviśuddhi* or of *śūnyatāyāṃ śūnyatā*.

As should already be evident, not all buddhalogical doctrine is generically metaphysical in this way. Some is; and when it is it typically explains the observed facts or postulated necessities of Buddha's presence to and relations with non-Buddhas by appeal to some changeless metaphysical facts about the fabric of the cosmos. Many examples of this strategy will be found in the next three chapters. But buddhalogical doctrine as found in the digests is almost equally often put not metaphysically but rather soteriologically, and is couched in terms of the practice of the path and of the attainment of particular powers at particular stages upon that path. These soteriological explanations are constitutively and necessarily temporal: they appeal to the possibility of change over time, to the removal of afflictions and so forth, while the metaphysical explanations are, by contrast, constitutively and necessarily atemporal. There is a tension between these modes of expounding buddhalogical doctrine, a tension capable of resolution finally only in metaphysical terms; this will become clear in chapter six. But it will prove useful in reading chapters four and five to keep in mind this distinction between metaphysically and soteriologically orientated approaches to buddhalogical doctrine.

In chapter seven I shall attempt a strictly philosophical analysis of the axioms of whose truth-conditions buddhalogical discourse provides an explanatory account; chapters four through six, in their exegetical parts, will provide a fairly detailed statement of the intuitions as to what counts as a great-making property that appear to be operative in the digests. It remains now only to say something about the place that properly buddhalogical discourse has in the systematic structure of the digests.

First, and obviously, it needs to be said that not all the digests are concerned with the same subject-matter, and that they therefore do not all have the same structure. Most generally, the digests with which I am concerned here tend to be of two kinds: those whose primary concern is to give a systematic account of their school's metaphysic, and whose scope is thus truly universal; and those whose primary concern is to give a systematic exposition of the path to Nirvana, and whose structure is thus determined by the stages of that path. This is not by any means a rigid division. Metaphysical texts often (though not always) devote an *adhikāra*, a chapter or section, to the path; and path-texts will inevitably devote a good deal of attention to strictly metaphysical matters.

I consider the path-texts first (including those parts of the metaphysical texts concerned explicitly with the path). Matters here are relatively straightforward: since awakening (*bodhi*) is the proper culmination of the path, expositions of what it is to be Buddha and analyses of the properties that Buddha must have in order to be Buddha come naturally at the end of such texts. They form the culmination of the whole work.[50] The location of the analysis of Buddha at the end of a systematic text that is not structured around the stages of the path is also common,[51] and in these cases, too, the point of locating buddhalogical discourse at the end of the work is the same: the systematic exposition of the metaphysic is brought to a culmination and conclusion thereby.

Buddhalogical discourse does not, however, occur always at the end of the digests. Some of them—those not entirely structured around the stages of the path—treat the path as a small subsection of a broader scheme, and expound their buddhalogy at the end of that section.[52] There are also at least two digests whose buddhalogy is effectively impossible to separate from the rest of their content.[53]

The systematic location of buddhalogical discourse in the digests shows its centrality to them. It is the key to both their metaphysic and their soteriology, providing the grounding and the culmination of their systems. It is thus the supreme doctrine among all doctrines, the doctrine greater than which none can be conceived. Just as the *buddhabhūmi* lies at the end of the path, so buddhalogical doctrine is the high point, the *bhūtakoṭi*, of all Buddhist doctrinal thought.

Chapter **4**

Buddha in the World

4.0 Prolegomena

Buddha seems, from time to time, to be active as a human person in worlds like ours, worlds containing other human persons. This is a central tenet of all buddhalogical doctrine. In this chapter I shall describe, in some detail, the doctrines used by the digests to describe this activity. I shall restrict the inquiry to those things done by Buddha in historical time in worlds more or less like this one, "worlds with four continents" (*caturdvīpaloka*) as Buddhist cosmologists would put it. For practical purposes this means that I shall be talking about the actions of Gautama Śākyamuni in India between two and two and half millennia ago, as these are understood by the digests. But it should be remembered that these actions are a paradigm for all actions undertaken by Buddha in all worlds of this kind; and since these are uncountably many, the actions described below have occurred on innumerably many occasions in the past, and will occur again on innumerable occasions in the future.

4.1 The Buddha-Legend

A developed form of the Buddha-legend[1] underlies and is presupposed by everything the digests say about the actions of Buddha in the world. These texts do not retell the legend; their genre and their audience make that both inappropriate and unnecessary, since the former does not permit the extensive and discursive narrative that would be necessary to do so, and the latter was entirely familiar with the story in any case. But the legend is very much present in the subtext of these digests, and occasionally surfaces when controverted doctrinal questions are discussed. I shall therefore offer a brief reprise of it here. Although the legend has Gautama Śākyamuni as its principal object, it should be remembered that a story with identical structure—and often with identical details—could be (and was) told about every Buddha active in a world of the proper kind.

Buddha has had many previous lives, during each of which it has developed one or more of the perfections proper to it; this reference to past lives is an indispensable part of the frame of reference of the Buddha-legend. While waiting for the proper circumstances in which to be born in its last life, the Buddha-to-be is located in one of the heavenly realms (typically the Tuṣita or Akaniṣtha heaven), from which it can survey events in some four-continent world and see when the proper circumstances obtain for its entry into a woman's womb and its subsequent birth. The digests often say, as also occasionally do the narrative presentations of the Buddha-legend, that Buddha is present in a heavenly realm as a body of communal enjoyment (*sambhogakāya*—to be discussed more fully in chapter five) before its descent into a woman's womb, and so is already fully Buddha before the occurrence of any of the events that make up the typical life of a *nirmāṇakāya*, a body of magical transformation.

When these circumstances do obtain, the Buddha-to-be is conceived, in Gautama's case in the womb of Queen Māyā, and is eventually born, in miraculous fashion, from her side while she is standing up. The birth is accompanied by various miraculous events, including an earthquake, the cleansing of the Buddha-to-be's newly born body with streams of water from the heavens, and so forth. These miraculous signs are generally meant both to inculcate astonishment in the reader or hearer of the legend, and to dramatize the surprise of the cosmos at the exceedingly rare event of the beginning of Buddha's life in a four-continent world.

Immediately upon being born, the Buddha-to-be is capable of both walking and talking. His body (I use the masculine pronoun advisedly now, for the Buddha-legend always presupposes that Buddha is present and acts in a four-continent world in a male body) is marked from the beginning with the thirty-two major and the eighty minor marks of a great person (*mahāpuruṣa*); and in many versions of the legend his first acts are to take seven steps and to say: "I have been born for awakening and for the well-being of the world: this is my last birth" (*bodhāya jāto 'smi jagaddhitārtham antyā bhavotpattir iyaṃ mameti*).[2]

The Buddha-to-be grows to maturity in wealthy surroundings; attains mastery over all the arts, sports, and other accomplishments in which skill is expected of someone in his social class; marries; and has a son. He then gradually comes to feel revulsion toward the life of luxury into which his upbringing has led him, revulsion that culminates in renunciation of that life. This renunciation is followed by attempts to find the answer to the problem of suffering, attempts that include study and religious practice under the direction of several different teachers at different times, some of whom recommend severe asceticism, including starvation almost to death. Finally, dissatisfied with such methods, and with everything else he has been able to learn from others, the Buddha-to-be seats himself under a tree and resolves that he will not rise from this posture until he has realized awakening and so become Buddha.

This, in short order, he does, after fighting off the temptations of Mara, the evil one, and his legions. Buddha's realization of supreme, perfect awakening (*anuttarasamyaksambodhi*) is, like his conception, birth, and renunciation, an event marked by cosmic appreciation and astonishment. There are the usual and obligatory earthquakes, showers of flowers from the heavens, and so forth. Then, shortly after becoming Buddha, Gautama sets in motion the wheel of doctrine (*dharmacakra*) by preaching his first sermon, and spends the rest of his life teaching others what he had discovered when he became Buddha. During his teaching career he attracts large numbers of disciples, including kings and other individuals with political power; and, in providing for them and ordering their communal life, founds the monastic order, the sangha. In this way the triple jewel (*triratna*), also called the triple refuge (*triśaraṇa*), of Buddhism is established: Buddha, doctrine, and monastic community, understood as the supremely effective realities, the best protections from suffering, evil, and repeated death.

Finally, after many years of teaching as a mendicant, Buddha dies. More precisely, he enters *parinirvāṇa*, complete and final Nirvana, yet another event of cosmic significance marked by homage done to him by both gods and human persons. The relics of his physical body are then divided, and *stūpas*, or memorial mounds, built to house and honor them. These relics become one of the centers of the community's ritual life, one of the means by which Buddha is made present to and efficacious for faithful Buddhists (though not, as we shall see, the only one; and, doctrinally speaking, not the most important one).

This, in bare outline, is the legend. The digests presuppose it, and are concerned to give a doctrinal account of it, to provide a set of concepts that can be used to make sense of it in light of their entire doctrinal system. Chief among these is the concept of *nirmāṇakāya*, or body of magical transformation, and to the digests' doctrines about this I now turn. But before doing so it is worth noting that if the Buddha-legend is taken as the frame governing the construction of buddhalogical doctrine, that doctrine will inevitably be soteriologically, and so also temporally, ordered. That the buddhalogical doctrine of the digests is largely not so ordered is one of the reasons why the Buddha-legend has not only to be explained by them, but also explained away.

4.2 Bodies of Magical Transformation

Buddha's actions as a human person in worlds like this are, according to the digests, always to be understood as actions of a body of magical transformation (*nirmāṇakāya*).[3] This body does not, however, appear and function in the world only as a human person. The digests are quite clear that it can appear as a nonhuman animal, a hungry ghost (*preta*), and the like, in addition to its appearances as human persons.[4] In fact, it can appear as whatever is most salvifically beneficial in a particular case. Neither does a body of magical transformation have to exhibit all the characteristics of a Buddha-in-the-world as described in the Buddha-legend. In the Tibetan Buddhist traditions, at least, it is common to hear the title *sprul-sku* (a translation of *nirmāṇakāya*, perhaps more familiar in the form 'Tulku,' a transliteration intended to render the sound of the word in modern Tibetan speech rather than its spelling in classical Tibetan) given to important teachers, and certainly to exalted Lamas such as the Dalai Lama.[5] But it is difficult to be sure when this extension of the term was made, and since the digests almost always discuss the body of magical transformation in the context of a stereotyped presentation of the events of Gautama Śākyamuni's life, my discussion will also proceed in that context, without paying attention to the interesting doctrinal possibilities generated by Buddha's appearance in the world as a non-human.

In defining this body the digests usually offer a schematic outline of the Buddha-legend, sometimes saying no more than *janmādi* ("birth and so forth"), and sometimes providing something a little more extended, like this outline:

> sprul pa'i sku ni . . . dga' ldan gyi gnas na bzhugs pa nas gzung ste/ 'pho ba dang/ bltam ba dang/ 'dod pa la spyod pa dang/ mngon par 'byung ba dang/ mu stegs can gyi gan du gshegs pa dang/ dka' ba spyod pa dang/ mngon par rdzogs par byang chub pa dang/ chos kyi 'khor lo skor ba dang/ yongs su mya ngan las 'das pa chen po kun tu ston pa/[6]

> The body of magical transformation manifests: (1) living in and descending from its palace in the Tuṣita heaven; (2) being born; (3) hedonistic behavior; (4) going forth [from home to homelessness]; (5) meeting with infidels; (6) harshly ascetical behavior; (7) perfect awakening; (8) turning the wheel of doctrine; and (9) entering into great final cessation.

This outline predicates nine properties of the body of magical transformation, each referring to one of the key events in the

Buddha-legend. The first refers to Buddha descending from its dwelling in one of the heavenly realms into a woman's womb in a four-continent world like ours. Beginning the account of Buddha's actions in its body of magical transformation in this way has some interesting implications. It suggests that before being so conceived, Buddha was already Buddha. More exactly, it is Buddha active as a body of communal enjoyment in a particular heavenly realm who "descends" therefrom into a womb. So we read:

> gang gi tshe dga' ldan na bzhugs pa las/ sangs rgyas mngal du gshegs pa de bzhin du dus de nyid kyi tshe na/ gnas brtan shā-ri'i-bu la sogs pa 'khor 'di dag kyang de bzhin du sprul pa'i gnas skabs kyis de dang der bzhugs par blta bar bya'o/[7]
>
> it should be understood that just when Buddha left his dwelling in the Tuṣita [heaven] and entered his mother's womb, the circle of his disciples, Śāriputra and the rest, came to dwell there [that is, where Buddha is] through their magical transformations.

It is not only Buddha who is already awakened before being born as a body of magical transformation in a four-continent world. The same is true of all the chief disciples, those who received and transmitted the doctrine preached by that body of magical transformation. The complex set of events set in train by such a birth, then, is simply a set of appearances for the benefit of living beings; it is not what it seems to be.

The other eight properties predicated of the body of magical transformation in the extract translated earlier should need little explanation. Buddha is born (2), he practices "hedonistic behavior" (3), which means that he gets married, fathers a son, and indulges the pleasures of the flesh. He then abandons this worldly life (4), studies under some "infidels" (5), teachers of practices that are supposed to lead toward awakening but in fact do not, and as a result engages in harshly ascetical practices (6), which almost lead to his death. But eventually the body of magical transformation engages in the correct practices, attains perfect awakening (7), teaches the doctrine to others (8), and then dies (9).

The digests, in explaining the events of Gautama's career, often say that the manifestation of these events is caused by the power of distinguished or excellent awareness (*jñānaviśeṣa*), and that it consists solely in "representations" (*vijñapti*), "appearances" (*pratibhāsa*), or "reflections" (*pratibimba*) in the minds of others. Consider the following verses, the subject of which is Buddha's appearance in the world as a body of magical transformation:

> pratibhāsaḥ sa cātyantam avikalpo nirīhakaḥ/ evaṃ ca mahatārthena lokeṣu pratyupasthitaḥ//
> svacittapratibhāso 'yam iti naivaṃ pṛthagjanāḥ/ jananty atha ca tat teṣām avandhyaṃ bimbadarśanam//[8]

> This appearance is completely free from constructive thought and effortful action;
> Its occurrence in the world nonetheless brings great benefit.
> Ordinary people do not know that it is an appearance in their own minds;
> Nonetheless, their vision of [Buddha's] reflected image is of great use to them.

This makes still more explicit what has already been said. The events that constitute a body of magical transformation's life exist solely as experiences had by non-Buddhas; such events appear to others to happen, they occur as modifications in the streams of experience that constitute non-Buddhas; but that is all. So, for example, when Gautama preached his first sermon, the sermon in which the wheel of doctrine was turned for the first time, no change of any kind occurred in Buddha. Buddha does nothing new, but new experiences—"representations"—occur for those others who hear this sermon. In fact, a complete account of what happens when the first sermon is preached can be given in terms of modifications in the mental continua of its hearers; and this is true also for all events in the life of a body of magical transformation.

Even this point might require modification if, as was suggested earlier, Gautama's close disciples are also bodies of magical transformation. For then, presumably, neither Gautama's act of preaching nor the acts of hearing and praising undertaken by those disciples require, for their explanation, reference to anything other than modifications in the mental continua of others. The magic-show is extended, on this view, beyond the speech and action of Gautama to that of his greatest hearers.

An iconographic analogue for this philosophical view may be found in the fact that, as far as we can tell, early Buddhism was resolutely aniconic in its presentation of Buddha as a body of magical transformation.[9] Just as Gautama, understood as such a body, is not understood as a center of identity with character-traits, intentions, volitions, fears, hopes, and goals, so also he is not depicted in the early traditions as a person but rather as a significant absence—an empty space or a footprint—whose importance lies precisely and only in the effects he has upon those others to whom he appears to be present.

There are a number of philosophical reasons for presenting the career of a body of magical transformation in this way. Primary among them is the need, on the part of buddhalogical theorists, to avoid predicating change of Buddha. I shall defer a full exploration of this until chapter six, when I come to discuss Buddha in its real body (*dharmakāya*). Subsidiary to this is the need to avoid predicating intention or volition of Buddha, and so also the need to give a causal account of Buddha's (apparent) actions in the world in terms not of Buddha's needs, goals, or intentions, but solely in terms of the needs and desires of non-Buddhas. I shall return to this below when I come to discuss Buddha's action in the world in more detail, and especially when I offer an analysis of what the body of magical transformation does with food as a paradigm of such action. But before doing this it is important to say a little more about how the digests understand the relation between Buddha's many bodies of magical transformation and its single real body.

They say again and again that the bodies of magical transformation are based (*āśrita*) upon the real body.[10] This is taken to mean that the body of magical transformation is identical with the real body in its aspiration and action, which in turn simply means that it, along with the other two bodies, aspires only for the benefit of all living beings; and that it does only those things that will bring about such a result. But it differs from the real body (and from the bodies of communal enjoyment) in that it has properties the real body cannot have. This point is typically put in terms of a discussion of a number of impossibilities, a number of claims that do not make sense and so cannot coherently be made, and yet which would have to be made were, counterfactually, the real body and the bodies of magical transformation strictly identical in the sense of having all their properties in common.[11]

One example will suffice. One of the properties of all bodies of magical transformation is that they appear at certain points in their career to be both ignorant of certain facts and not in possession of certain skills. This is evidenced by the fact that in the Buddha-legend Gautama Śākyamuni is represented as having to learn basic skills such as reading and writing, which suggests that there was a time when he was, or appeared to be, illiterate. Such ignorance cannot be predicated of the real body since, as I shall show, that body is strictly omniscient. So we read: "It is not possible that those bodhisattvas who remember their previous births should not have complete understanding of writing, calculation, mathematics, and so forth" (*byang chub sems dpa' skye ba dran pa rnams ni yi dge dang/ rtsis dang/ grangs la sogs pa mi mkhyen pa ni mi rigs te*).[12]

This is a reductio argument: it is absurd to say that a Buddha-to-be, one who has practiced the path intensively for many lives to such good effect that he was living in an exalted and delightful palace in the Tuṣita Heaven immediately prior to his birth in a four-continent world, and who has reached such a stage of spiritual advancement that he can remember all of his previous lives, yet knows neither how to add two and two nor any of the many Sanskrit words for 'lotus.' And yet such things must in some sense be said, for it is integral to the Buddha-legend that the Buddha-to-be should pass through all the stages of life mentioned in the brief summary quoted earlier, including the stages, proper to human children, of ignorance about basic skills. This conundrum is resolved by denying that any properties suggestive of imperfection or ignorance are to be attributed to the real body in any way whatever, and by affirming that such properties may be predicated of the bodies of magical transformation, but only in the following manner: Buddha, in its bodies of magical transformation, seems to living beings to possess properties indicative of such imperfection if and only if there is benefit to such living beings in such seeming. Another way to understand such arguments, this time in terms of the distinctions made in chapter three, is to say that they show the move toward using atemporal metaphysical explanations to subsume temporal and soteriological ones.

It is this large—perhaps infinitely large—range of properties of apparent imperfection that differentiates Buddha in its bodies of magical transformation from Buddha in its real body. Another way of saying this is to say that all temporally indexed relational properties indicative of imperfection, all properties of the forms *seems to S to be possessed of imperfection I at time t,* belong to Buddha only in its bodies of magical transformation. Buddha in its real body has no relational properties at all (to be discussed further in chapter six); and Buddha in its bodies of communal enjoyment has relational properties, but none that indicate imperfection (to be discussed further in chapter five). The bodies of magical transformation, then, are unique in possessing the kind of property under discussion here; and this is the point made by the digests when they use reductio arguments to differentiate Buddha in the world from Buddha in its real body.

Further, it is I think defensible (though the digests do not put matters in quite this way) to say that the only properties Buddha has in its bodies of magical transformation that are of interest to the digests are apparently relational properties, properties of the form *seems to S to be P,* or, derivatively, properties of the kind *is caused by S to seem to S to be P*; and that these properties are further divisible into two kinds: seeming to be (or being caused to seem to be) possessed of imperfections of various kinds. This is indicated (though not stated) by the vocabulary used in the digests to describe the bodies of magical transformation. Verbs of appearance or manifestation are common, most often causatives of the root *dṛś-* (*sandarśayati, darśayati,* and the like), and such verbs necessarily require an object, someone or something for whom or to whom the appearance occurs; they thus indicate relational properties.

I am tempted to claim that such apparently relational properties are the only properties that Buddha can be said to have in its bodies of magical transformation. But this will not quite do, since such bodies have also the property of being identical in aspiration (*samāśaya*) with the real body and with the bodies of communal enjoyment, together with others of like kind. But such properties as these are not what interest the digests when they come to discuss the bodies of magical transformation: these bodies are of interest to them only as a conceptual tool of use to explain how it is that Buddha can act in the world. They are concerned, that is to say, almost exclusively with these bodies as instruments of unmatched salvific power (*vimocane mahopāya*), and for this the apparently relational properties are the only ones that count. This point is emphasized in the technical language of the digests by the connection they draw between the bodies of magical transformation and the achievement of what benefits others (*parārtha*).[13]

4.3 *Buddha's Perfections of Appearance in the World*

I referred briefly to Buddha's perfections of appearance in chapter three; I mentioned there its thirty-two major defining characteristics and its eighty minor marks as one of the elements in the standard list of Buddha-properties.[14] There is some difficulty in the interpretation of these lists: most of the digests do not clearly predicate the marks of a particular Buddha-body, and so do not make it clear whether they are to be understood to belong to Buddha in the world or Buddha in heaven.[15] But in some digests that may be later it is clearly stated that these marks belong not to the bodies of magical transformation, visible in worlds like this, but rather to those of communal enjoyment, available only in the heavenly realms.[16] By placing my discussion of these marks in this chapter rather than the next I am treating the marks as though they belonged to the bodies of magical transformation rather than the bodies of communal enjoyment. I do not intend by doing this to suggest anything definite as to the resolution of a complex question in the history of Buddhist doctrinal development; for my purposes the resolution of the historical question does not matter very much, for the philosophical points I wish to make do not depend upon deciding which bodies have these marks. Treating them as properties of the bodies of magical transformation is in accord with what most of the digests say, as well as with a good deal of iconographical evidence.

Buddha's physical appearance is presented in this list as maximally physically pleasing, which is to be expected of a maximally great being. Listing the physical perfections that Buddha has in the world appears to serve two purposes. The first is to indicate that the other kinds of perfection possessed by Buddha have their analogues in its physical appearance. So, for example, the fact that Buddha has firmly placed feet and walks evenly upon the ground represents or incarnates the firmness or evenness of its mastery over the doctrine, as well as of its self-possession, self-control, or equanimity (this last represented by the evenness of stride). And the fact that Buddha has thousand-spoked wheels, complete with hubs and rims, on the soles of its feet and the palms of its hands clearly indicates Buddha's mastery over the dharma and its function in setting the wheel of doctrine turning, which is to say in making it known to other living beings.

But I doubt whether all the perfections of appearance are straightforwardly symbolic in this way. Some of them appear to present Buddha simply as being maximally pleasing to the senses of others, and by being so to be maximally efficacious in encouraging those others to express their devotion and so to begin the practice of the path. So, for example, we are told that Buddha's eyes are intensely blue, and that its eyelashes are like a cow's (that is, long and elegantly curled). These physical marks are both auspicious and pleasing: they are therefore necessarily possessed by Buddha. On this second function of the perfections of appearance we read:

> atra lakṣaṇānuvyañjanānāṃ bhagavati mahāpuruṣatvasampratyayena darśanamātrāt pareṣāṃ prasādajanakatvaṃ karma sandarśitam/[17]
>
> Here [i.e., in a verse just quoted] the activity of the major and minor marks is shown to be the engendering of devotion in others, since merely by seeing [Buddha] they are convinced of the blessed one's greatness.

Here again it is easy to see that these perfections of appearance are relational properties of the kind *seems to S to be P*. An account of the benefits produced for non-Buddhas by seeing these physical perfections would therefore be an exhaustive account of both their coming into being and of their nature and functions.

Here is a full list of the thirty-two major physical perfections of Buddha in the world:

> (1) A great person has firmly placed feet and walks evenly upon the ground (supratiṣṭhitapādo mahāpuruṣaḥ samam ākramati). (2) Upon the soles of his feet there are thousand-spoked wheels with hubs and rims, complete in every aspect (adhasthāt pādatalayoś cakre jāte sahasrare sanābhike sanemike sarvākāraparipūrṇe). (3) The great person has long fingers (dīrghāṅgulim mahāpuruṣaḥ). (4) He has broad heels (ayātapādaparṣṇiḥ). (5) His hands and feet are soft and delicate (mṛdutaruṇapāṇipādaḥ). (6) His hands and feet are weblike (jalapāṇipādaḥ). (7) His ankles are hidden (uccaṅgacaraṇaḥ). (8) His legs are like those of an antelope (aineyajaṅgaḥ). (9) His body does not bend (anavanātakā). (10) His penis is sheathed (kośagata-vastiguhyaḥ). (11) He is round, like a banyan tree (nyagrodhaparimaṇḍalaḥ). (12) He has a halo extending as far as his arms can reach (vyāmaprabhaḥ). (13) His body hairs point upward (urdhvaṅgaroma). (14) His body hairs are separate; each separate [hair] grows in its own pore and is blue, curled, and turned to the right (ekaikaroma/ekaikam asya romakupa jātaṃ nīlaṃ kuṇḍalakajātaṃ pradakṣiṇavartam). (15) His skin is golden (kañcanasannibhatvāk). (16) His skin is smooth; because of the smoothness, dust and dirt do not stick to his body (ślakṣaṇatvāt tvace rajo malasya kāye nāvatiṣṭhate).

(17) His body has seven protuberances: two on his hands, two on his feet, two on his shoulders, and one on his neck (saptodsādakāyaḥ/ kāye jātaḥ dvau hastayor dvaur pādayor dvav asamyor eko grīvāyām). (18) The front of his body is like a lion (simhapūrvārdhakāyaḥ). (19) His torso is well-rounded (susamvṛttaskandhaḥ). (20) He has no hollow between his shoulders (citāntarāṃśaḥ). (21) He is straight and tall (bahudṛjugātraḥ). (22) He has forty even teeth (catvāriṃśat samadantaḥ). (23) His teeth have no spaces [between them] (aviraladantaḥ). (24) His teeth are very white (suśukladantaḥ). (25) His jaw is like a lion's (simhahānuḥ). (26) His tongue is long and thin; because of the length of his tongue, when he sticks it out he covers his entire face up to the edge of his hair (prabhutatanujiḥvaḥ/ prabhutatvāj jiḥvāyāḥ mukhāj jiḥvaṃ nirnamya sarvamukhamaṇḍalam avacchādayati yāvantakaṃ keśaparyantam). (27) He has obtained an excellent sense of taste (rasarasāgraprāptaḥ). (28) His voice is like Brahma's: it speaks as delightfully as a Kalaviṅka bird's (brahmasvaraḥ kalaviṅkamanojñābhāni). (29) His voice is like the sound of a magical drum (dundubhīśvara-nirghoṣaḥ). (30) His eyes are intensely blue and his eyelashes are like a cow's (abhinīlanetraḥ gopakṣamaḥ). (31) His head is like a turban (uṣṇiṣaśīrṣa). (32) The hair growing between his eyebrows is white, soft, and turned to the right (ūrṇa cāsya bhrūvor madhye jāta svetā saṅkhanibhā pradakṣiṇavartā).[18]

There is a connection between Buddha's perfections of appearance and the meditational practice of recalling or paying attention to (*anusmṛ-*) Buddha's physical properties. There can be little doubt that the lists of Buddha's defining marks and the detailed descriptions of Buddha's appearance in the heavenly realms were used as aids to such practice; and they were also represented iconographically in painting and sculpture. A full treatment of the marks would require a detailed analysis of the iconographical evidence, but that is beyond the scope of this study.

A final note. It is obviously necessary, in order for Buddha to possess perfections of appearance, that Buddha should possess—or, better, appear as—a physical body. I shall show in chapter six that the localization in time and space that appearing as a body entails is not an essential property of Buddha, from which it follows that none of the perfections of appearance are essential properties either. This does not mean that they are unimportant; they may indeed be essential to Buddha's fulfilment of its properly salvific functions. But it does mean that they are not part of Buddha's essential nature, its *svabhāva*. They are instead strictly relational properties of the usual kind: Buddha in its body of magical transformation *seems to S to be P*, which in this case means that Buddha in the world seems to those who perceive it to be maximally beautiful, and by so doing engenders in them awe, devotion, and (ideally) a desire for religious practice.

4.4 Buddha's Perfections of Action in the World

These have already been briefly described in chapter three: Buddha does whatever living beings in a world like ours will most benefit from. Here I shall concentrate not so much upon the details of what Buddha does—for these will, after all, differ according to the conditions and needs of the living beings in the world-realm in which Buddha acts—but rather upon the philosophical account given by the digests of the nature of this action. For it is necessarily in such an account that the doctrinal dimension of discourse about Buddha's action becomes most apparent.

Buddha's action in its body of magical transformation is given a technical description by the digests. It is associated with the "awareness that does what needs to be done" (*kṛtyānuṣṭhānajñāna*), an awareness defined programatically in the following way:

> kṛtyānuṣṭhānajñānaṃ nirmāṇaiḥ sarvadhātuṣu/
> citrāprameyācintyaiś ca sarvasattvārthakārakam//[19]

> The awareness that does what needs to be done
> Effects what benefits all living beings in all world-realms,

> Through an inconceivable and immeasurable variety
> of magical transformations.

A number of commentators on this verse use the image of a medicinal drug that cures all diseases as an illustration of the nature of Buddha's action in the world.[20] More concisely yet, in another of the digests we read: "The awareness that does what needs to be done is that by which Buddha's action is effected" (*bya ba sgrub pa'i ye shes ni . . . sangs rgyas kyi mdzad pa sgrub pa'o*).[21]

More precisely and technically, Buddha appears to act in the world physically (through its *kāya*), verbally (through its *vāc*), and mentally (through its *citta*). These instruments are used, of course, because only in these ways is communication with embodied living beings a possibility. Every act done in one of these three ways by Buddha in its body of magical transformation is then itself classified as an instance of magical transformation (*nirmāṇa*), and the digests take considerable trouble to analyze and classify the possible types of transformation.

One such classification divides the physical and verbal acts of a body of magical transformation into three kinds, and its mental acts into two kinds. The division is according to what it is that appears to act: the possibilities are that it is the body of magical transformation itself; some other body; or a nonsentient object. So, for instance, a body of magical transformation's verbal acts, its speech, may appear to emanate directly from the body of magical transformation itself, as when Gautama Śākyamuni preached the doctrine to his followers in India; or it may appear to emanate from nonsentient objects, as when the wind is magically transformed into a voice preaching doctrine. Similar examples are given for the three kinds of physical action attributed to the body of magical transformation, though only two kinds of mental action are recognized, presumably because in order to have an instance of Buddha's mental actions appearing to be performed by a nonsentient object, one would have to postulate the absurdity of a nonsentient mind.[22] It is interesting to note that at this level of specificity and precision the digests are not quite in accord. While they all agree that the body of magical transformation manifests only two kinds of mental activity, some postulate the three kinds of physical and verbal activity mentioned in the preceding paragraph,[23] while others seem to acknowledge only two.[24] Whatever position is taken on this issue, the point of such classifications is to indicate that Buddha can act in its body of magical transformation in any way that the needs of living beings make beneficial, and that the mode of its action in a particular case is causally determined entirely by the kind and extent of those needs.

For the purposes of this study, the most significant properties possessed by every instance of Buddha's action in its body of magical transformation are two: spontaneity or effortlessness on the one hand, and endlessness or uninterruptedness on the other. I shall treat these in turn, though they overlap considerably and are often difficult to disentangle from one another in the treatment given them in the digests.

4.4.1 Spontaneity and Effortlessness

The spontaneity of Buddha's action in its bodies of magical transformation involves at least the following: first, the absence of any intentions or volitions (*cetanā, abhisamskāra*) on Buddha's part as causes of that action;[25] second, following from the first, the absence of any effort (*yatna, ābhoga*) or deliberation involving constructive or analytical thought (*vikalpa*) informing or guiding that action;[26] and third, as a corollary of the first and second points, the absence of any possibility of wrong action, of making mistakes.

Buddha in its body of magical transformation always and everywhere does the right thing, the most salvifically efficacious thing, and does only that. A key verse here is the following:

> na buddhānām evaṃ bhavati mama pakvo 'yam iti
> cāprapācyo 'yaṃ dehī api ca adhunā pacyata iti/
> vināsamskāraṃ tu prapācam upayaty eva janata.[27]

Buddhas do not say 'I have brought this one to maturity,'

> Or, 'This living being needs to be brought to maturity,'
> Or, 'I am now bringing this one to maturity.'
> Instead, living beings advance to maturity without volitional action [on Buddha's part].

The digests make two points in their elucidations of this verse. The first is expressed by piling up terms for effort, contrivance, volition, intention, and exertion, and then negating them all: Buddha has none of these things.[28] The second is to connect the absence of effortful exertion in Buddha's action with the absence of discriminative or deliberative thought informing that action.[29] The connection is clear: effort, intention, and the rest require the forming of ideas about what should be done and plans as to how best to do it, and such ideas require in turn discriminative thought, the distinguishing of one goal from another, and the judgment that one goal is preferable to another. The digests therefore have to reject the possibility that Buddha in its bodies of magical transformation can make such discriminations; only in this way can the claim that Buddha's action is strictly spontaneous be preserved.[30]

A number of similes are then employed to give the student of these texts some idea of what the actions of a body of magical transformation are like if they are really free from effort and deliberation, properties that in ordinary discourse, Buddhist or other, are taken to be necessarily possessed by all actions of any living being. I shall say something about only four of these similes in connection with spontaneity, although many more are used: Buddha's action is said to be like a divine drum (*dundubhi*), like a wish-fulfilling jewel (*cintāmaṇi*), like an echo (*pratiśrutkā*), and like the magical appearance of Indra (*śakrapratibhāsa*) in the world.

The divine drum is used largely as a simile for Buddha's voice teaching the doctrine.[31] The drum sounds in the divine realms without any living being in those realms intending that it should or doing anything to make it sound. Its sounds result from the past actions of those living beings who inhabit those realms, even when they are unaware of anything they have done to bring this about. Similarly for Buddha's voice teaching doctrine in the world: it says what it says because of the actions of those who live in the world, and it is audible only to those who are ready to hear it.[32] So the utterance of key doctrine-expressing sentences such as *all conditioned things are impermanent* by a body of magical transformation in a world-realm like this one is subjectless and free from volition (though certainly not meaningless or without effect).

Buddha's action is also like a wish-fulfilling gem (*cintāmaṇi*).[33] A wish-fulfilling gem, like Aladdin's lamp or any of the other wish-granting objects so common in fairy-stories, gives what is wished for without deliberation, because it must. It does this in virtue of properties inherent in it: it is in the nature of wish-fulfilling gems to be radiant and to grant wishes, and in just the same way it is in the nature of bodies of magical transformation to manifest appropriate activities of body, speech, and mind for the benefit of others. So Buddha in the world "benefits others to the extent that they are worthy, without effort" (*tathā munir yatnam ṛte yathārhataḥ parārtham ātiṣṭhati*).[34] Also, both Buddhas in the world and wish-fulfilling gems are exceedingly rare, to be prized and treasured when found.

Buddha's action is also like an echo (*pratiśrutkā*).[35] A complete causal account of the arising of an echo can be given by mentioning the occurrence of some sound and describing the configuration of the physical environment in which that sound is made. No reference to intention, discrimination, or effort is necessary. So also for Buddha's action in the world; it is "free from constructive thought, without effort, and has nothing upon which to stand, inside or out" (*nirvikalpam anābhogaṃ nādhyātmaṃ na bahiḥ sthitam*).[36]

Buddha's action is, finally, like the appearance of Indra in the world.[37] Here, the appearance of Buddha in the world is likened to the appearance of Indra, with all his appurtenances and retinue, as a reflection in the polished surface of a gemstone. Just as people seeing Indra's reflection would be moved to virtuous conduct and to acts of homage, so people seeing Buddha in the world as a body of magical transformation will, "filled with eagerness, yoke themselves to the attainment of Buddhahood" (*taṃ ca dṛstvābhiyujyante buddhatvāya spṛhānvitaḥ*).[38] But in both cases that to which people respond is just an appearance (*pratibhāsa*). Its appearance or disappearance, and all changes in the way it is seen, are due not to any change in it, but rather to the condition of the mind perceiving it; hence Buddha in the world is just an appearance in the mind of the perceiver.[39]

The corollary of these ways of presenting the spontaneity of Buddha's action is that Buddha, in its body of magical transformation, can neither do any wrong nor be subject to any fear or apprehension that it might do wrong. To think that it could be in such a condition would be as absurd as thinking that an echo might be worried about the accuracy and appropriateness of its reproduction of sounds. This point is made explicit in the digests in a number of ways, but most often through the categories of the four confidences (*vaiśāradya*) and the three guardlessnesses (*arakṣya*).[40] These categories are used to explain that Buddha in its body of magical transformation is fully confident of its own complete awakening, and that it therefore does not have to guard its actions against inappropriateness in any way. So we read:

> bsrung ba med pa'i gsum ni/ de bzhin gshegs pa'i sku'i phrin las dang gsung dang thugs kyi phrin las bsrung ba med pa ste/ bsrung ba med pa gsum kyis ni de bzhin gshegs pa'i nyes pa mdzad pa 'chab pa rnam pa thams cad spangs pa 'di yongs su bstan to/ gang yang dgra' bcom pa la brgya lam na res 'ga' zhig brjed nas ngan par byas pa/ lung du ma bstan pa cung zad tsam yod pa de yang/ de bzhin gshegs pa la thams cad kyi thams cad du mi mnga' bas de'i phyir de bzhin gshegs pa ni ji ltar zhal gyis 'che ba de lta bu'i ngo bo nyid yin no/[41]

> The three guardlessnesses are [comprised in] the Tathāgata's physical, verbal, and mental conduct, none of which need to be guarded. These three guardlessnesses explain the Tathāgata's abandonment of all inappropriate acts that need to be hidden. For *arhat*s, by contrast, there is the possibility of performing some inappropriate or [ethi-

> cally] neutral act as a result of momentary forgetfulness; but such things do not occur at all for a Tathāgata, since its essential nature is in accord with its assertions.

4.4.2 Endlessness and Omnipresence

Buddha's endlessness (*apratiprasrabdhatva*) and omnipresence (*sarvagatatva*) are discussed very widely in the digests.[42] Just as Buddha's action in the world is spontaneous, so it is also endless, uninterrupted, always the same, present everywhere. More precisely, Buddha's maximally efficacious salvific actions occur whenever and wherever there are living beings to benefit from them: the existence of living beings is both necessary and sufficient condition for Buddha's action in the world to become apparent. Here is one way of putting this:

> de bzhin gshegs pa rnams . . . sems can gyi don du sku dang gsung dang thugs sprul pa'i phrin las rgyun mi 'chad par 'byung ngo . . . sems can skal ba yod pa'i dus na ni sprul pa'i skus mngon par sangs rgyas pa la sogs pa ston pas na skye bar snang ngo/[43]

> Tathāgatas . . . uninterruptedly give rise to magical transformations of body, speech, and mind for the benefit of living beings . . . wherever there are living beings for whom it is appropriate, [Buddha] appears to be born in its body of magical transformation, showing [in that body] the attainment of awakening and the rest.

Since there are, in effect, always living beings for whom it is appropriate that Buddha be active in the world, Buddha is always in some sense so active. But it is important to realize that Buddha is not always active in the world precisely as a body of magical transformation, one whose career is described in the Buddha-legend. Buddha may also be active in other ways, notably through the teaching of the doctrine carried on by the monastic establishment, in the relics of a dead body of magical transformation, and through the visions of bodies of communal enjoyment obtainable by virtuoso meditators in world-realms like ours. But these kinds of activity and presence are not the focus of interest in this chapter.

Buddha's action in the world is therefore strictly omnipresent. It has the properties of *sarvagatatva,* literally 'having-gone-everywhere-ness.' and *abhinnatva,* literally 'not having been split-up-ness.' These properties are sometimes explicitly mentioned and argued for in the digests, but again they are also often suggested by the use of similes. The most common among these are: the rain that falls from clouds upon all living beings everywhere;[44] the sun that shines without differentiation upon all living beings everywhere;[45] the earth, which nourishes the roots of all plants everywhere and without exception;[46] and the moon, whose radiance illuminates everything.[47] There is also the simile of space (*ākāśa*), which is used to make similar points, but does so in a rather more abstract fashion. Consider the following:

> yathāmbaraṃ sarvagataṃ sadā mataṃ tathaiva tat sarvagataṃ sadā matam/
> yathāmbaraṃ rūpagateṣu sarvagaṃ tathaiva tat sattvagaṇeṣu sarvagam//[48]

> Just as space is always considered to be omnipresent,
> So also this is always considered to be omnipresent;
> Just as space is omnipresent among physical forms,
> So also this is omnipresent among the hosts of living beings.

This verse created some divisions among the commentators, principally about the referent of the pronoun 'this.'[49] It is clear that something is being compared to space, and that this something is said to be like space in that both it and space are omnipresent. But the verse does not immediately make clear what the subject of this comparison is. Some take it to be Buddhahood; others, the purified ground of reality (*dharmadhātuviśuddhi*); and yet others, the real body (*dharmakāya*). These differences have significance for the detailed history of Buddhist use of terms for the absolute, as well as for a full understanding of the finer scholastic distinctions made in buddhalogical discourse,[50] but for the purposes of this study it will suffice for now to say that in spite of their differences the commentators agree that omnipresence is a property of Buddha as it is in itself: it is not taken to be a relational property, and so is not of central importance to the digests when they come to analyze Buddha's action in the world. It needs to be mentioned here because the omnipresence of Buddha in its real body is a presupposition for and an explanation of the way in which Buddha acts in the world. Buddha can respond ceaselessly, uninterruptedly, to the needs of living beings in the world in the way that the digests claim it does just because of this metaphysical fact. But the metaphysical fact does have relational significance, since Buddha's omnipresence is necessarily experienced by living beings in the world.

Two related points are made by the digests in this connection. The first is that while Buddha is, strictly, present to all living beings in the same way and to the same extent at all times, it is also the case that Buddha in its body of magical transformation seems to be present to different living beings in different ways and to different extents. That is, Buddha in the world has a large set of properties of the following kind: *seeming to S to be present and available to extent E at time t,* where E is determined entirely by the condition of S and not at all by alterations in Buddha. Both points are made through the use of similes, just as was the case with the property of spontaneity.

The sameness and universality of Buddha's presence are illustrated most commonly with the already-mentioned similes of rain and sunshine. Rain falling to the ground has a single taste, savor, color, and texture, and falls everywhere; similarly, the sun sheds its light everywhere in the same way and to the same degree. These same images are used to illustrate why it is that Buddha in its bodies of magical transformation does not seem to be equally present and available to all: neither rain nor sun reaches every point on the ground in the same way, nor do they remain always the same in their properties when they have reached the ground. For example, rainwater becomes salty where there is salt on the ground, and in just the same way the doctrine takes on many different tastes and varieties "because of the differences in the conditions of living beings" (*santānasthānabhedāt*).[51] Sunshine also is not everywhere equally visible and does not always have the same effects. So also with Buddha's action: some living beings receive more of it because of their merits, just as high mountains get more of the sun's light;[52] and some living beings respond positively to it and some negatively, just as some lotus plants open themselves to the sun's rays while others close their petals.[53] The obverse of the same point is made when bodhisattvas are exhorted to become like a cloudless sky, for although the moon shines everywhere in the same way, it is only fully visible in a sky without clouds.[54]

4.4.3 Excursus: Buddha's Consumption of Food

It may be helpful at this point to look at an example of Buddha's action in the world in order to see how the theoretical points made above play out in a particular case. I choose the example of Gautama Śākyamuni's apparent ingestion and digestion of food. This is an important example in a number of ways, most obviously because the donation of food to worthy recipients and its ingestion and digestion by them is one of the most important religious acts that a lay Buddhist can perform. It makes merit—the amount made is dependent largely upon the worthiness of the recipient—and so conduces to a good rebirth and eventually to the attainment of that awakening that is the notional goal of all Buddhist practice. For most lay Buddhists, Buddha in its body of magical transformation is not available as a recipient of gifts of food; for them, members of the monastic order, the sangha, are the best recipients. But for those face to face with a body of magical transformation there can be no better recipient, none whose acceptance of food will bring more merit to the donor. The narrative versions of the Buddha-legend are therefore replete with stories about feasts given for Gautama Śākyamuni, and it is largely because of this that the digests give the attention they do to the question of the consumption of food.

Consider the following overtly paradoxical verse, the last line of which mentions Buddha's consumption of food:

skye med sangs rgyas skye ba ste/
mi gnas pa la rab tu bzhugs/
lhun gyis grub par thams cad mdzad/
zhas bzhi po ni gsol ba lags//[55]

The unborn Buddha is born,
Abides in nonabiding,
Does everything spontaneously,
And eats the four foods.

This verse occurs in a section of one of the digests that treats four of Buddha's "profundities" (*gambhīrya*), namely, those of birth ("the unborn Buddha is born"), abiding ("abides in nonabiding"), action ("does everything spontaneously"), and sustenance ("eats the four foods").

The first two of these four profundities offer a prima facie contradiction: Buddha is born and not born, remains and yet does not remain. That these are not really intended as contradictory claims but rather as rhetorical devices with a certain shock value is clearly shown by the way the digests treat them: Buddha is unborn in the sense that it is not subject to defiled or passionate birth, but is born in the sense that it descends into Queen Māyā's womb and appears to be born from her side; Buddha does not abide in the sense that it is not firmly or fixedly located anywhere—neither in Samsara nor in Nirvana; but it does abide in the sense that it continues precisely in that condition of not being fixed.[56]

The third and fourth among the profundities are less overtly and dramatically paradoxical. The third ("does everything spontaneously") has already been sufficiently treated, and is in a sense the topic of this whole chapter; its paradox consists in the fact that action normally requires deliberation and effort, so that the idea of spontaneous action comes close to being self-contradictory. But it is the fourth profundity that concerns me here: Buddha's profundtiy of sustenance is that it eats the four foods. What is meant by this?

Buddhist scholasticism has a good deal to say about the four foods.[57] The standard list says that the four foods are: (1) "Food that fills the mouth" (*kavaḍikāra*), quantities of edible or drinkable stuff that have smell and taste. A slice of avocado or a glass of wine would meet the description, though the digests more commonly give "honey, molasses, meat, and fish"[58] as examples. (2) "Contact" (*sparśa*), a term that refers to a "meeting of the three," which is to say a meeting between sense-organ, sense-object, and sensory consciousness. This term thus labels a mental event produced by sensory input of any kind, for example, seeing a particular color or smelling a particular odor. (3) "Volition of thought" (*manaḥsañcetanā*), a term that refers to any intentional action of the mind based upon the sensory inputs labeled by the term 'contact.' And finally, (4) "consciousness" (*vijñāna*), a generic term for any intentional mental event, which is to say any mental event with an (apparent) object. This last category can include examples of what western cognitive psychologists would call affect, conation, and cognition, in addition to the types of mental event mentioned in (1) and (2).

These things are all food—although only the first would usually be called so in English—in the sense that they are all nourishment for existence (*bhavāpoṣaṇā*). Material food, obviously, nourishes the body and so makes continued existence possible; the three kinds of mental food do the same for the continuum of the mental life. The following story from one of the digests explains how sensory inputs, volitions and the like, extend both physical and mental life.[59] A poor man with his two young sons leaves his home country, where there is famine, and begins to travel to a place where he hopes there will be more food. Exhausted, and feeling that he is about to die, he fills a sack with ashes, places it on a wall, and tells his two sons that it is full of food. Then he dies. Given encouragement and hope by the thought that there is food in the sack, the boys live for a long time; but then a passer-by opens the sack and shows them that it contains only ashes. The boys die in despair.

The point is that the mental condition of the two boys—specifically their *manaḥsañcetanā,* their conation—extends their life and so acts as a kind of food. In fact, ingestion of the third and fourth kinds of food, which is to say the perpetuation of consciousness by the continued occurrence of volition, is specifically linked with rebirth by the digests.[60] The round of death, birth, redeath, and rebirth is thus nourished in large part by the occurrence of affective mental acts (responding with liking or repulsion to some sensory input), and conative mental acts (willing or intending some desired goal).

Given this background it is now possible to return to the question of Buddha's consumption of the four foods, and to ask again what it might mean to say that it ingests food, and whether it is really the case that it ingests every kind of food.

The digests substantially agree in saying that Buddha, in its bodies of magical transformation, appears to be sustained by all four kinds of food. That is, such bodies appear to consume material food by putting it into their mouths, and they appear to have sensory experiences, volitions, and various kinds of consciousness. But the digests also agree in emphasizing that this is only an appearance. So we read that Buddha uses the food given to it in its bodies of magical transformation "as though" to sustain a physical body; it does this to gladden those living beings who make donations to it, and to allow them to make merit; but the food so consumed does not perform the functions of real food (*āhārakṛtya*) for Buddha. Instead, "the gods take it from Buddha and give it to other living beings, thereby leading them to attain awakening" (*sangs rgyas las lha rnams kyis blangs nas gzhan sems can rnams la sbyin par byed de*).[61]

So, although Buddha appears to be sustained by the four foods, it does not actually consume them and thus is not really sustained by them, even though they appear to be consumed and Buddha appears to be sustained. The digests give the following list of ten reasons why Buddha appears to be sustained by food when it is active as a body of magical transformation:

> rnam pa bcus na sangs rgyas zas kyi bya ba mi mdzad kyang sku zas kyis gnas par ston te/ (1) sems can rnams kyi bsod nams bsags pa'i phyir dang/ (2) chos mthun pa nyid du yang dag par bstan pa'i phyir dang/ (3) rigs pa la longs spyod par rjes su bslab par bya ba'i phyir dang/ (4) chags pa med par bslab par bya ba'i phyir dang/ (5) mchod pa nye bar bsdu ba'i phyir dang/ (6) brtson 'grus brtsams pa yang dag par shes par bya ba'i phyir dang/ (7) dge ba'i rtsa ba yongs su smin par bya ba'i phyir dang/ (8) bdag nyid chags pa med par bstan par bya ba'i phyir dang/ (9) las la grus pa nye bar bstan par bya ba'i phyir dang/ (10) smon lam 'byung ba yongs su rdzogs par bya ba'i phyir ro/[62]
>
> There are ten reasons why Buddha does not perform with food that function which is proper to food, even though its body appears to be sustained by food. (1) To accumulate merit for living beings. (2) To agree with custom. (3) To train [living beings] in the enjoyment of reason. (4) to train [living beings] in detachment. (5) To gather offerings. (6) To bring about the beginnings of effort [in religious practice]. (7) To bring the roots of virtue [belonging to others] to maturity. (8) To manifest attachment [to living beings]. (9) To inculcate respect for action. (10) To fulfil initial vows.

The "function proper to food" is to give sustenance to the body and so to maintain life. Buddha's apparent ingestion of food in its bodies of magical transformation cannot have anything to do with this function, since each of these ten reasons for its apparent use of food has to do with the needs of living beings other than itself. These beings need to amass the merit produced by donating food to Buddha and having it eaten; they need to learn to develop and inculcate the joy that comes from seeing and hearing Buddha in its bodies of magical transformation, and since such seeing and hearing are dependent upon such a body seeming to be physical (which entails appearing to be sustained by food), they must see it consume food. And so forth.

This example should drive home the point made above. All the significant properties possessed by the bodies of magical transformation are relational, and all can be couched in terms of appearance, in sentences of the form *seems to S to be P at T.* A complete causal account of what Buddha does in the world can therefore be given in terms of the needs of the living beings who constitute that world; there is never any need to appeal to the needs of Buddha *in se*. In the case of the ingestion, digestion, and evacuation of food, this means that a complete account of Buddha's use of food can be given in sentences of the following kind: *Buddha seems to Ānanda to chew in the morning; Buddha seems to Mahākāśyapa to digest in the afternoon; Buddha seems to Śāriputra to defecate in the evening*—and so forth. But, for Buddha in its body of magical transformation, in no case do any of the physiological processes that normally result from the ingestion of food actually occur. And this conclusion can be generalized to all of Buddha's actions in the world.

4.5 Buddha's Perfections of Cognition in the World

In chapter three I divided Buddha's perfections into five kinds: appearance, action, cognition, attitude, and control. In the immediately preceding sections of this chapter I have tried to show what account the digests give of perfections of the first two kinds as they pertain to Buddha in the world. In this section I shall make some brief comments about Buddha's perfections of cognition in the same context. My comments will be relatively brief here because, as I shall show subsequently, the perfections of cognition are, paradigmatically, perfections that belong to Buddha in its real body, and a full analysis of what it means to say, for example, that Buddha is omniscient can only be given in the context of a discussion of that body. But there are some perfections of cognition among those listed in chapter three that are properly predicated of the bodies of magical transformation, and I shall treat as examples of these the third and fourth of the four kinds of specific or analytical understanding (*pratisamvit*), which portrays Buddha in the world as knowing all logical and practical possibilities. There are, naturally, other perfections of cognition that could be analyzed in this context—and which should be if a complete account were to be given. But the main components of the account offered of these two can be generalized to the others.

4.5.1 Omnilinguality

The four specific or analytical understandings possessed by Buddha are treated in most of the digests.[63] The last two of these say that Buddha has specific or analytical understanding of the intensional meanings and grammatical forms of words (*nirukti*), and of eloquent discourse (*pratibhāna*). This amounts to saying that Buddha possesses complete and perfect skill in speaking every natural language. Understanding of words is connected, obviously, with speech; more specifically it involves knowledge of the various languages spoken in different countries. Among the requirements for such a skill appear to be the following. First, Buddha must have a complete lexical knowledge of all natural languages; the digests usually put this by saying that Buddha knows all synonyms (*paryāya* or *adhivacana*) both within one natural language and across many. So, for example, it is said that knowing synonyms (*paryāyajñāna*) involves knowing all those words (*nāma*) whose object, referent, or meaning (*artha*) is the same.[64] Then, Buddha must also have a complete grammatical and syntactical understanding of all natural languages, an understanding that entails the ability to provide a complete grammatical analysis of any lexical item.[65] These things together issue in complete mastery over eloquent discourse, by means of which Buddha says just what needs to be said in just the words of the natural language best suited to its hearers.[66]

I note parenthetically that this is not the same as what is said to have happened to the disciples of Jesus of Nazareth at Pentecost. There, or so it appears, a single set of sounds uttered by the disciples was heard as a set of well-formed sentences in different natural languages by different hearers at the same time[67]—though in fact the New Testament account is not entirely clear about this. Buddha's omnilinguality, in any case, does not consist in its ability to utter such a (translingual?) single set of sounds, but rather, as the occasion demands, to speak well-formed sentences in different natural languages seriatim.

The digests do not give a very clear account of what it is for a non-Buddha to possess the ability to speak a natural language. It is, therefore, necessarily somewhat speculative to offer an account of just how, cognitively and practically, Buddha in the world possesses and uses its omnilinguality. But I think it can be said with a reasonable amount of certainty that the model in play here must accord with what has been said above about Buddha's action understood generically. That is, if spontaneity and the absence of deliberative thought and effort are the hallmarks of all instances of Buddha's action, they must also be properties of its utterance. And if this is right, all of Buddha's utterance in all natural languages must be understood in a manner very different from that in which we usually understand our own utterance.

Our utterance is usually marked with deliberation and choice; sometimes also, especially in formal or unfamiliar settings, or when struggling with a language other than our native tongue, with painful effort. Perhaps the only truly spontaneous, choiceless, effortless utterances that most of us ever make are scarcely utterances at all, but rather subverbal grunts of agony or ecstasy, moans of appreciation, and the like. These, usually, are not characterized by effort and deliberation; they also, of course, generally communicate across the boundaries of natural languages. Some few of us, perhaps, in the grip of afflatus, may do more: we may compose poetry, prose, or speak ad hoc in a manner which, in terms of its phenomenal properties at least, appears to us to be spontaneous and effortless in just the way that Buddha's utterance must be. But such instances are for us atypical, mysterious even to those who experience them, while for Buddha they are all that is possible. The semantic connection in Sanskrit between Buddha's eloquent discourse (*pratibhāna*) and poetic inspiration is significant here.

Buddha's possession of omnilinguality, then, should not be understood on the model of an enormously large computer, programmed with the lexica, grammar, and syntax of all natural languages, and with a perfectly efficacious translation program. Such a computer, when faced with a well-formed sentence in some natural language, could translate it into any (and every) other natural language very fast by making all the right choices in the right order. But Buddha, in performing the same feat, could make no choices at all and could undertake no deliberations at all; there would be neither hardware nor software behind the scenes, as it were, to guarantee the production of the correct sentences. Instead, as with all of Buddha's actions in the world in its bodies of magical transformation, a complete causal account of the occurrence of its utterance in any natural language can be provided in terms of the needs and situations of living beings who are not Buddhas and who form the context for the utterance in question.

In terms of cognition (for I am, recall, considering Buddha's omnilinguality as an example of its perfections of cognition in the world), it is therefore speaking with the vulgar to say that Buddha 'knows' the lexica of all natural languages. It would be more proper to say that what the possession of such knowledge on Buddha's part means is just and only that in certain theoretically specifiable situations Buddha will utter sentences in whatever language is understood by its interlocutors. Here, then, what appears at first sight to be a perfection of cognition reduces to a perfection of action: Buddha possesses no linguistic knowledge or artistry other than what is evident in its linguistic behavior in the world.

4.5.2 Awareness of What Is Possible and What Is Impossible

Buddha in the world possesses ten powers (*bala*), abilities that issue from various kinds of knowledge and awareness. The first of these is called the power that springs from an awareness of what is possible and what is impossible (*sthānāsthānajñānabala*).[68] This power involves being fully aware of the range of practical possibilities in the world, of what can follow from what and what cannot. Many examples are given in the digests. Some have to do with practical or logical impossibilities, as when we are told that it is not possible (*asthāna*) for a woman to realize Buddhahood, while it is possible for a man to do so,[69] or when possibilities and impossibilities are discussed in terms of causal theory.[70] But most of the examples given involve matters of more direct salvific significance.[71] We are told, for example, that Buddha is aware that good rebirths come from accumulated good actions in the world, while bad rebirths come from accumulated bad actions,[72] and that Buddha uses the power that comes from this awareness to overcome those who would teach something that contradicts such claims. More specifically, Buddha uses this power to both rebut and refute such erroneous teachings as that everything occurs without cause, or that everything is caused by God (*īśvara*);[73] it then replaces these teachings with standard Buddhist doctrine on the dependently originated nature of all reals.

Again, though the basis for this power is clearly presented as a perfection of cognition, the interests of the digests in expounding it are located firmly in its salvific effects upon non-Buddhas. They do not at this point give a detailed analysis of what it might mean to say that Buddha possesses omniscience in regard to all propositions predicating causal relations of any kind between two or more existents; that has to wait for the analysis of the awareness possessed by Buddha in its real body. Instead, they focus exclusively upon how this awareness is used; and since this use is, for the most part, a verbal one—consisting usually in a rebuttal and refutation of false doctrinal claims made by others—a full and proper account of it can be given in terms of the effortless spontaneity of action described already. And, as a result, here too, what appears at first sight to be a perfection of cognition reduces to a perfection of action: Buddha's knowledge of what is possible and what is impossible is understood exclusively in terms of the actions that Buddha appears to engage in.

4.6 One Body of Magical Transformation at a Time? A Controversy

I have just given a sketch of Buddha's activity in the world. In it, I emphasized that the kind, extent, and quality of this activity are all determined by the needs of the living beings who provide the context for it; and that the various perfections possessed by Buddha in the world share the property of being maximally salvifically effective for those beings. If this sketch is correct in its essentials, a number of pressing questions come at once to mind. The two to be dealt with here are: First, if Buddha's presence in the world, an instantiation of the relational properties of seeming in terms of which an account of Buddha in the world can almost exhaustively be given, is indeed of maximal salvific effect, why is a body of magical transformation not always present in all worlds? Why, that is, does there ever seem to be an occasion on which such a body is absent? Second, would not the salvific effect of Buddha's presence in the world be magnified by multiplying the number of bodies of magical transformation available at a particular time? That is, why could there not be two or more bodies of magical transformation present in the same world at the same time? More imaginatively yet, why could there not be an infinity of such bodies present and active in a world at a time, perhaps one for each unawakened living being? This scenario, it would seem, could truly maximize Buddha's salvific effect, since its actualization would permit the custom-tailoring of uninterrupted teaching by each body of magical transformation for every individual non-Buddha.

But the digests reject all such scenarios in favor of what became the standard position: only one body of magical transformation in a world at a time. But there were other possibilities that were seriously canvassed, as is evident by the fact that the digests offer arguments against them. The digests typically begin such arguments by affirming that there must be more than one body of magical transformation, though not necessarily more than one at the same time. A number of arguments are offered here, among which I distinguish the following four as the most important.[74]

First, there is a plurality of lineages and a plurality of names for different bodies of magical transformation. This means that different bodies are named differently by us—they are, for example, called 'Gautama Śākyamuni' or 'Vipaśvin,' the last two bodies of magical transformation to appear in this world-realm;[75] and they have different histories, different sets of practices by means of which they became awakened. Therefore, there cannot be just one body of magical transformation.

Second, an enormous variety of bodhisattvas, Buddhas-to-be, is always in the process of amassing stores of religious merit by following the path. This merit would be "useless" (*vaiyarthya*), or would go to waste, if those bodhisattvas did not severally and separately achieve awakening at different times and in different places. Therefore, there cannot be just one body of magical transformation.

Third, the actions of Buddha in the world are supposed to bring all non-Buddhas to awakening. Since the career of one body of magical transformation evidently does not bring about that end, and since it is also the case that Buddha always achieves its ends, there cannot be just one body of magical transformation; many—perhaps infinitely many—will be required to bring all non-Buddhas to awakening.

Fourth, and finally, there is an argument that purports to demonstrate the necessity of there having been more than one body of magical transformation from the fact of there having been any at all. The occurrence of awakening that constitutes the coming into being of a particular such body has among its necessary conditions a prior accumulation of merit and wisdom; and this in turn requires the person accumulating the merit and wisdom to have been in contact with a body of magical transformation teaching the doctrine at some time in the past (usually during a past life). All this entails both that there cannot have been a first or original Buddha (*ādibuddha*)—in the sense of a first body of magical transformation before which there had existed no other such body—and that, if there have been any bodies of magical transformation at all, there must have been more than one. The antecedent of this last conditional is then affirmed, and the conclusion follows.

All these arguments proceed by drawing out conclusions from the contradictory of the claim to be demonstrated (in this case the contradictory is *there is at most one body of magical transformation*) which are clearly incompatible with matters of fact about which, in the digests, there is no dispute. So, in the case of the first argument, the claim *there is at most one body of magical transformation* is shown to issue in the (conventionally) unacceptable conclusion that proper names such as 'Gautama Śākyamuni' and 'Vipaśvin' have an identical referent. And in the case of the third argument, the unacceptable conclusion that Buddha fails in its goals is shown to follow from the same claim.

The thesis that there are and have been many bodies of magical transformation is thus not a controversial one for the digests. They all agree on it. But it is important to note the arguments used to support that thesis, since they inform and are presupposed by the arguments used to decide a genuinely controverted issue: that of whether it is possible for more than one body of magical transformation to be present and active in the same world-realm at the same time. Given that one can—must—have multiplicity, can one also have simultaneity?

In the digests I have found two arguments for the possibility of the simultaneous presence of two or more bodies of magical transformation; five arguments against simultaneous presence in the same location; and a resolution that acknowledges the desirability of admitting simultaneous presence, but rejects the possibility of simultaneous presence in the same place.[76]

The two arguments for the possibility of simultaneous presence do not mention the issue of whether this presence can or should occur at the same place; they are effectively neutral on that question. The first argument is little more than an assertion. It is claimed that since there are infinitely many living beings in need of Buddha's salvific actions at any particular time, these beings would be better and more effectively served if more than one body of magical transformation were always available to them.

The second argument is a little more developed. It begins from the premise that at any time infinitely many bodhisattvas are practicing the path and so accumulating the merit and wisdom that will permit them eventually to become Buddha. From this fact it is taken to follow that at any particular time many such practitioners will have completed their practice, and so will be ready to become Buddha. Such practitioners should awaken to Buddhahood simultaneously; the only other option is that they will, metaphorically or actually, stand in line somewhere awaiting the end of the career of one body of magical transformation before their own career as such can begin. This option is taken to offend against both common sense and the pan-Buddhist view that Buddhahood follows immediately upon completion of the path. It therefore follows that numerous bodies of magical transformation must function at the same time.

These arguments are not seriously questioned anywhere in the digests: simultaneity is taken to be as desirable and as well-established as multiplicity so far as bodies of magical transformation are concerned. The five negative arguments are not concerned to refute the idea of simultaneity but rather the idea of the simultaneous presence of more than one body of magical transformation in the same place. Four of these arguments claim that if such simultaneous presence were to occur, specifiable undesirable results would follow. The fifth is of a different kind: it has to deal with a sacred text, a Sūtra, which appears to claim straightforwardly that the simultaneous presence in one world-realm of two or more bodies of magical transformation is impossible (*asthāna*), that there is no scope (*anavakāśa*) for such a thing. I shall deal with these five arguments briefly and seriatim.

The first argument against the possibility of simultaneous presence in one place concerns the bodhisattva's vow, a formulaic declaration attributed to those who undertake eventually to become Buddha. One of the forms used for this vow includes the intention to function as Buddha in a world-realm without any Buddha present in it (*avinayako lokadhātu*). If some particular bodhisattva were to be active as a body of magical transformation in a world where another such body was already present, the terms of the vow would not be fulfilled.

The second argument has to do with salvific overkill. A single body of magical transformation, it is argued, can do everything Buddha needs to do in a particular world-realm at a particular time; the simultaneous presence of a second would therefore be entirely superfluous.

The third and fourth arguments may be treated together since they both have to do with the kinds of response that should be generated by the presence of a body of magical transformation in the world. This response has two dimensions: first, living beings should respond to such a body with awe, amazement, and reverence; second, they should respond with zeal and enthusiasm for the practice of the path, and for the eventual attainment of Buddhahood on their own behalf. Both kinds of response, it is argued, would be inappropriately diluted by the presence of more than one body of magical transformation in one place at one time. People would, if they could be in the presence of more than one such body at once, become blasé, and so would be neither sufficiently reverential nor sufficiently zealous. The theorists who produced the digests seem to have been very alive to the dangers of overexposure.

The fifth argument hinges upon a rather more complex issue of scriptural exegesis, and is found more frequently than the other four as well as usually being treated in more detail.[77] The scriptural text in question appears to deny the possibility of the simultaneous presence of two or more bodies of magical transformation in one world-realm (*lokadhātu*);[78] and while the digests are quite happy to affirm, as this text implies, that two or more bodies of magical transformation are indeed not found in immediate spatial continguity at one time, and to use this very scriptural text as an argument against such a possibility, they are much less happy with the text's other implication, which is that simultaneity not involved with such continguity is also to be ruled out. As I have already shown, the digests uniformly want to affirm this kind of simultaneity. How then to deal with this text?

The digests fasten upon a crucial ambiguity in the term 'world-realm,' the spatial locus in which the simultaneous presence of two or more bodies of magical transformation is denied in the text in question. Two meanings are distinguished, based upon a standard division in Buddhist cosmology. The first takes 'world-realm' to mean *caturdvīpaloka*, a 'four-continent world' with all its accompanying heavens and hells; while matters are rather more complex than this will make them sound, it seems fair to say that a four-continent world is roughly analogous in Buddhist cosmology to a planet in contemporary western cosmology. That is, it is a relatively self-contained system (or at least appears to be such to its inhabitants) which is, from the perspective of those inhabitants, large, but from that of the universe as a whole, infinitely small. The second takes 'world-realm' to mean *trisāhasramahāsāhasralokadhātu*, a 'great trichiliocosm'; this consists of one thousand million four-continent worlds,[79] and is thus perhaps analogous to a galaxy in western cosmology.

Suppose 'world-realm' in the disputed text has the first meaning. The simultaneous presence of more than one body of magical transformation upon a single planet is then denied. This is the position taken by most of the digests. It is relatively easy to see why: the simultaneous presence of two or more bodies of magical transformation in such a (relatively) small space could easily lead to the kind of immediate contiguity rejected by the digests in the four arguments just discussed. So they prefer to take the disputed text as denying simultaneous presence in one four-continent world, a denial that leaves open the possibility of affirming such simultaneity in a great trichiliocosm. More specifically, if this line is taken it becomes possible to affirm the serial presence of several bodies of magical transformation in a single four-continent world, each of which may be functioning simultaneously with some other body of magical transformation in some other four-continent world within the same trichiliocosm. The required maximum level of salvific effect is thus assured.

The standard position derived from all this argumentation then includes the following claims: simultaneity coupled with immediate spatial contiguity is not possible for bodies of magical transformation; simultaneity not so coupled is not only possible but necessary; and every four-continent world (every planet, that is to say) has had, now has, or will have (or all three) a body of magical transformation active in it. All of this has one other important implication: that the absence of a body of magical transformation in a particular world-realm, brought about by its apparent death, is a necessity if its salvific aims are to be properly realized.

Recall the third and fourth arguments against the possibility of simultaneous presence in immediate contiguity. There it was suggested that such a state of affairs would make the development of proper reverence and zeal on the part of non-Buddhas close to impossible. A similar argument is used to show that an endless presence of some particular body of magical transformation would have the same effect: if, say, Gautama Śākyamuni had never appeared to die, to pass, as the digests put it, into final Nirvana, then zeal for the practice of the path would have been transferred by living beings to devotion to that body, and they would, as a result, never have reached final awakening themselves. Six arguments are offered in the digests for the conclusion that bodies of magical transformation must appear to die;[80] they all focus upon the difficulty of making efforts toward one's own awakening if a body of magical transformation is always before one, or upon the dangers of developing excessive attachment to the beauties and glories of such a body if it is continuously present. It is essential to the standard position, then, that each body of magical transformation should be present for only a short time, no more than a long lifespan at most.

I have tried to show in this chapter how the digests understand Buddha in the world. In the course of the exposition, and especially in the analysis of Buddha's perfections of action and cognition, it became evident that the doctrines about these perfections—doctrines that emphasize the effortlessness, spontaneity, choicelessness, and complete effectiveness of Buddha's action and cognition in the world—have complex truth-conditions that are neither fully stated by the digests in those contexts in which they discuss Buddha in the world, nor given systematic defense by them there. To put this another way: the central doctrinal claim that the only properties of interest that belong to Buddha in the world are relational properties of the kind *seems to S to be P at t* is grounded in and given sense by the metaphysics of Buddha's real body (*dharmakāya*), of the nonrelational properties of Buddha as it is in itself. And so it is in chapter six, in the context of an analysis of those nonrelational properties, that a fuller explication of the metaphysical context for and explanation of Buddha's action in the world will be given.

Chapter 5

Buddha in Heaven

5.0 Prolegomena

Buddha is active and available not only in its bodies of magical transformation in worlds like ours, but also in its bodies of communal enjoyment (*sambhoga*) in heavenly realms that often appear very unlike this world.[1] In this chapter I shall explore what the digests have to say about such worlds and such bodies. I can be relatively brief here since many of the philosophical points made in the preceding chapter about the nature of Buddha's actions in the world apply to Buddha's actions in heaven as well. Here, as there, Buddha possesses a wide range of properties of the kind *seems to S to be P at t*; the specific kinds of seeming predicated of Buddha in its bodies of communal enjoyment are different from those predicated of it in its bodies of magical transformation, but the properties are of the same logical kind. I shall begin by describing the heavens inhabited by Buddha, and shall pass from there to an analysis of buddhalogical doctrine about the actions of bodies of communal enjoyment.

But first some explanation of the term *sambhoga* and of why I choose to translate it 'communal enjoyment.' *Bhoga* is a nominal item derived from the verbal root *bhuj-*; the semantic range of this terms spans those of 'consume' and 'enjoy' in English, largely because consumption understood in its broadest sense—of sensory inputs of all kinds, but most commonly of food and sex—is taken in Indic texts to be pleasurable by definition. Since this is not the case in English (if anything, 'consumption' and associated terms have come to have largely negative connotations), *bhoga* might be translated 'pleasurable consumption.' But because this seems a little clumsy I prefer, along with most other scholars, to use simply 'enjoyment' for *bhoga*, leaving the object of such enjoyment to emerge from the contexts in which it is used.

In the case of *sambhoga*, a prefix (*sam-*) is added to the nominal item, and it is this that I translate 'communal.' The prefix suggests, most often, connection, simultaneity, or reciprocity; most generally it indicates that something is occurring together with something else. Hence my translation.[2] This is not, though, the translation used by most scholars working in this field. They tend to ignore the prefix altogether, and translate *sambhoga* simply as 'enjoyment'; some, influenced by the Tibetan translation (*longs spyod rdzogs*), which understands the prefix to suggest completeness or definitiveness, translate 'complete enjoyment' or the like. But this Tibetan translation seems to me misleading. It is preferable to emphasize that what the *sambhogakāya* does is precisely and always done in community, in the midst of a retinue of bodhisattvas drawn up around the lion-throne on which a body of communal enjoyment is seated. The digests often emphasize these communal facts when they gloss the term.[3] As I shall show, the object of the communal enjoyment of the *sambhogakāya* and its audience is paradigmatically the dharma, the doctrine whose flavor is unsurpassed. This doctrine is consumed at a communal meal, and in the act of consumption unparalleled pleasure and unparalleled salvific benefit are produced.

5.1 *Ornamenting Heaven*

A body of communal enjoyment, as Paul Masson-Oursel put it long ago, is "un Bouddha se rendant 'participiable' . . . aux bodhisattvas."[4] That is, Buddha makes itself available to advanced practitioners of the path, practitioners who are themselves almost Buddha, mostly in its *sambhogakāya*, its body of communal enjoyment. Buddha does this, paradigmatically, in a

Buddha-field (*buddhakṣetra*), a heavenly realm not directly or easily accessible to embodied living beings in a world-realm like ours. Indeed, the digests often define Buddha-fields and bodies of communal enjoyment interchangeably: the former is where the latter are found, and the latter are found where the former is.[5]

What then is a Buddha-field? The Sūtras are full of stories about them,[6] but these stories are rarely sufficiently precise to be of use in sorting out questions that concern me here. But some general cosmological points are clear. A *buddhakṣetra* is usually said to be identical with a great trichiliocosm (*trisāhasramahāsāhasralokadhātu*), a cosmic system consisting of one thousand million four-continent worlds (*caturdvīpaloka*), or planets, with all their attendant heavens, hells, and living beings of various classes and kinds. Spatially, a great trichiliocosm is thus roughly equivalent to a galaxy in western cosmology. Since every four-continent world is part of a great trichiliocosm, it follows that every four-continent world, even the most apparently unpleasant, is actually part of a Buddha-field. But some Buddha-fields appear to be more pleasant than others; some, for instance, contain no apparently impure worlds like ours.

In buddhalogical terms a Buddha-field is the *gocara* or sphere of influence of some particular Buddha, who may be manifest in it either as a body of magical transformation or as a body of communal enjoyment.[7] A number of the digests place considerable emphasis upon the connections between reaching a certain stage of the path and gaining the ability to manifest (*sandṛś-*) a Buddha-field to non-Buddhas.[8] They typically say that such an ability is obtained at the eighth stage (*bhūmi*) of the practice of the path, since it is at that stage, when those following the path are very nearly Buddha, that their spheres of influence are sufficiently purified by their meditational and ethical training to make this possible. Notice that at this stage of practice, a particular body of communal enjoyment does not yet take up residence in a particular Buddha-field; what is obtained is rather the capacity (*śakti*) to do so. The actuality obtains later, when the path has been followed to its proper conclusion. The question of when a particular body of communal enjoyment with its Buddha-field comes into existence is a variant of a larger set of problems about attributing temporal change to Buddha at all. I shall discuss this further in chapter six. At this point it will suffice to say that what causes a particular Buddha-field to come into existence is the complete purification (*pariśodhana*) of a particular practitioner's environment through the practice of the path.

The vocabulary used by the digests to discuss the capacity to manifest a Buddha-field is similar to that used to analyze the activities of bodies of magical transformation. I commented in chapter four on the importance in such contexts of the use of *sandṛś-* and its derivatives, especially in the causative forms; precisely the same terminology is used in contexts where Buddha-fields are the topic, and once again the significance of these terms—meaning literally 'to cause to see' and so 'to manifest' or 'to make apparent'—is that it shows the properties of Buddha, in its bodies of communal enjoyment, clearly to be best understood as properties of the kind *seems to S to be P*.

A particular Buddha-field, then, is caused to come into being by the completion of some practitioner's religious path, which is the same as to say that it is caused by—or, better, consists in—the fulfilment of the religious vows (*praṇidhāna*) that marked the beginning of the path for that practitioner. More specifically, the attainment of the ability to manifest a Buddha-field is connected by the digests with the gaining of sufficient flexibility of mind (*cittakarmaṇyatva*) on the part of the practitioner to do so; this flexibility is attained through the meditational practice that disposes of obstacles to the completion of the path, and most especially of the obstacle of volition or effort; once one has got rid of this, one can make Buddha-fields of various kinds appear in spontaneous response to the needs of those living beings who will inhabit them.[9]

This last point is important: the digests are, for the most part, concerned to reject the idea that the gorgeously ornamented heavens in which the bodies of communal enjoyment are active are real places with spatial location. That their existence is dependent upon the mental flexibility of those practitioners of the path who are capable of manifesting them at will strongly suggests that they are mental projections, appearances resulting from modifications of the mental stream (*cittasantāna*) of such practitioners. The point is driven home when the digests say that Buddha-fields are in fact nothing other than representations (*vijñapti*) or mental images designed to have desired salvific effects upon the minds of those who experience them: there are no mind-independent objects of any kind in them.[10]

There was, no doubt, a polemical context for such assertions: then, as now, many Buddhists appear to have taken the descriptions of Buddha-fields found in the sacred texts to be descriptions of real places, places in which they could hope to be reborn after an appropriately good life. The digests are concerned, in contrast, to present entry into Buddha-fields and interaction there with bodies of communal enjoyment as meditational possibilities, not as places in which one might find a new spatial location after the death of whatever body one might happen to have. The Buddha-fields, like the appearances of bodies of magical transformation in worlds such as ours, are produced entirely by the needs of living beings; it would therefore be a conceptual error, and a salvifically damaging one, to think of them as desirable places in which to be reborn. They are, rather, from the viewpoint of the digests, salvifically beneficial possibilities theoretically experienceable now. The obverse of this point is that apparently pure Buddha-fields are just like apparently impure and unpleasant four-continent worlds, such as the one we inhabit, in at least the following important respect: they are exclusively products of the salvific needs of non-Buddhas, and so are ontologically on a par with one another.

The tension between metaphysical and soteriological explanation, noted already in chapters three and four, is evident here as well. On the one hand, the emergence of some particular Buddha-fields is linked with some practitioner's attainment of Buddhahood, and so is indexed to a time and to the practice of the path; on the other, Buddha-fields are explained metaphysically as atemporal, changes in Buddha's activity that are only apparent and not indexed to a particular time. The digests do not attempt a resolution of this tension in the context of their discussions of Buddha-fields; it can only be resolved finally by a full analysis of Buddha's eternality and changelessness, a matter to which I shall return in the next chapter.

The digests do not in fact typically provide the detailed and ornate literary descriptions of the Buddha-fields found in more discursive sacred texts devoted to that purpose. Rather, they presuppose such descriptions and provide analytical categories and schemata with which to make sense of them. It is on these that I shall focus in the comments that follow, though wherever necessary I shall try to explain them by reference to these more detailed descriptive presentations.

A Buddha-field is often presented descriptively as containing (or even as consisting in) a great palace, a palace in which the body of communal enjoyment takes up residence in order both to enjoy the dharma itself and to communicate such joy to the bodhisattvas who gather in its retinue. This palace is given enormously detailed description in many Sūtras, and is alluded to descriptively in terms of its perfections of color (*varṇa*) and configuration (*saṃsthāna*) in the digests.[11] Typically, the digests say that the great palace in which Buddha resides in its body of communal enjoyment is ornamented with seven kinds of precious metal and gemstones; its radiance fills the entire galaxy; and its divisions and apartments are perfectly designed for its purposes. The discursive descriptions of Buddha's palace are much more lyrical, adding flowers, thrones, canopies, parasols, banners, garlands, lights, and so forth, as explanations of its perfections of color and configuration. The following, a description of Buddha's lion-throne in one such palace, is quite typical:

> There a hundred trillion tiers all around it, with a hundred trillion gold webs, a hundred trillion flower curtains, a hundred trillion jewel curtains, a hundred trillion garland curtains, and a hundred trillion incense curtains hung above it. Garlands of flowers hung down, their scent perfuming everywhere. A hundred trillion canopies of of flowers, a hundred trillion canopies of garlands, and a hundred trillion canopies of jewels were held by various celestial beings arrayed in rows on all four sides. A hun-

> dred trillion precious robes were spread on it. A hundred trillion balconies radiantly adorned it, with a hundred trillion nets of pearls and a hundred trillion nets of jewels covering above, while a hundred trillion nets of necklaces hung down on all four sides.[12]

Part of the point of such descriptions is meditational and part motivational. That is, reciting or hearing recited such hypnotically repetitive descriptions is itself a tool intended to produce a vision of the Buddha-field in question, and so to bring the meditator into direct contact with the body of communal enjoyment around which and for which the field is constituted. Recall that the digests typically give their descriptions of Buddha-fields in the context of an analysis of *buddhānusmṛti*, the active and attentive recollection of the good qualities of a body of communal enjoyment, which are inseparable from the adornments of the heaven within which such a body is to be found. But the descriptions are also motivational: they are intended to depict a place of such overwhelming beauty and desirability that the hearer will intensify her religious practice in an attempt to become one of the advanced bodhisattvas ecstatically assembled around the body of communal enjoyment as it teaches.

But it should also be clear from what was said in chapter four about the similes used to represent the spontaneity, effortlessness, and omnipresence of Buddha's action in the world, that similar points are being made here through these immensely detailed descriptions of kinds of precious stones, lights, flowers, and so forth, in which each Buddha-field is said to consist. Such descriptions are designed to show the spontaneous variety of Buddha's teaching of the dharma in its bodies of communal enjoyment. In these bodies also, as in its bodies of magical transformation, Buddha's teaching activity is spontaneous and appears differently to different recipients; hence the great variety of jewels, flowers, and the rest. The Buddha-field is a phantasmagoria of salvifically effective ornaments, changing from moment to moment according to the needs of living beings. And in bearing such a relation to the needs of living beings, it does not differ from the considerably less exciting four-continent world in which we live.

5.2 Bodies of Communal Enjoyment

I have shown, briefly, where the bodies of communal enjoyment are to be found. Something now needs to be said as to how the digests define these bodies.[13]

Some scholastic technicalities will be unavoidable here. Consider the following verses:

> svābhāviko 'tha sāmbhogyaḥ kāyo nairmāṇiko 'paraḥ/
> kāyabhedā hi na buddhānāṃ prathamas tu dvayāśrayaḥ//
> sarvadhātuṣu sāmbhogyo bhinno gaṇaparigrahaiḥ/
> kṣetraiś ca nāmabhiḥ kāyair dharmasambhogacṣṭeitaiḥ//[14]

> The body of Buddhas is differentiated according to the body in its essence, in its communal enjoyment, and in its magical transformation. The first is the basis of the other two.
> In all spheres, the body in its communal enjoyment is differentiated according to the crowds it gathers, fields, names, bodies, communal enjoyment of doctrine, and actions.

My translation here suggests that the body of Buddhas is singular, but that it can be differentiated according to different functions.[15] The commentaries on these verses make this abundantly clear: there is a single body (*kāya*) belonging to all Buddhas, and it is this single body that is called the "body in its essence." But functionally speaking it makes sense to speak of two other bodies: the "body in its communal enjoyment" and the "body in its magical transformation." The body of Buddhas is thus numerically single but functionally multiple; when three bodies are spoken of, or, more commonly, when a threefold body (*trividhakāya*) is spoken of, the intended referent is not three separate entities, but rather a single entity with three kinds of function. This interpretation is both supported and clarified by the fact that a threefold-body theory is expounded under the rubric of Buddha's function (*vṛtti*), a category discussed in chapter three.

It is evident from the verses translated above that when Buddha is considered in its bodies of communal enjoyment it is multiple in the sense that instances of such functioning both can and must be differentiated according to a variety of categories. The following comments on the verses from one of the digests will make these differentiations clearer:

> de la mang po yongs su sdud pa zhes bya ba ni 'khor sdud pa la bya ste/ rdzogs longs spyod pa'i 'khor mang po yang tha dad do/ ji lta zhe na/ rdzogs longs spyod pa'i 'khor kha cig ni byang chub sems dpa' blo gros mi zad pa zhes bya ba la sogs pas bskor la/ rdzogs longs spyod pa'i 'khor kha cig tu ni byang chub sems dpa' kun tu bzang po dang/ spyan ras gzigs kyi dbang po zhes bya ba la sogs pa byang chub sems dpa'i 'khor gzhan gyis bskor ba'i phyir ro/ zhing tha dad pa ni sangs rgyas kyi zhing gis gzhi kha cig shel gyi kha dog tu gnas/ kha cig ser dang bai-dū-rya la sogs pa'i kha dog tu gnas pa'i phyir ro/ ming tha dad pa ni rdzogs longs spyod pa'i sku kha cig gi mtshan rnam par snang mdzad ces bya/ kha cig snang ba mtha' yas zhes bya/ kha cig kun tu bzang po zhes bya ba la sogs pa mtshan tha dad pa'i phyir ro/ sku tha dad pa ni kha cig sku mdog gser du snang ba dang/ kha cig shel dang/ kha cig dngul du snang ba dang/ kha cig ni sku tshad che/ kha cig ni sku tshang cung ba'i phyir ro/ chos la rdzogs par longs spyod pa tha dad pa ni kha cig gi rdzogs longs spyod pa'i 'khor na sa bcu'i theg pa chen po 'chad/ kha cig ni lang-kar-gshegs pa 'chad/ kha cig ni shes rab kyi pha rol tu phyin pa 'chad pa'i phyir ro/[16]

> "[Differentiation according to] the crowds it gathers" means that the assemblies gathered for communal enjoyment are differentiated. This in turn means that some of the assemblies gathered for communal enjoyment encircle a bodhisattva such as Akṣayamati, while others encircle bodhisattvas such as Samantabhadra and Avalokiteśvara. As to "differentiation according to fields": some Buddha-fields are the color of crystal, while others are of gold or lapis lazuli. As to "differentiation according to names": the body in its communal enjoyment is differentiated in its defining characteristics, and so is called 'Vairocana,' 'Samantabhadra,' 'Amitābha,' and the like. As to "differentiation according to bodies": [the body in its communal enjoyment] is sometimes radiant with a golden color,

> sometimes with a crystal color, and sometimes with a silver color; sometimes it is very small and sometimes very large. As to "differentiation according to communal enjoyment of doctrine": in some assemblies gathered for communal enjoyment the *Mahāyāna-Daśabhūmika* is taught; in others the *Laṅkāvatāra*; and in yet others the *Prajñāpāramitā*.

According to these comments (and others like them), the body of Buddha exhibits at least five formal features whenever it functions as a body of communal enjoyment: it gathers a crowd around it; it is located in a Buddha-field; it has a particular name; it has a particular body with recognizable features; and it teaches the dharma surrounded by its crowd, in its Buddha-field, with its body to which a particular name is attached. Each body of communal enjoyment, though it has these formal features in common with every other such body, differs from every other in its particulars. So Amitābha differs from Vairocana in name (obviously), Buddha-field, appearance, assembled audience, and particular teachings.

Some interesting features of the lengthy passage just quoted need further explanation. The first has to do with the sacred texts mentioned as examples of the dharma enjoyed and consumed by specific bodies of communal enjoyment together with their audiences. These are all famous and influential works, but their promulgation is attributed to different speakers, and the nature of these speakers shows something of how the bodies of communal enjoyment are understood by the digests. The first work mentioned, *The Sacred Text on the Ten Stages Belonging to the Mahāyāna* (*Mahāyāna-Daśabhūmikasūtra*), contains extensive and detailed teaching on the stages of the bodhisattva's religious path. It represents itself as being spoken by one Vajragarbha, a bodhisattva, under the persuasion and by the influence of many Buddhas, including Gautama Śākyamuni.[17]

The voluminous *Perfection of Wisdom* (*Prajñāpāramitā*) literature is, by contrast, attributed to Gautama himself, speaking from the Vulture Peak to an assembly including (usually) Śāriputra and Ānanda, and (often) Avalokiteśvara and other assorted bodhisattvas.[18] The *Sacred Text on the Descent into Laṅkā* (*Laṅkāvatārasūtra*) is similarly said to have been spoken by Gautama,[19] though this time on the island of Sri Lanka rather than on the Vulture Peak. These facts are also of interest, since Gautama's teaching activity is usually thought to be best understood as the work of a body of magical transformation. So this may suggest that the boundary between what can properly be said to be an action of a body of magical transformation, on the one hand, and an action of a body of communal enjoyment, on the other, is not well defined. I shall return to this.

The idea that a body of communal enjoyment need not, in the strict sense, be Buddha, but can instead be a bodhisattva far advanced along the path of religious practice, is confirmed by the examples given. Among these, Amitābha and Vairocana are Buddha; but Samantabhadra, Akṣayamati, and Avalokiteśvara are bodhisattvas, and are explicitly said to be such in the extract under discussion here. How is this possible?

Two conceptual distinctions are being ignored—or at least blurred—in these identifications of Gautama Śākyamuni's teaching activities with those of a body of communal enjoyment, and of bodhisattvas as bodies of communal enjoyment even though they are not yet Buddha. One very broad explanation will serve to deal with both: following the claim that everything well-spoken is spoken by Buddha (discussed in chapter two), it might be said that all salvifically beneficial action is performed by Buddha, and that it therefore makes little difference whether Gautama's teaching is categorized as having been done by a body of magical transformation or one of communal enjoyment; nor whether bodhisattvas should be talked of as bodies of communal enjoyment. The truth is that all actions of the appropriate kind are Buddha's actions. Categorizing some of them as performed by bodhisattvas or Buddhas-to-be like Avalokiteśvara or Maitreya (or indeed by Gautama before he became an awakened one), some by bodies of magical transformation, and some by bodies of communal enjoyment, is useful for the purposes of scholastic analysis (which may in itself be salvifically beneficial), but making such distinctions is, in the end, of only instrumental significance: it can be abandoned when it needs to be, since the distinctions in question are not rooted in Buddha itself, but are, rather, distinctions in Buddha's modes of appearance to non-Buddhas.

To put this somewhat differently: the truth is that all actions of Buddha, whether they appear to occur in a four-continent world like this one or in a golden Buddha-field adorned with vast and imaginative floral arrangements, are representations in the minds of living beings whose occurrence is explicable without remainder in terms of the needs of those beings. Such representations typically fall into two broad categories: the first consists of the kinds of activities discussed in chapter four, activities of an apparently more-or-less human body in a world much like this one; the second consists of the kinds of activities discussed in this chapter, activities of an obviously nonhuman body in a world dramatically unlike this one.

But some Buddha-actions fall somewhere uneasily between these two categories, and when this happens it becomes clear that the category-system is entirely conventional: it matters as little whether a specific Buddha-action is said to belong to one or another category as it does whether something said by a specific individual who is both spouse and professor is said to be spoken by a spouse or by a professor. There are certain things said by that individual, perhaps endearments whispered to the spouse, which it seems sensible to categorize as spousal; just as there are others, perhaps formal lectures given, which are better characterized as professorial. But there will be cases (expounding philosophy to the spouse, say) where either categorization is possible and appropriate. Just so with Buddha-actions. Some are obviously, paradigmatically, actions of a body of communal enjoyment, and some are equally obviously to be predicated of a body of magical transformation. But others, like the actions of Maitreya in the Tuṣita heaven, or of Śākyamuni on Ghṛdhrakuṭa (though for different reasons in each of these cases) can appropriately be characterized as either.

Maitreya's actions in the Tuṣita heaven may be taken as paradigmatic of the actions of an advanced bodhisattva, more precisely a bodhisattva whose religious practice has taken him as far as the tenth stage (*bhūmi*) of the path. They are not, therefore, actions of Buddha in the strict sense. Yet they are certainly productive of salvific benefit, and so can by that criterion be classified as actions of Buddha. The question then becomes whether to think of them as actions of Buddha in a body of communal enjoyment or in a body of magical transformation. And here it is clear that they are much more like the former: they occur in a heavenly realm whose physical properties are very unlike those of this one (even though Maitreya's heaven is strictly to be understood as a part of this impure four-continent world and not as a Buddha-field), and they consist in teaching the dharma. (It might be useful at this point to recall that the corpus discussed at some length in chapter two is attributed in part to Maitreya.) Hence such actions are said by the digests to be the actions of Buddha in its body of communal enjoyment. In general, the more exalted bodhisattvas—among whom Maitreya and Avalokiteśvara are the best examples[20]—are given functional status as Buddha by the tradition. They give teachings treated as (and said to be) Buddha's word; there is a religious cult surrounding them; and they inhabit and act in heavenly realms that, while technically distinguishable from Buddha-fields, are describable in terms that make such distinctions impossible to discern. It is therefore scarcely surprising to find their actions being talked of by the digests as actions of bodies of communal enjoyment.

A similar explanation can be given—though rather more briefly—for the judgment that Gautama Śākyamuni's preaching at Vulture Peak is an action of a body of communal enjoyment rather than one of magical transformation. A case could certainly be made for judging it to be the latter, but the important respect in which it is more like the former lies in its retinue, the audience to which it speaks. This audience typically consists not only of monks and *arhat*s, but also of extremely large crowds of bodhisattvas;[21] this fact alone is enough to make Buddha's actions in such a context best characterized as actions of a body of communal enjoyment, for it is precisely characteristic of such bodies to enjoy the dharma in their Buddha-fields surrounded by just such a retinue.

What has been said to this point about the bodies of communal enjoyment is confirmed by a list, found in one of the digests, of properties that distinguish these bodies from the single essential or real body.[22] Most of these differences are entirely straightforward: the body in its essence is not physical, whereas the bodies of communal enjoyment appear to be physical; the bodies of communal enjoyment appear to change because they appear differently to different audiences as the aspirations and needs of those audiences change, while this cannot be true of the body of Buddha in its essence; and the bodies of communal enjoyment are intrinsically relational in that it is only in and through them that Buddha can be related to the bodhisattvas, divine beings, and others who make up its typical audience. So we read, in a passage commenting upon traditional formulations of the differences between the real body and the body of communal enjoyment:

> da ni gang las dgongs nas ngo bo nyid kyi sku longs spyod rdzogs pa'i sku ma yin zhe na/ de bstan par bya ste/ de gzugs kyi skur snang ba dang zhes bya ba la/ sangs rgyas ni chos kyi sku yin la/ de ni gzugs su mthong ba'i phyir ro/ chos kyi sku ma yin te/ de lta bu ni chos kyi sku ma yin pas/ de'i phyir na chos kyi sku ma yin no/ longs spyod rdzogs pa'i sku de ni sangs rgyas kyi 'khor gyi dkyil 'khor tshad med pa dag na tha dad par snang la/ chos kyi sku la ni tha dad pa med do/ de'i phyir tshul 'dis kyang longs spyod rdzogs pa'i sku ngo bo nyid kyi sku ma yin no/ mos pa ji lta ba bzhin du longs spyod rdzogs pa mthong bas kyang ste/ ji ltar mdo las/ kha cig ni kha dog ser po/ kha cig ni kha dog sngon po zhes bya ba la sogs pa rgyas par 'byung ba'i phyir ro/ de bzhin du longs spyod rdzogs pa'i sku ni ma nges pa'i ngo bo nyid du snang ba yin gyi/ ngo bo nyid kyi sku ni ma nges pa'i ngo bo nyid du mi rigs te/ de'i phyir tshul des kyang longs spyod rdzogs pa'i sku ni ngo bo nyid kyi sku ma yin no/ yang longs spyod rdzogs pa de ni gcig nyid yin na yang gzhan dang gzhan du mthong bar 'gyur la/ yang de nyid kho na de las kyang gzhan du mthong bar 'gyur bas de ni gyo ba'i ngo bo'i ngo bo nyid yin pa'i phyir ngo bo nyid kyi sku yin par mi rigs te/ de'i phyir na yang ngo bo nyid kyi sku ma yin no/ yang longs spyod rdzogs pa de ni lha la sogs pa'i 'khor dang rtag tu 'dres shing bskor nas gnas pa yin gyi/ ngo bo

> nyid ni 'dres par mi 'gyur te/ de'i phyir na yang ngo bo nyid kyi sku ma yin no/[23]
>
> Now, if it is asked in what sense the essence body is different from the body of communal enjoyment, this is explained in the words "it appears to be a physical body." Buddha is a real body and it appears as a physical body; but since it is not the real body that appears in such a way, [these words] do not refer to the real body. It is the body of communal enjoyment that "appears differently among the innumerable Buddha-assemblies." There is no differentiation in the real body, and so the body in its communal enjoyment is not the essence body. Furthermore, it is the body of communal enjoyment that is "seen in accordance with the aspirations [of living beings]," which means, in short, that some see it as golden in color and others as blue. In this way the essence of the body of communal enjoyment appears to be undetermined, but this is not true of the essence body. For this reason, too, the body of communal enjoyment is not the essence body. And if the body of communal enjoyment and the essence body were one and the same, then the essence body [like the body of communal enjoyment] would have a changeable essence because it would be seen in a variety of ways. But one cannot say this of the essence body. Also, the body of communal enjoyment functions in relation to the assemblies of divine beings and so forth, while the essence body is not relational. For this reason too [the body of communal enjoyment] is not the essence body.

This passage points to a series of differences in the ways that bodies of communal enjoyment are capable of appearing to living beings—as golden, as blue, and so forth. These appearances are changeable: a body of communal enjoyment can *seem to S to be P at t*; and then can *seem to S to be Q at t + 1*. Alternatively, it can *seem to S to be P at t* while also *seeming to T to be Q at t*. None of these are properties capable of being predicated of the essence body. Perhaps more important, all the properties possessed by a body of communal enjoyment are relational: it has no properties other than those that relate it to its assembled audience in the Buddha-field wherein it functions. And this too is not true of the essence body.

There is a further important difference between the bodies of communal enjoyment and the essence body, a difference made clear by those among the digests that adopt and deploy a particular theory as to the nature and kinds of consciousness (*vijñāna*), a theory associated above all with the scholasticism of the Yogācāra. This theory, to state it briefly and without attention to any of its many implications that have nothing directly to do with Buddha, divides consciousness into eight kinds.[24] The first six of these comprise the 'active' or 'functioning' (*pravṛtti*) consciousnesses, which are visual, auditory, olfactory, gustatory, tactile, and thinking. The first five of these are kinds of consciousness brought into being by sensory inputs through the five physical senses, while the sixth is brought into being by the exercise of the organ of thought (*manas*). The scholasticism of the digests makes no distinction of kind among these six: each is understood as a product of consuming and enjoying (*bhuj-*) what appears as the external world, and that one of them is (by the standards of western scholasticism) mental and the other five physical is not taken to be important. In addition to these six there is a seventh called the 'afflicted organ of thought' (*kliṣṭamanas*), a consciousness whose main function is to act as an explanatory category for some difficult problems in soteriology; it will not detain me further here. Finally, there is an eighth consciousness, the 'store-consciousness' (*ālayavijñāna*), a nonintentional consciousness whose main function is to act as a repository or storehouse for the results of past actions, and so to explain various complex issues in causal theory.

All these consciousnesses are capable of a radical transformation. It is soteriologically necessary for the digests to say this since it is axiomatic for them that the usual functions of these consciousnesses are undesirable: the presence of passions and afflictions of various kinds issues in improper doxastic and affective habits, which means that the beliefs formed on the basis of this ordinary functioning, together with the associated habitual emotional responses to those beliefs, are entirely antipathetic to progress along the religious path. If such progress is to occur, then, the ordinary functions of the eight consciousnesses must be capable of profound and complete transformation. The digests usually designate this transformation by the word *parivṛtti* (or sometimes *parāvṛtti*), a term meaning something like 'turning around,' 'transformation,' or 'reorientation.'[25] I shall adopt this last translation.

With this set of conceptual distinctions in mind, the point that concerns me here is that the operations of the bodies of communal enjoyment are said to be connected especially with the radical reorientation of the sensory consciousnesses. This radical reorientation produces mastery (*vibhutva* or *vaśitā*) over all sensory objects in the sense that a particular sense-organ—say, the ear—is no longer limited to experiencing auditory objects, but can now experience visual objects, olfactory objects, and so forth.[26] This is to say that each sense-organ can freely experience all sensory objects with complete spontaneity.

While it is a little difficult to imagine what such a condition might be like for its possessor—what the phenomenal properties of such an erasure of the boundaries between the different modalities of sensory experience might be (a matter about which I shall say more in chapter seven)—it seems clear that the point of making a claim like this for the bodies of communal enjoyment does not, for the digests, lie in the realm of phenomenology. Rather, the point is to explain how the bodies of communal enjoyment are able to produce and magically transform at will the sensually gorgeous Buddha-fields.

The objects of the sensory consciousnesses and the consciousnesses themselves are, for the digests, correlative concepts. That is, when mastery over one is obtained—when one can, at will, transform experience in one sensory mode into experience in another—so is mastery over the other: the objects of sensory experience can also be transformed at will. Here is one way of putting this:

> sārthodgrahaparāvṛttau vibhutvaṃ labhyate param/
> kṣetraśuddhau yathākāmaṃ bhogasandarśanāya hi//[27]

When apprehension together with its objects is transformed,

> One obtains supreme mastery over manifesting enjoyment at will in a pure field.

On which one of the digests comments:

> don gyi sgra ni gzugs nas chos kyi bar du yul drug la bya'o/ 'dzin pa'i sgras ni mig gi rnam par shes pa nas lus kyi rnam par shes pa'i bar du rnam par shes pa lnga'i tshogs la bya ste/[28]
>
> The word "objects" denotes the six kinds of sensory spheres, beginning with physical form and ending with the objects of the organ of thought. The word "apprehension" denotes the group of five sensory consciousnesses, beginning with the visual and ending with the tactile.

The digests typically treat the reorientation of the sixth sensory consciousness (*manovijñānaparāvṛtti*) separately, since discussion of it involves an analysis of *vikalpa*, with which it is usually identified.[29] The extract continues:

> yul drug dang rnam par shes pa'i tshogs dag ste/ gnas gzhan du gyur na/ 'byor pa dam pa rnam pa gnyis 'thob par 'gyur ro zhes bya ba'i don to/ zhing yang 'dod bzhin dag pa dang/ longs spyod shin tu ston par ro/ zhes bya ba la/ phyi'i yul rnams gzhan du ma gyur pa'i dus na ni ngam grog dang/ tsher ma dang/ gseg ma dang/ gyo mo la sogs pa lta bur ma dag pa snang la/ nam dag par gyur pa'i dus na ji ltar 'dod pa bzhin du bai-dū-rya dang/ shel dang gser la sogs pa'i kha dog gi sa gzhi lta bur dag par snang bar 'gyur te/. . . . rnam par shes pa lnga'i tshogs ma dag pa'i dus na ni mig gi rnam par shes pas kyang gzugs la dmigs shing gzugs la longs spyod byed pa tsam las mi nus te/ so so'i yul nyi tshe la 'jug pa tsam las lhag par mi nus pa las rnam dag ste gnas gyur pa na rnam par shes pa lnga la sangs rgyas kyi zhing de dag na bdud rtse'i rdzing dang/ dpag bsam gyi shing la sogs pa'i longs spyod rnam pa sna tshogs ston te/ 'dzin pa gzhan du gyur pa las ni 'byor pa'i mchog thob par 'gyur ro/[30]
>
> When the six sensory objects and the group of [five] sensory consciousnesses are radically reoriented, one obtains two kinds of supreme mastery [among which the

> first is] "manifesting enjoyment at will in a pure field." [This means that] when sensory objects are not yet reoriented, they appear as impure objects such as ravines, thorns, pebbles, and bricks. But when they are reoriented they appear "at will" as pure objects, like places with the color of lapis lazuli, crystal, or gold. . . . When the group of five sensory consciousnesses is not yet purified, this means, for instance, that the visual consciousness can enjoy only physical objects, and can turn itself toward those for no more than a short time. But when the five sensory consciousnesses are purified—which is to say reoriented—various kinds of enjoyment are manifest in the Buddha-fields: of ponds of nectar, wish-granting trees, and the like. From the radical reorientation of apprehension, then, supreme mastery is obtained.

Only the first supreme mastery is dealt with here; there is a second, dealt with immediately after the extract quoted, but it goes beyond the scope of my discussion at this point. This lengthy quotation shows that radical reorientation of the sensory consciousnesses together with their corresponding objects is therefore what makes possible the communal sensual pleasures shared by bodhisattvas and bodies of communal enjoyment. This is the doctrinal explanation given for the perceived necessity of having Buddha available in a Buddha-field as a body of communal enjoyment. Recall that this analysis is typically offered by the digests in the context of showing how the (many) bodies of communal enjoyment differ from the (single) real body. The need is therefore for an explanation of apparent multiplicity in the context of actual unity.

This is a need that presses upon the digests throughout their explanations of Buddha's apparent functioning (*vṛtti*) in both heaven and on earth. I have tried to show in this chapter for Buddha's presence and activity in heaven, as I did in the previous chapter for Buddha's presence and action in its body of magical transformation in worlds like ours, that the most prominent kind of explanation offered is couched in terms of the needs of non-Buddhas as causal determinants upon the phenomenal properties of Buddha. It is largely in this way that the ornamentation of heaven and the gorgeous appearance of the bodies of communal enjoyment is explained. These are broadly metaphysical explanations, based as they are upon certain views as to the properties of Buddha considered *svabhāvataḥ*, as it is in itself. This explanation is, structurally at least, the same for both Buddha in the world and Buddha in heaven.

But there are also temporally indexed soteriological explanations offered, principally in terms of powers gained at particular points upon the practice of the path. So, for example, the analysis just given of the bodies of communal enjoyment in terms of specific kinds of awareness is *both* a properly metaphysical explanation—because, as I shall show, Buddha's awareness is a changeless fact about the fabric of the cosmos; *and* a properly soteriological explanation—because the awarenesses in question are got by a particular practitioner at a particular time in the course of practicing the path.

It remains difficult, though, to see how the metaphysical grounding of doctrines about the bodies of communal enjoyment can be held together with these temporally indexed soteriological explanations. If communal enjoyment of doctrine on the part of Buddha and bodhisattvas is explained in terms of changeless facts about Buddha, can it also be explained by temporally indexed facts about the practice of the path? This is a variant upon a deep problem in the whole of Buddhist theory: that of whether in fact any changes genuinely occur upon the path, of whether, that is to say, awakening occurs suddenly (*yugapat*) or gradually (*krameṇa*).[31] This problem, in turn, is an aspect of a still deeper question: Does temporal change of any kind occur? How are the indubitable appearances of change in time—of which Buddha's actions in the world and in heaven may be taken as paradigmatic instances—to be related to the metaphysical fact of changelessness? To see how this is done in terms of buddhalogical doctrine I must now turn to a consideration of Buddha *svabhāvataḥ*, or Buddha in eternity.

Chapter **6**

Buddha in Eternity

6.0 Prolegomena

In chapters three through five I showed how the digests understand buddhalogical doctrine in general, and how in particular they present Buddha's action—its *karman* and its *vṛtti*—in the world and in heaven. I emphasized throughout these chapters that both soteriological and metaphysical explanations are offered for this action; the former are couched largely in terms of the efficacy of the path, while the latter are couched largely in terms of changeless metaphysical facts about Buddha in itself, Buddha understood *svabhāvataḥ*. I now want to focus in more detail upon the second kind of explanation, principally by looking at what the digests say about the real body (*dharmakāya*), the third of Buddha's three bodies—or, more exactly, Buddha as Buddha really is, not as Buddha appears to non-Buddhas.

I suggested in chapters four and five that Buddha's actions in the world and in heaven can be interpreted in terms of properties of the kind *seems to S to be P at t*, where *S* is some non-Buddha, *P* some mode of appearance, and *t* some time. In this chapter, by contrast, I shall show that all properties predicated of Buddha *svabhāvataḥ* are nonrelational; I shall offer an explanation of why this is at the end of the chapter, and shall provide a more detailed analysis of it in chapter seven.

It will become clear in what follows that the digests, in defining and discussing Buddha as it is in itself, deploy predicates of two kinds. The first I shall call metaphysical and the second epistemic. This is not a distinction the digests clearly make. In their definitions and analyses they mix the two kinds in a fashion that stresses their inseparability. But there are elements in the rhetoric and explanatory strategies of the digests that are at least congruent with, and may even be taken actively to support, my classification of the predicates. The metaphysical predicates, broadly speaking, are used when Buddha as it is in itself is homologized with everything there is just as it is: in such contexts Buddha is spoken of as eternal, changeless, pure, omnipresent, and so forth. These predicates correlate naturally with the metaphysical explanations of Buddha's action in the world and in heaven. The epistemic predicates, by contrast, are used when the digests want to speak of Buddha as consisting in a particular kind of awareness (usually called *jñāna*); these predicates correlate with the soteriological explanations of Buddha's action as resulting from the completion of the path. Whether and in what fashion these two kinds of predicate can be brought together into a single coherent account will be a question running through this chapter.

The mixing and separation of the two kinds of predicate can be seen to advantage in the following lengthy passage. The passage is explaining what it means to identify Buddha's real body with the "stage of attainment" (*prāptyavasthā*)—this is one of the terms used for the final stage of the path; in so doing it brings together the metaphysical and the soteriological explanations with their corresponding predicates.

> prāptyavasthā buddhānāṃ dharmakāya iti sarvāvaraṇaprahāṇāt/ tatpratipakṣānāsravadharmabījapracayāc cāśrayaparāvṛttyātmakaḥ sarvadharmavaśavartī/ anālaya iti buddhānāṃ dharmakāyaḥ/ tena dharmaprativedhaniṣṭhādhigamanāt prāptyavasthety ucyate/ anye tu niḥśeṣāgantukamalāpagamāt suviśuddho dharmadhātur eva dharmatākāyo dharmakāya iti varṇayanti/ sarvasminn api jñeye 'saktāpratihatapravṛttiviśiṣṭajñānaṃ dharmakāya ity apare/[1]

> To say that the real body of Buddhas is the "stage of attainment" means that it consists in radical reorientation,

> which is to say that it gains mastery over all good qualities as a result of abandoning all obstacles; it does this by accumulating the seeds of the undefiled good qualities that are their antidotes. And so the real body of Buddhas is said to be free from the storehouse-[consciousness], and is identified with the stage of attainment because its realization is founded upon a penetration to what is real. Others describe the real body as the body of reality, and identify it only with the well-purified ground of the real; this is because they see it as completely free from adventitious taints. Yet others identify the real body with a special kind of awareness that ranges without attachment or obstruction over all objects of awareness.

This passage will bear fairly extensive explication since it presents alternative (perhaps opposed, perhaps complementary) understandings of the real body with unusual clarity. It begins by explaining the sense in which the real body is to be identified with the stage of attainment; in doing so it uses a set of terms that clearly belong to the realm of soteriological explanation. The real body is said to be "radical reorientation," a soteriological term that denotes the final removal of all cognitive and affective obstacles, and so also the completion of the religious path. It is because of this radical reorientation that the real body can be said to be free from all obstacles, and so to have "gained mastery" over all good qualities.[2]

This much is standard. What makes this passage so useful for my purposes are the two opinions stated at the end. The first, using the strongest metaphysical language, identifies the real body (*dharmakāya*) as the body of reality (*dharmatākāya*). *Dharmatā* is an abstract noun formed from *dharma*, literally 'dharma-ness' or 'dharma-hood': the condition of being dharma. I render the term 'reality' to indicate that *dharmatā* refers to what all reals have in common, 'the dharma-hood of all dharmas' (*sarvadharmāṇāṃ dharmatā*) or the reality of all reals, to use a tag frequently found in the digests. The term thus picks out whatever it is in virtue of which everything there is is what it is. And so Buddha's real body is understood as the embodiment or assemblage of what there really is: this is what "body of reality" means. The first opinion cited in the passage then goes on to identify this body as nothing other than the "ground of the real" (*dharmadhātu*)—another important metaphysical term denoting that which grounds or makes possible the reality of everything that is. The term 'ground' (*dhātu*) is usually interpreted by the digests to mean 'cause' (*hetu*).[3] This makes it still clearer that the digests are making a strong claim about the relationship between the ground of the real and all other reals.

But this first opinion goes further. The real body is not just the ground of the real, but also the "well-purified" (*suviśuddha*) ground of the real. This is to say that the ground of the real can be purified from "taints" (*mala*) that belong to it adventitiously, that come upon it by accident (*āgantuka*) as it were, and that when this happens it is proper to identify it with the real body. I shall return to this interesting complex of metaphysical terms later in this chapter. For the moment I note that this first opinion about the real body suggests the strictly metaphysical doctrine that Buddha *in se* is identical with everything there is as it really is. This is not the same, of course, as saying that the real body is identical with everything as it appears, because things generally appear as if impure, and no impurity can be predicated of the real body.

The passage quoted mentions another opinion as well, the opinion that Buddha in its real body is identical with a "special kind of awareness" (*viśiṣṭajñāna*), a kind of awareness whose proper scope or domain is simply everything—or at least everything that is a possible object of awareness (*jñeya*). This amounts, as I shall try to show, to a claim that the real body just is omniscience. This appears at first sight to be significantly and interestingly different from (and is also perhaps not compatible with) the claim that Buddha in its real body is identical with everything; whether this is really so will be a central topic of this chapter, though it is certainly true that the author of the passage in which these two opinions are quoted does not suggest that they are irreconcilable—though neither is any attempt made to harmonize them.

6.1 Epistemic Predicates

The epistemic predicate most often used of Buddha as it is in itself is *jñāna* which, for reasons to be explained, I shall translate 'awareness.' A large number of technical terms are employed by the digests to attribute special kinds of awareness to Buddha; among these I shall concentrate upon the following: 'awareness without construction' (*nirvikalpajñāna*) and its correlate, 'subsequently attained awareness' (*pṛṣṭhalabdhajñāna*); 'mirror-awareness' (*ādarśajñāna*); and a variety of terms used to designate Buddha's awareness of everything (omniscience, with the reservations to be expressed below), principally 'awareness of all modes of appearance' (*sarvākārajñāna* and cognates). But first some general comments on awareness simpliciter as understood by the digests.

6.1.1 Awareness Simpliciter

Jñāna is most often translated into English as 'knowledge.' This is not necessarily objectionable. 'Knowledge' covers a very broad semantic field in English, some parts of which overlap interestingly with the equally broad and complex field of *jñāna* in Sanskrit. But 'knowledge' also has a more precise and technical usage in contemporary anglophone philosophy, a usage that diverges in important ways from the technical use of *jñāna* in the digests. And since I am interested here primarily in uncovering with as much precision as I can the properly doctrinal import of buddhalogical discourse, I prefer to distance *jñāna* from 'knowledge' by generally eschewing the latter as a translation of the former.

'Knowledge' is frequently taken by contemporary anglophone philosophers to denote a propositional attitude, an attitude had by some subject toward some proposition, for example, the proposition expressed by the sentence *Buddha is aware of everything*. The attitude may be paradigmatically dispositional, as Gilbert Ryle claimed;[4] or it may be occurrent. Knowledge is also often taken to be a species of belief (which is also a propositional attitude). Attempts to differentiate it from belief are most often made (though not without a good deal of difficulty) in terms of the epistemic situation of the knower vis-à-vis that of the believer (the former is justified in her belief while the latter need not be); and in terms of the properties of the proposition or propositions that are the object of knowledge as distinct from those made the object of belief: the former must be true, while the latter need not be. It is arguable that Plato intended some distinctions such as these in his discussion of true opinion in the Meno (97c–98a); and it is almost certain that Kant did when, in the First Critique (A820–31; B848–59) he made distinctions among having opinions (*Meinen*), having beliefs (*Glauben*), and having knowledge (*Wissen*). Debates about the possibility and the details of making such distinctions have dominated epistemology in the anglophone world for most of this century.[5]

While I do not wish to give the impression that there is anything approaching a consensus among anglophone philosophers about epistemological procedures (much less about substantive conclusions), it is true that the debates by such philosophers about these matters evidence a tendency significantly different from that visible in Indic discussions of *jñāna*. The latter tend to see *jñāna*—or, better, instances of it—as episodic mental events with cognitive significance, rather than as (dispositional or occurrent) propositional attitudes.[6] The term occurs in the digests perhaps most often in connection with discussions of the path. For instance, the "path of vision" (*darśanamārga*, one of the divisions of the meditational path) is defined in part in one of the digests as "the awareness of the identity of what takes a mental object and what is taken as such an object" (*dmigs par bya ba dang dmigs par byed pa mnyam pas mnyam par shes pa*).[7] The practitioner on the path of vision learns to perceive the nature of things directly by developing a certain kind of awareness: in this case an awareness in which, phenomenologically speaking, there is no separation or distinction between perceiving subject ("what takes a mental object") and perceived object ("what is taken as such an object"). There is no hint here that *jñāna* is being used to describe assent to the claim that there is no separation between subject and object (though of course if the awareness in question is veridical this claim must be true). Instead, it denotes a mental episode with specifiable phenomenal properties, properties that match or reflect those of its putative object (though, given the example cited, it is not quite proper to say that the awareness in question has an object; it would be better to say that precisely in the absence of differentiation between subject and object it is homologous with the way things are); this example is entirely representative of other uses of the term *jñāna* in soteriological contexts.[8]

An episode of awareness understood in this sense must, furthermore, have some phenomenal properties that are sufficiently specific and definite to be capable of description.[9] A mental event without such properties would, according to pan-Indian scholastic thought, best be characterized not as an instance of awareness (*jñāna*), but rather as one of doubt or uncertainty (*saṃśaya* and the like). An instance of *jñāna* is thus typically an episodic mental event with intentional structure and phenomenal properties; if it is veridical (*tathya* rather than *mithya*) its structure and properties will be homologous with those of its apparent object. This is the view of awareness presupposed and deployed by the digests. It is, of course, a phenomenon not limited to Buddha. I am having a succession of instances of awareness as I write these words. But Buddha has, or on some readings just is, a special kind of awareness, a kind not accessible to me under normal conditions, and in describing this the digests test the limits of the understanding of *jñāna* that they presuppose.

6.1.2 Buddha's Awareness

Veridical awareness is taken by the digests to be a good. Buddha is understood by them not only to possess all goods, but to possess them maximally. It follows, then, that Buddha *in se* must possess (or, according to some interpretations, simply be) maximal veridical awareness, awareness whose scope is universal and whose content is free from imperfection. The digests attempt to capture this fact when they attribute various perfections of cognition to Buddha. One way of elucidating what it might mean for Buddha to possess (or be) this kind of awareness is to consider the limitations and imperfections that usually characterize the awareness of non-Buddhas, and to describe Buddha's awareness as free from those. The clearest case of this method is found in the discussions given by the digests to *vikalpa* or constructive mental activity as a property that the awareness of non-Buddhas almost always possesses, and which is entirely absent from the awareness of Buddhas.

Vikalpa is derived from a verbal root, *klṛp-*, whose semantic range runs from the functions of ordering, arranging, and adapting, to those of ornamenting and embellishing. A derived nominal form (*kalpana* or *kalpanā*) is often associated with literary creation: *kavikalpanā* denotes a poet's literary creation. Adding the prefix *vi-* to produce the nominal form *vikalpa* gives a distributive sense to the term: it can often mean to create or contrive options, to set up anitheses, to ornament by opposing, and so forth. Uses of *vikalpa* in the digests preserve many of these semantic connotations, but are concerned more closely with the conceptually constructive and classificatory activities of the mind, activities like those of the poets in that they create an inhabitable fictional world, one that does not exist as it appears. In some contexts, 'imagination' is a defensible translation; but in the more strictly philosophical contexts that concern me here, 'construction' or (adjectivally) 'constructive' seems preferable.[10]

The digests provide fairly extensive analyses of *vikalpa*. One of these divides the constructive activity of the mind into eight categories.[11] The first three are "construction of essences" (*svabhāvavikalpa*), "construction of distinctions" (*viśeṣavikalpa*), and "construction of the apprehension of material forms" (*piṇḍagrāhavikalpa*). These are connected with what the digests take to be the mind's construction of a world of distinct material objects, of substances with properties both theoretically and practically separable one from another—the material universe, that is, of everyday experience. The construction of such a world is taken to be both itself a function of *vikalpa* and to allow the proliferation of further *vikalpa*: *vikalpa* consisting this time in language, the separation and designation of those existents that *vikalpa* has itself created. The fourth and fifth kinds of *vikalpa* are "construction concerning 'I' " (*aham iti vikalpa*) and "construction concerning 'mine' " (*mameti vikalpa*). These have to do with the construction of a sense of personal identity, the root of the conceit—in both the sense of arrogance and that of literary flourish—that the perceiving subject exists (*asmimānamūla*), and of the false view that persons exist. The final three kinds of *vikalpa* are "construction of what is pleasant" (*priyavikalpa*), "construction of what is unpleasant" (*apriyavikalpa*), and "construction of what is neither" (*tadubhayaviparītavikalpa*). Dividing and classifying our percepts into things we like, things we don't like, and things to which we are indifferent is, thus, also a function of *vikalpa*: these kinds of constructive mental activity generate affect by aiding our attraction to those things that appear desirable to us, and our revulsion from those that appear unpleasant.

This classificatory analysis of *vikalpa* is intended as a complete though schematic account of the various ways in which we construct for ourselves the world of everyday experience, the world of subsistent subjects experiencing persistent objects and reacting to such experiences with various kinds of affect. It should be clear that *vikalpa* understood in this way is unambiguously salvifically negative for the digests. That it characterizes the awareness of non-Buddhas is unfortunate for those of us numbered among them, and its removal is one of the most important goals of the path; it is clear that the awareness belonging to (or constituting) Buddha cannot be of this kind, and so we read:

> paśyatāṃ kalpanāmātraṃ sarvam etad yathoditam/
> akalpabodhisattvānāṃ prāptā bodhir nirūpyate//[12]

> Bodhisattvas who are free from construction and who see all this [sc. the entire cosmos] just as it has been described, as nothing but construction, are said to have attained awakening.

The awareness belonging to Buddha, then, is free from construction. But what, positively, could such awareness be like?

The digests are concerned to eliminate a number of possible errors in thinking about awareness without construction.[13] The first of these is the error of judging such awareness to be identical with simple unconsciousness, a simple absence of mental activity. If it were, such absence would be easy to attain: a sharp blow to the head produces unconsciousness; and there are various meditational practices that dispose of many kinds of mental activity at an early stage of the practice of the path.[14] But it is obvious that the absence of constructive activity that characterizes Buddha's awareness is not so easily attained. Neither is it the case, according to the digests, that Buddha's awareness is epistemically, phenomenally, or soteriologically as uninteresting as deep sleep or a drunken stupor.

More interestingly, the digests also negate the idea that unconstructed awareness is to be identified with a much more exalted meditative state called the 'attainment of cessation' (*nirodhasamāpatti*) or the 'cessation of sensation and conceptualization' (*saṃjñāveditanirodha*).[15] This is a condition attained by complex and difficult meditational practice, a condition wherein there are no mental events of any kind. It is not death; but it is not distinguishable from death by any phenomenal properties. The only difference between the two is that the attainment of cessation can be emerged from, while death cannot (not, at least, without various complications caused by the need to take on a new body and the like, complications that need not detain us here). Buddha's construction-free awareness is distinct even from this exalted condition, and the digests put this in formal terms by denying that Buddha's awareness could be identified with the attainment of cessation, because if it were it would not be an instance of awareness (*jñāna*) at all, which its name requires it to be, for awareness cannot occur where there are no mental events of any kind.[16] The point here is the simple logical one that awareness is a species of mental event, from which it follows that no instance of awareness can be identified with a condition in which there are no mental events.

It is worth pausing here to consider what the negation just mentioned implies. On its face it seems to suggest that Buddha's construction-free awareness is a species of mental event, that it is, to use the technical terminology of the digests, to be categorized as belonging to the class-category 'mind and mental concomitants' (*cittacaitta*). And yet it isn't difficult to find places in the digests where it is explicitly denied that Buddha's awareness involves the operations of the mind and its concomitants.[17] What is to be made of this tension? Definitionally it is clear that Buddha's awareness must, like all instances of awareness, be classified as a mental event; and in contexts like the one under discussion, in which the goal is to show that Buddha's construction-free awareness is not the same as a simple absence of mental activity, this is indeed emphasized. But there are other contexts in which it is rhetorically and logically important for the digests to emphasize that Buddha's awareness is different in almost all its significant defining characteristics from any other mental event, and in such contexts stress on these differences may lead to a denial that Buddha's awareness is a mental event at all. The issue, in the end, is one of where to draw a definitional line: the digests do not disagree significantly as to which properties should be predicated of Buddha's awareness; they do sometimes disagree as to whether to call it a mental event or not.

I return to the negations through which the digests define Buddha's construction-free awareness. The most important among these for gaining understanding of the phenomenology and epistemic significance of Buddha's awareness is the negation of the claim that this awareness comprises any volitional turning of the mind toward its objects (*ālambanābhisaṃskāra*). This is not the same as denying that Buddha's awareness has content, or consists of events with phenomenal properties; it is simply a denial that the phenomenal properties of its apparent objects are, or can be, things with which it can be involved in a sustained and intentional way.[18] In so far as what appears in the mind does so with phenomenal properties, those properties do not lead the Buddha-mind to fasten upon them, to follow after them,[19] or to make judgments that a particular thing with particular properties is now being experienced.

For example, suppose Buddha sees a blue pot. One way of reading the negation described in the preceding paragraph is to say that Buddha has a spontaneous (that is, effortless, nonvolitional) moment of awareness (*jñāna*) consisting of a mental object or image (*ālambana, nimitta*) whose phenomenal properties (*ākāra*) consist of a complex list of things such as 'transient-blue-pot-here-now'; in English such an occurrence is best described adverbially by saying that Buddha is appeared to transient-blue-pot-here-now-ly. Sanskrit is more comfortable using abstract nouns (*anityatva, nīlatva,* and so forth) as qualifiers of the instance of Buddha's awareness in question. But in either case the important distinction between Buddha's blue-pot awareness and mine is that Buddha neither does nor can judge that it is being appeared to blue-pot-ly, whereas I, other things being equal, inevitably do. Buddha, moreover, does not engage in the constructive activity of manipulating and massaging its mental images; it has no affective response to them, and, above all, no concern for their endurance, cessation, or repetition. The digests sometimes express this by saying that Buddha does not behave like an artist toward the objects of its awareness;[20] this appears to mean that Buddha does not intentionally create a variegated and beautiful picture from the objects of its awareness (recall the connection between *kalpanā* and poetic literary creation). But more often the point is made by saying that the object of Buddha's awareness is always pure. Consider the following:

> saṃvṛttyā na tu paramārthataḥ/ tasya nirvikalpatvāt/ tad anena cāviparyāsena bodhisattvo viśuddhyālambana-kuśalo bhavati/ nirvikalpajñānaviṣayatvāt/ viśeṣaḥ sāmānyalakṣaṇasvalakṣaṇayoḥ ko vidyate/ abhilāpa-svabhāvasamāropitatvasya pratipakṣeṇānabhilāpya-svabhāvata paramārthalakṣaṇam/ parikalpitasvabhāva-nairātmyaṃ punaḥ sarvadharmāṇāṃ prakṛtir iti sāmānyalakṣaṇam/ evaṃ darśanabhedavaśād viśeṣo bhavati na tv arthād/[21]

> [Buddha's awareness] is ultimate rather than relative, because of the absence of construction in it. It is in virtue of just this absence of cognitive error that a bodhisattva becomes skilled in [the discernment of] pure mental objects: [such skill is possible] because [such mental objects] are the sphere of operation of construction-free

> awareness. What is the distinction between the defining characteristic possessed in common [by all reals], and that which is specific [to particular reals]? The ultimate defining characteristic, which is also the defining characteristic possessed in common [by all reals], is the realization that by nature all reals are without a self, which means that they are without an imagined essential nature; also, [it is the realization that] the essential nature of all reals is to be inexpressible, [which realization functions as] an antidote to the imputation of an expressible essential nature [to reals]. Hence, the distinction between [the defining characteristic possessed in common by reals and that specific to each real] is epistemic rather than ontological.

To have a "pure mental object" (*viśuddhyālambana*), according to this passage, is the same as not making cognitive errors about the images that appear in one's mind. These images may appear as if related causally to a world of individuatable objects, objects with essential properties unique to themselves, but such appearances have no rooting in reality. This is what the passage means by saying that the distinction between what all things have in common ("the defining characteristic possessed in common [by all reals]") and what is unique to specific existents ("that which is specific [to particular reals]") is "epistemic rather than ontological." Awareness that makes use of construction creates an impression in its possessor that the objects of her consciousness are genuine images of specific images with particular properties; but this is, according to the digests, an interesting fact about the epistemic situation of non-Buddhas, not a fact that communicates anything of use either about reality (*dharmatā,* the totality of reals or dharmas) or about the epistemic situation of Buddha. It is only from those epistemic situations in which *vikalpa* is implicated that cognition of such individuatable particulars seems to be possible.

It follows from these claims about construction-free awareness that Buddha's awareness cannot be implicated with speech; nor with any unvocalized use of concepts that reflects and presupposes acquaintance with lexical items in any natural language. The digests put this most simply by saying that Buddha's construction-free awareness is dumb;[22] but they also often say that construction-free awareness is inexpressible (*nirabhilāpya*), or that it is free from conceptual proliferation (*niṣprapañca*)—meaning thereby that it does not engage in the ceaseless multiplication and elaboration of conceptual systems whose function is to provide a conceptually interesting and aesthetically pleasing (recall, again, the negation of the claim that Buddha functions like an artist) system for the elucidation and control of experience.[23]

The digests must claim that construction-free awareness is not implicated with language because deployment of words is taken by them to be among the more important functions of *vikalpa*: words separate, analyze, sort, and construct, none of which Buddha's awareness does. More precisely and more technically, to deny that construction-free awareness is implicated with language involves, according to the digests, the following argument: in order to know that the object of one's awareness is of a particular kind, one must already know a lexical item in some natural language that one takes to designate it.[24] But such a lexical item, when functioning as a designans (*abhidhāna*), is clearly not the same as its designatum (*abhidheya*): there is a difference in kind (*bhinnalakṣaṇatva*) between them; and this means that the activity of knowing and deploying words requires just the kind of mental activity ruled out by the presence of construction-free awareness. Knowing that one is appeared to transient-blue-pot-here-now-ly requires both that one know the words 'blue,' 'pot,' and so forth, and that one judge the phenomenal properties of one's experience be appropriately designated by those words.

It is because construction-free awareness lacks these kinds of knowledge that its implication with language is denied. This is far from a crass or radical claim to ineffability: the digests do not want to say that construction-free awareness is ineffable in the sense that all statements with it as their putative referent are epistemically equivalent. Since such a position is dramatically incoherent,[25] it is fortunate that this is not the goal. The more interesting claim made in the digests is that some of the formal properties of Buddha's awareness—for example, its difference from simple unconciousness, discussed above—can be expressed; but that its phenomenal properties cannot be directly and fully described, and that its occurrence and operation are not implicated with language in any way.

The radical conclusion drawn from this by the digests (as also often by the wider tradition) is that Buddha *in se* does not speak. Consider the following famous passage from one of the digests:

> yadi buddhair bhagavadbhir nātmeti deśitaṃ nānātmeti kiṃ tarhi deśitam iti// ucyate/ *nivṛttam abhidhātavyaṃ nivṛtte cittagocare/ anutpannāniruddha hi nirvāṇam iva dharmatā//* <xviii.7> iha yadi kiñcid abhidhātavyaṃ vastu syāt tad deśyeta/ yadā tv abhidhātavyaṃ nivṛttaṃ vācāṃ viṣayo nāsti tadā kiñcid api naiva deśyate buddhaiḥ/ kasmāt punar abhidhātavyaṃ nāstīty āha/ nivṛtte cittagocara iti/ . . . gocaro viṣaya ālambanam ity arthaḥ/ yadi cittasya kaścid gocaraḥ syāt tatra kiñcin nimittam adhyāropya syād vācāṃ pravṛttiḥ/ yadā tu cittasya viṣaya evānupapannas tadā kva nimittādhyāropo yena vācāṃ pravṛttiḥ syāt// kasmāt punaḥ cittaviṣayo nāstīti pratipādayann āha/ anutpannāniruddhā hi nirvāṇam iva dharmatā/ yasmād anutpannāniruddhā nirvāṇam iva dharmatā dharmasvabhāvo dharmaprakṛtir vyavasthāpitā tasmān na tatra cittaṃ pravartate/ cittasyāpravṛttau ca kuto nimittādhyāropaḥ/ tadabhāvāt kuto vācāṃ pravṛttiḥ/ ataś ca na kiñcid buddhair bhagavadbhir deśitam iti sthitam avikalam/[26]

> If Buddhas taught neither that there is a self nor that there is no self, what then did they teach? "When the mind has no more scope, there is nothing to refer to; reality, like Nirvana has neither arisen nor ceased" <xviii.7>. If there were anything capable of being referred to, then this could be taught. When, however, there is nothing capable of being referred to, when there is no sphere within which speech can operate, then there is nothing whatever for Buddhas to teach. But how can there be nothing to refer to? This is so when the mind has no scope . . . which is to say, no sphere of operation, no mental object. If the mind had any such scope, then speech could function by imputing to

> it a mental image with a specifiable character. But when the mind has no sphere of operation at all, then how can there be any imputation to it of a mental image with a specifiable character in virtue of which speech might function? The line "reality, like Nirvana has neither arisen nor ceased" explains how it is that there is no sphere of operation for the mind. It is because reality, the essence or true nature of reals, is like Nirvana in neither having arisen nor ceased, and so the mind cannot function in relation to it. And when the mind does not function, how can there be imputation to it of a mental image with a specifiable character? And in the absence of that, where can the functioning of speech come from? Therefore, the conclusion that the blessed Buddhas have taught nothing at all is established beyond doubt.

This passage drives home the points I have been making. Buddha teaches nothing because there is, precisely, no designatum, nothing capable of being referred to and so nothing capable of being taught. There is certainly a sense, therefore, in which Buddha does not speak; but there must also be a sense in which it is proper to say at least that Buddha appears to speak. Recall the discussion of Buddha's omnilinguality in chapter four. There, I made the point that a key part of Buddha's action in the world is its ability to appear to speak all natural languages perfectly. So Buddha possesses at least the property of seeming to speak to its hearers in world-realms like this one. This is also at least partly true of the properties possessed by Buddha when it acts as a body of communal enjoyment in its Buddha-fields. The denial that Buddha teaches anything at all must then be compatible with these claims about Buddha's omnilinguality, just as must the denial that Buddha's construction-free awareness is implicated with language. It is relatively easy to see how these things can be held together. If speech is defined as dependent upon the deliberative application of concepts to the flow of experience, the proliferation of ideas for the manipulation and categorization of percepts, then Buddha's construction-free awareness precludes it. This is the sense in which Buddha is dumb, or in which Buddha teaches nothing; this is what is meant by denying that Buddha's awareness is implicated with language. But if speech is equated with utterance, with the simple vocalization of lexical items in sentence-patterns, then Buddha's construction-free awareness is entirely compatible with it, and may even be said to require it. For utterance may occur without accompanying mental effort and volitional activity, and so also without *vikalpa*. When it does, of course, the semantic content of what is uttered is not present to the mind of the utterer; instead, the utterance occurs spontaneously in response to some theoretically specifiable set of causes and conditions; and this was just the interpretation I gave to Buddha's omnilinguality in chapter four.

This interpretation of the relations between Buddha's awareness and its use of natural language is compatible with all of the digests. Some of them, though, are a little more specific in their attempts to account for these relations.[27] They distinguish, that is, between a "fundamental" (*maula*) construction-free awareness, Buddha's awareness as it is at the moment when Buddhahood is realized, and a "subsequently attained" (*pṛṣṭhalabdha*) construction-free awareness. These two are sometimes also called "transcendent" (*lokottara*) and "worldly" (*laukika*). The former is like a dumb person who finds something she has been looking for; the latter is like that same person with the faculty of speech. Alternatively, the former is like a person with his eyes shut; the latter is like that same person with opened eyes. Or, finally, the former is like empty space; the latter is like that space filled with colors and forms.[28] For the digests that make such a distinction, it is the second of these two kinds of construction-free awareness that makes possible Buddha's apparent speech and action. But postulating two kinds does not alter in any way the account just given of how it is that Buddha can seem to speak; what it does do is suggest the possibility of change or transition within Buddha's awareness, from a moment of fundamental construction-free awareness, in which not only is *vikalpa* absent, but also all content, all phenomenal properties, to a sequence of moments in which there is rich and variegated content. To call this second variety of construction-free awareness "subsequently attained" certainly suggests some such reading.

But there are some obvious difficulties with such a reading. I shall note two of them here, and shall adjudicate the problem when I come to engage in doctrinal criticism in chapter seven. The first is that if the possession of subsequently attained construction-free awareness is required for the apparent occurrence of Buddha's speech and action in the world and in heaven, if there is any time (even a moment) when Buddha is still Buddha (that is, possesses Buddha's awareness) and yet is incapable of acting salvifically toward non-Buddhas (that is, seeming to them to say and do salvifically beneficial things), as would be the case were Buddha ever in possession only of fundamental construction-free awareness and not also of the subsequently attained variety, then the awkward conclusion that there is a time when Buddha is Buddha and is yet a salvific surd cannot be avoided. The second is that the division of Buddha's awareness into phenomenologically distinct types requires that Buddha *in se* be both temporally and epistemically differentiated: Buddha is not always in the same epistemic condition. Whether such conclusions can be accepted by the digests as bearing doctrinal force remains to be seen.

Buddha's awareness, then, is definitively and completely free of constructive activity; this is what the digests mean by calling it *nirvikalpa*. Another technical term is used by them with almost equal frequency to describe the same thing. This is *ādarśajñāna*, "mirror-awareness," a term whose meaning is summarized in the following verse:

> ādarśajñānam amamāparicchinnaṃ sadānugam/
> sarvajñeyeṣv asaṃmūḍhaṃ na ca teṣv āmukham sadā//[29]
>
> Mirror-awareness is without anything of its own;
> It is not demarcated and it always follows;
> It is free from confusion about objects of awareness;
> And never confronts them.

Here a number of properties are said to belong to mirror-awareness. First, it is "without anything of its own," literally "without mine," without any possessions or possessiveness. Then, it is "not demarcated," without boundary, not marked off from other things, without shape. The term "always follows" is ambiguous as it stands; it could have either a spatial or a temporal reference, but the digests generally give it a temporal one (they read it *kālataḥ*), and understand it to mean that mirror-awareness is present in all times. Then, it is "free from confusion about objects of awareness," which is taken to mean that its awareness is always veridical. Finally, mirror-awareness is said not to "confront" objects of awareness, not to place itself face-to-face with them, not to direct itself toward them. One of the digests, in commenting upon this verse, explicitly says that mirror-awareness does not engage in (epistemic) confrontation because it is without "modes of appearance" (*ākāra*).[30] This is an important term; what does it mean to deny that Buddha's awareness possesses "modes of appearance"?

Etymologically, *ākāra* is a nominal form derived from the root *kṛ-*, 'to do, to make,' together with the prefix *ā-*. In conjunction with verbal forms this prefix can sometimes suggest 'back' or 'toward'; so *āgacchati* from *ā* + *gam-* (a root meaning 'to go') often means 'to come' ('to go back,' 'to go toward'). With *kṛ-*, the prefix *ā-* sometimes gives the sense 'to bring near' (toward), or 'to confront.' This derivation had some effect upon the ways in which *ākāra* is used in the digests; it often has the sense 'to confront' or 'to bring face-to-face with.'[31]

In nontechnical Sanskrit, *ākāra* often denotes simply something's shape or external appearance: to be *ākāravat* is to be shapely. In Pali texts the adjectival form *ākāravatī* is often used to modify *saddhā*: an appropriate translation might be 'well-formed confidence' and an appropriate gloss 'confidence with the right components in the right configuration.' A cognate term *ākṛti*, also a nominal form derived from *ā* + *kṛ*, is extremely important in Mīmāṃsā and Vedānta theories of meaning and reference. A word's *ākṛti* is "a sort of composite, class-contour or concrete universal in virtue of which members of a particular class become individuated."[32] It would not, perhaps, be misleading to think of this "concrete universal" as having a shape (*ākāra*) in virtue of which it is the universal it is and not some other. Indeed, based upon this use of *ākṛti,* adherents of the Mīmāṃsā regard a word as producing an *ākāra* in its speakers and hearers. This *ākāra* is, as Madeleine Biardeau puts it, "l'object direct de la perception,"[33] a meaning which, as I shall show, is in some respects close to the technical Buddhist usage.

Among Buddhist uses of *ākāra* the most significant for the purposes of this study is its use in basic Buddhist theory of cognition. It was (and is) part of the technical lexicon of this theory, and in one of the digests it is defined thus: "*ākāra* is that mode under which every instance of mind and mental events apprehends objects" (*sarveṣāṃ cittacaittānām ālambanagrahaṇa prakāra ākāra iti*).[34] The implication is, as this work goes on to state, that every mental event that has an object also has an *ākāra,* a mode of appearance.[35] Further, according to the basic theory, every mental event does in fact have an intentional object, variously called *ālambana, viṣaya, vastu,* and so forth.[36] These terms are not quite synonymous, but the subtle differentiations among them do not need to be explored here. The important point is that every mental event necessarily has some particular phenomenological characteristic or set of such, some flavor. Every mental event has (or, perhaps better, is) a particular way of appearing to its subject. This is its *ākāra,* its mode of appearance.

Presuppose this understanding of 'mode of appearance' as a term denoting the phenomenal content of a particular instance of awareness; presuppose also the comments already made about Buddha's construction-free awareness, in which I suggested that the best reading of what the digests have to say about this awareness is not to deny that it has content, but rather to deny that the kind of content it has is capable of engaging the attention of the possessor of the awareness in question; what then is to be made of the apparent denial in the digests that Buddha's mirror-awareness has any modes of appearance?

One of the digests explains the statement that Buddha's mirror-awareness never confronts its objects of awareness because it has no modes of appearance in this way:

> shes bya dag la gzugs la sogs pa la dmigs pa bzhin du dmigs pa'i bye brag gam/ sngon po la sogs pa'i rnam pa'i

> bye brag gis 'jug pa ma yin pa'o de ni dmigs par bya ba dang dmigs par byed pa mnyam pas mnyam pa rnam par mi rtog pa de bzhin nyid la dmigs pa'i ngo bo nyid de/[37]
>
> [The mirror-awareness] does not function in accordance with the division of objects into such things as form/color, nor in accordance with the division of modes of appearance into such things as blue. This is because it is a construction-free awareness in which what takes a mental object and what is taken as a mental object are identical; also, its mental object is actuality.

A comment on the same issue from another of the digests reads:

> me long gyi dkyil 'khor du rnam pa gzugs brnyan rnam pa du mar rnam pa mang po skye ba yang me long gi dkyil 'khor de la de dag med de/ me long gyi dkyil 'khor de la ched du 'jug pa med cing mngon par 'du byed pa med pa de bzhin du de bzhin gshegs pa rnams kyi me long lta bu'i ye shes kyi gzugs brnyan rnam pa du mar rnam pa mang po snang ste/ me long lta bu'i ye shes la gzugs brnyan med de/ me long lta bu'i ye shes kyi gzugs brnyan de la ched du 'jug pa med cing mngon par 'du byed pa med do zhes gsungs so/[38]
>
> In a mirror-maṇḍala there are many and varied modes of appearance, and yet there are no modes of appearance therein. Also, in a mirror-maṇḍala there is neither effort nor volitional mental activity. In just the same way, the reflected images in the mirror-awareness belonging to Tathāgatas have many and varied modes of appearance, and yet there are no reflected images at all in this mirror-awareness. Also, the reflected images belonging to the mirror-awareness are free from effort and volitional mental activity.

There is play with paradox in these comments. If, in order to have phenomenal properties or modes of appearance, awareness must be characterized by effortful acts of attention toward specific objects (as it certainly must in most instances of ordinary awareness), then it is proper to say that Buddha's awareness is *nirākāra*, 'free from modes of appearance.' But if possessing modes of appearance can be understood through the simile of reflections on the surface of a mirror, then it is reasonable to say that Buddha's awareness does have them—for a mirror, like Buddha's awareness, does not engage itself with or focus upon specific 'reflectables'; it simply reflects, spontaneously, perfectly, and without distortion, everything that passes before it. It is in this sense, I think, that the digests intend us to understand Buddha's awareness.[39]

So much, then, for the phenomenology of Buddha's awareness. What of its scope, its range? The thrust of the digests toward presenting Buddha as maximally great requires the scope of Buddha's awareness to be maximized: if it is a good to have unconstructed awareness, then the temporal and spatial range of this awareness cannot be restricted or limited in Buddha's case: it must be, as the digests claim it to be, strictly universal in scope.[40] Buddha must therefore be, in some important sense, omniscient; and the digests make this claim by deploying and defining some technical terms that typically contain an epistemic term (usually some derivative of *jñā-* or *budh-*), and a universality term (usually *sarvam*, 'all'), as well as sometimes a middle term specifying what kinds of things Buddha is aware of when Buddha is aware of everything. Most commonly we find the term *sarvākārajñatā*, the 'awareness of all modes of appearance,' used to denote the universal scope of Buddha's awareness; but other terms, such as *sakalārthabodha*,[41] 'understanding all objects,' are also sometimes used.[42]

The digests agree, then, that Buddha's awareness must be maximal; they agree also, as a result, in predicating omniscience of Buddha. But because saying that Buddha is aware of everything raises deep and intractable metaphysical problems, they do not agree as to exactly how such predications should be understood. The controversies cluster around questions of proper limitation. Given that the scope of Buddha's awareness is maximal, which means that Buddha has directly present to it everything that can be an object of awareness, what are the restrictions in the scope of Buddha's awareness forced by logic? It is clear that there must be some. Buddha cannot be aware of nonexistent objects, or of states of affairs that have not, or do not, or will not obtain. So, since an existent called a 'barren woman's son' or an 'eternal self'[43] cannot be the object of anyone's awareness—they cannot, technically, have the term *jñeya*, 'object of awareness,' applied to them since they have neither actual nor possible existence—it follows a fortiori that Buddha cannot be aware of them either. But how far does this limitation extend? Can Buddha, for example, be aware of past or future events? (One's decision about this will depend on whether one takes past and future events to be possible objects of awareness.) Can Buddha be aware of what it is like to experience unbridled lust? Can Buddha have memories, if the having of memories entails the presence of false judgments as to the nature of the relations between the rememberer and its past? And so forth.

There are at least two radical views about the limitedness of Buddha's universal awareness argued in the digests. The first claims not that the universality of Buddha's awareness is actual, but that it is potential, a capacity that Buddha possesses. Here is one way of putting this view:

> naiva ca vayaṃ sarvatra jñānasaṃmukhībhāvād buddhaṃ sarvajñam ācakṣmahe/ kiṃ tarhi/ sāmarthyāt/ yā hy asau buddhākhyā santatis tasyā idam asti sāmarthyaṃ yad ābhogamātreṇāviparītaṃ jñānam utpadyate yatreṣṭam/[44]

> But we do not assert that Buddha is aware of everything in the sense that its awareness is directly present everywhere. Rather [we assert that Buddha is aware of everything] in the sense that Buddha is capable [of being aware of anything at all]. The term 'Buddha' designates a certain mental continuum; to this continuum belongs the capacity [in question], a capacity that causes accurate awareness to occur wherever Buddha wishes, simply upon the basis of a [mental] effort.

This says that Buddha can be aware of anything Buddha wishes to be aware of just by turning its mind toward it. But this view runs into difficulties because it requires both intentional effort and change to be predicated of Buddha's awareness, properties that I have already shown to be consistently denied to Buddha elsewhere in the digests. Indeed, the Sanskrit term translated "[mental] effort" in the extract above (*ābhoga*), is exactly that denied to Buddha when its spontaneity and effortlessness are at issue. This is a splendid example of a limitation placed upon maximal greatness by the incompatibility of two great-making properties: one cannot have both maximal effortless spontaneity and universal awareness as a capacity; and since the former is higher in the hierarchy of great-making properties for the digests, the latter is asserted only occasionally, and then only as a marginal and idiosyncratic position.

The second radical view of Buddha's universal awareness is that which understands the universality-terms used to describe it (*sarva, sakala,* and so forth) to denote not strictly 'everything,' but rather 'everything important.' That is, to say that Buddha is aware of everything is just to mean that Buddha is aware of everything that pertains to the attainment of awakening. While this view is mostly expounded and defended in texts that are earlier and of a different genre than the digests,[45] it is also mentioned in the digests,[46] though not, so far as I can tell, defended there. The reasons for its unpopularity in the digests should be obvious: if Buddha is aware only of what is relevant to the attainment of awakening, this could mean that Buddha is aware of as little as I am about, say, the quickest way to get from Madras to Delhi. And this does not sit well with judging Buddha to be maximally epistemically great.

Once these two radical views have been dismissed, the standard view of the digests is that the scope of Buddha's awareness is universal in a very strong sense. Consider the following, in which a distinction is made between Buddha's 'awareness of all modes of appearance' (*sarvākārajñāna*) and its 'awareness of everything' (*sarvajñāna*):

> rnam pa thams cad mkhyen pa thob/ ces bya bas/ ye shes phun sum tshogs pa bstan te/ de yang rnam pa thams cad mkhyen ces bya bar sbyar ro/ de la mi rtag pa dang/ sdug bsngal ba dang/ stong pa dang/ bdag med par de lta bur phyin ci ma log par shes pas ni rnam pa thams cad mkhyen pa zhes bya'o/ phung po dang khams la sogs pa'i chos kun ma lus par mkhyen pas na thams cad mkhyen pa zhes bya ste/[47]

> 'Attainment of the awareness of all modes of appearance': this refers to accomplishment in awareness, which should be understood to mean awareness of all modes of appearance. Here, in virtue of having accurate awareness of impermanence, unsatisfactoriness, emptiness, and absence of self, one has awareness of all modes of appearance. In being aware of all reals without exception—[reals] such as the aggregates and the spheres—one has awareness of everything.

Here it is claimed that Buddha is aware of all particulars without exception, as well as of all the modes in which they are capable of appearing. The only limitation acknowledged in this view, inevitably, is that Buddha's awareness cannot contain modes of appearance implicated with any kind of error, cognitive or affective.[48] So, for instance, Buddha's awareness cannot be said to contain modes of appearance such as 'lust' or 'greed'; but it can (and must) contain all nondelusive modes of appearance.

In the light of this material, I suggest that a formal restatement of what it means for Buddha to have universal awareness would require at least these two claims:

1. All the phenomenal properties (*ākāra*) of Buddha's awareness (*jñāna*) are veridical (*aviparīta*).
2. All states of affairs (*dharma, tattva*) not implicated with conceptual or affective error (*prapañca, viparyāsa, kleśa,* or more generally *abhūtaparikalpa*) are directly present (*sākṣātk-, saṃmukhībhū-*) to Buddha's awareness.

I will expand upon this a little. By "phenomenal properties of an instance of awareness" I mean the properties that constitute how it seems to its possessor to have it; or, in the absence of a possessor, the properties that would (counterfactually) constitute how it would seem to its possessor to have it, were there one. So, for instance, the phenomenal properties of a visual image of a blue pot in a dust-free and perfect mirror would all be described subjunctively: they would be qualia were there an experiencing subject to have them. I take a phenomenal property to be "veridical" if it reflects, images, or makes available a state of affairs to its experiencing subject without distortion (or would so make it were there an experiencing subject). In (2) I take a state of affairs being "directly present" to mean at least: (i) that it is not mediated by conceptual or imaginative activity (this is required by the rejection of *vikalpa* as a property of Buddha's awareness); and (ii) that it is reflected or made available fully in the phenomenal properties of the instance of awareness in question. (1) and (2) together, then, at a fairly high level of abstraction, I take to encapsulate the doctrinal commitments of the digests about the nature and scope of Buddha's awareness.

There remain the problems of time, tense, and change. Is Buddha's awareness subject to time in the sense that it changes from moment to moment? Is it tensed in the sense that it is appropriately expressed in tensed sentences? The digests' positions on these difficult matters are partly dependent upon the position they take on the strictly metaphysical position of whether what there is changes. If it does, then it might seem that since Buddha's awareness reflects it veridically, Buddha's awareness too must change (I shall show later that this conclusion can be avoided); if it does not, the contradictory might seem to apply. I shall explore this more fully in a moment, when I turn to the metaphysical attributes predicated of Buddha; but there are some preliminary observations to be made here.

The digests generally agree that Buddha's universal awareness is not brought about by causes, since this would entail its contingency: if the proper causes had not obtained, its universal awareness would not have obtained. And this cannot be correct: Buddha's awareness has always (*sadā*) and necessarily (*avaśyam*) existed.[49] Another way of putting this is to say that Buddha's universal awareness is neither obtained (*prāpyate*) nor engages in the act of obtaining anything (*prāpnoti*).[50] There is also the emphasis on the simultaneous apprehension of everything in a single moment (*ekakṣaṇika*) that is characteristic of Buddha's awareness, and the corresponding denial of a gradual (*krameṇa*, 'by stages') apprehension of objects of awareness by Buddha.[51] When Buddha knows things as they are, then, in virtue of the unchangeability (*akopyatva, ananyathātva*) of all things, it is incapable of change (*anyathākartuṃ aśakyatvam*); this entails the conclusion that when Buddha sees one existent it must also see them all.[52]

These comments, and others like them, strongly suggest that the digests want to commit themselves doctrinally to the claim that Buddha's awareness is not subject to change. Its scope is universal, both temporally and spatially; and so tense and change cannot be predicated of it. This position is held together—with some difficulty—with the view that Buddha's universal awareness comes to be at a particular time, as a result of the practice of the path. When the digests speak in this latter way they are speaking soteriologically, and so necessarily with and for the vulgar. There is a tighter link between the epistemic predicates and the soteriological manner of speaking than between the latter and the metaphysical predicates; indeed, as I shall now try to show, the properly metaphysical commitments of the digests turn their soteriological discourse (and so also much of their epistemic disourse) into a façon de parler.

6.2 Metaphysical Predicates

'Buddha'—or more often 'Buddhahood'—is one of a series of terms used by the digests to gesture lexically at what they take to be ultimately and finally real, at the way things actually are rather than the way they appear. I say that the digests use these terms to make lexical gestures rather than to make reference to, designate, or describe what is ultimately and finally real because an important strand of the metaphysical discourse deployed by the digests denies that what is finally real can be an object of designation (*abhidheya*): it is, instead, in a limited and formal sense, inaccessible to discourse (it is *nirabhilāpya*). But this restriction in no way inhibits the richness and complexity of the gestures the digests do make, so I shall likewise feel free to make such gestures.

The more important among the terms used for this purpose—many of which have received passing mention already in this study—are 'actuality' (*tathatā*); 'reality' (*dharmatā*); 'the ground of the real' (*dharmadhātu*); 'the purity of the ground of the real' (*dharmadhātuviśuddhi*); 'emptiness' (*śūnyatā*); 'the ultimate' (*paramārtha*); 'the summit of existence' (*bhūtakoṭi*); 'the imageless' (*animitta*); and, of course, *buddhatā* or *buddhatva* itself.[53] These terms are not strictly synonymous, although the digests often use them as glosses for one another. One of the digests, after listing and commenting upon some of these terms, which it calls "synonyms" (*paryāya*), offers the following explanation of what it might mean to consider them in this way:

> paryāya idānīm ucyate tathatā bhūtakoṭiś cānimittaṃ paramārthatā/ dharmadhātuś ca paryāyāḥ śūnyatāyāḥ samāsataḥ/ <i.14> iti paryāyo nāmaikasyārthasya bhinnaśabdatvaṃ pratyāyayati/ paryāyārthābhidhānam iti paryāya ucyate . . . naite śabdā gauṇāḥ kiṃ tarhy anvarthā iti/[54]

> In brief, the synonyms of emptiness are: (i) actuality; (ii) the summit of existence; (iii) the imageless; (iv) the ground of the real; (v) the ultimate <i.14>. The term 'synonyms' here indicates that a variety of words brings one thing to mind; this is to say that synonyms designate objects synonymously . . . these words are not figurative; rather, they relate to the same meaning.

I shall not attempt a detailed study of each of these terms. Rather, I shall take each to be functionally identical in that each can be used in certain contexts to gesture at what is finally real. I shall then offer a brief discussion of what I take to be the chief metaphysical affirmations implied by these terms (or directly stated in what is predicated of them), and shall understand these affirmations and predications to be made of Buddha.

First, there is a series of claims made about purity. Buddha is always and changelessly pure (*viśuddha, śukla,* and so forth), in the sense that it is never proper to predicate of it any afflictions or taints (*kleśa, mala*). Here is one analysis of what it means to predicate purity of Buddha:

> tatra viśuddhiḥ samāsato dvividhā/ prakṛtiviśuddhir vaimalyaviśuddhiś ca/ tatra prakṛtiviśuddhir yā vimuktir na ca visaṃyogaḥ prabhāsvarāyāś cittaprakṛter

> āgantukamalavisaṃyogāt/ vaimalyaviśuddhir vimuktir visaṃyogaś ca vāryādīnām iva rajojalādibhyaḥ prabhāsvarāyāś cittaprakṛter anavaśeṣam āgantukamalebhyo visaṃyogāt/[55]
>
> Purity is, in brief, of two kinds: natural purity, and the purity that consists in the absence of stains. Of these, natural purity is liberation but not separation; this is because although the mind is naturally radiant, it is not [always] separated from adventitious stains. The purity that consists in the absence of stains is both liberation and separation; this is because the naturally radiant mind is completely separated from adventitious defilements, just as such things as water are separated from such things as dust and dirt.

The distinction made here between "natural purity" and "purity that consists in the absence of stains" parallels the distinction I have been making between metaphysical and soteriological explanation. To say that Buddha is naturally pure is to say something about Buddha *in se*: natural radiance is a changeless fact about Buddha. This is a metaphysical claim. But Buddhahood may also be characterized as pure in the sense that it is "completely separated from adventitious defilements." This is a claim that makes sense only in the context of talk about the salvific efficacy of the path, for the path is designed precisely to remove all obstacles, impurities, and defilements. There is one sense, then, in which purity can be described as something that happens at a time: the time when a particular practitioner removes all impurities and so becomes Buddha. But there is also a sense in which purity is an atemporal property of Buddha: to speak of its attainment at a time is not to speak of its coming into being at a time, but rather to say that some incidental or adventitious relational properties that it has—or, better, appears to have—vanish at a time.

Some of the digests use a fourfold analysis of Buddha's purity, as in the following example:

> rnam par byang ba'i chos rnam pa bzhi la/ (i) rang bzhin gyis rnam par byang ba ni 'di lta ste/ de bzhin nyid dang/ stong pa nyid dang/ yang dag pa'i mtha' dang/ mtshan

> ma med pa dang/ don dam pa ste/ chos kyi dbyings kyang de yin no/ (ii) dri ma med par rnam par byang ba ni 'di lta ste/ de nyid sgrib pa thams cad dang mi ldan pa'o/ (iii) de thob pa'i lam rnam par byang ba ni 'di lta ste/ byang chub kyi phyogs dang mthun pa'i chos thams cad dang/ pha rol tu phyin pa la sogs pa'o/ (iv) de bskyed pa'i phyir dmigs pa rnam par byang ba ni 'di lta ste/ theg pa chen po'i dam pa'i chos bstan pa ste . . . rnam pa bzhi po 'di dag gis rnam par byang ba'i chos thams cad bsdus pa yin no/[56]
>
> There are four kinds of pure real: (i) Natural purity, which is to say actuality, emptiness, the summit of existence, the imageless, the ultimate, the ground of reality. (ii) Purity as a result of the removal of stains, which is to say precisely that [first kind of purity] when it is free from all obstacles. (iii) Purity of the path that leads to the attainment of that [second kind of purity], which is to say all those qualities favorable to the attainment of awakening,[57] such as the perfections. (iv) Purity of mental object, which produces that [third kind of purity], which is to say the true doctrine taught by the Mahāyāna . . . all pure reals are comprised in this fourfold division.

This schema is basically the same as the twofold one, but it explains with a little more precision the relations between the metaphysical fact of Buddha's changeless purity and the processes that bring about the (apparent) removal of those things that (apparently) defile this purity. The four purities are arranged hierarchically: the first makes the metaphysical claim; the second describes how this fundamental reality can appear to be free of stains (there is no reference to anything ontologically distinct); and the third and fourth purities refer in more detail to the salvific process that leads to the realization of the first (natural) purity. In both the fourfold and the twofold schema the metaphysical claim is basic: it denotes a necessary and changeless state of affairs upon which the soteriological explanations are parasitic, and from which they are detachable.

The digests are quite unambiguous in their claims that Buddha in its essential purity is not subject to change, and has no beginning or end in time. Consider the following example:

> de bzhin nyid don dam pa chos bdag med pa rgyu dang bcas pa ma yin pa dang rgyu las byung ba ma yin pa dang/ 'dus byas ma yin pa dang/ don dam pa ma yin pa ma yin pa dang/ don dam pa de'i don dam pa gzhan yongs su btsal bar bya mi dgos kyi de bzhin gshegs pa rnams 'byung yang rung ma byung yang rung ste/ rtag pa rtag pa'i dus dang ther zhug ther zug gi dus su chos gnas par bya ba'i phyir chos rnams kyi chos nyid dbyings de ni rnam par gnas pa kho na yin pa/[58]

> Actuality, the ultimate, the absence of self in things—this is not produced causally and is not compounded; it is the ultimate, and there is no need to seek another ultimate beyond it. Whether Tathāgatas come into being or not, the ground of the real, which is to say the reality of reals, continues in permanent and everlasting[59] time, so that reals might continue.

This insistence on permanence and everlastingness may seem surprising given the traditional Buddhist emphasis on impermanence as one of the three defining characteristics of all conditioned things (the other two are 'unsatisfactoriness' [*duḥkhatā]* and 'lack of an enduring self' [*anātmatva]*). But there is a sense in which claims about Buddha's permanence are not only not suprising but are actually natural and to be expected. There is a strictly philosophical reason for this. Suppose that (i) each specific existent or real (*bhāva, dharma*) is characterized by the property of impermanence—or, more radically still, of momentariness (*kṣaṇikatvam*), of ceasing to be as soon as it comes into existence; (ii) the relations among these strictly momentary existents are causal and temporal (that is, the relations 'being a cause of,' 'being an effect of,' 'being earlier than,' and 'being later than' are all instantiated); and (iii) the causal process has neither beginning nor end in time. It then follows that the causal nexus itself is beginningless and endless, so that it may properly be characterized as 'permanent,' 'eternal,' and the like. Even if no specific existent is eternal, the causal process that links them must be if it is beginnngless and endless.

Putting matters in this way suggests that a theory of types is the best conceptual tool to explain what is going on here.

Every member of the set of all existents has causal and temporal properties; these are first-type existents, bearing first-order properties. They are the reals, the dharmas. All these first-type existents have, among others, the first-order property 'being impermanent.' But the members of the second-type set of all universally applicable first-order properties of this kind, that is, the members of the set of first-order properties that apply to all first-order existents, do not themselves possess the properties that they are. So, for example, the property 'being produced causally' (*pratītyasamutpannatva*) is not itself produced causally. This is quite normal; the property 'being a president of the United States' is not itself a president of the United States (though, of course, every possessor of it is). Simply put, for the digests, the universally applicable first-order properties through which the standard claims about impermanence are made are themselves atemporal states of affairs. They obtain, if they do, atemporally, which is to say permanently and everlastingly (I take these predicates to deny beginning, end, and change, and so not to be temporal properties at all, but rather to deny temporality to their possessors), "so that reals might continue" as the extract translated above put it.

This point can also be made grammatically. The properties in question—*anityatā, duḥkhatā, pratītyasamutpannatva,* and so forth—are denoted in Sanskrit by abstract nouns, suggesting that the properties so denoted obtain in all times (*trikāleṣu*). It seems best, in light of this argument, to take the term *dharmatā,* another abstract noun that I am translating 'reality,' to denote all properties shared by all reals (dharmas); hence one can conveniently and lucidly translate the frequently occurring phrase *[sarva]dharmāṇāṃ dharmatā* as 'the reality of all reals.' Similarly for *tathatā,* 'actuality,' which is often synonymous with *dharmatā*: it, also an abstract noun, denotes the reality of all reals properly understood (*yathābhūta*).[60] So also for *dharmadhātu,* translated as 'the ground of the real';[61] this denotes that in virtue of which all existents can be what they are, and it too is of necessity beyond time and change.

So much for the first philosophical argument in favor of predicating permanence and eternality of Buddha. The second argument returns us to the sphere of soteriological explanation. Consider the following:

> rtag pa'i mtshan nyid ces bya ba ni ther zug gi mtshan nyid do/ de bzhin nyid rnam par dag pa de ni rtag pa ste/ gzhan du na de bzhin nyid ces bya ba yang med par 'gyur ro/ sngon gyi smon lam gyi shugs kyi phyir zhes bya ba ni des sngon 'di skad du sems can tshad med pa dag yongs su mya ngan las bzla'o zhes smon lam btab pa yang rtag pa nyid med du zin na de grub par mi 'gyur ro/ smon lam btab tu zin kyang sems can mtha' yas pa'i phyir bya ba yongs su rdzogs par mi 'gyur te/ sems can ji srid par gnas pa'i phyir rtag pa nyid do/[62]

> 'The real body has the characteristic of permanence' means that it is characterized by everlastingness. Pure actuality is permanent. Otherwise, what is referred to as 'actuality' would not exist. To say that it [sc., the real body] is under the impulse of former vows means that even though [Buddha] has previously made vows that it will deliver innumerable living beings from suffering, such a [vow] could not be accomplished were [Buddha] not eternal. Even if [Buddha] were to have made such a vow, it could not be fulfilled because of the limitless number of living beings. So, because [the real body] endures as long as there are living beings, it is permanent.

This, along with many other similar passages,[63] links Buddha's permanence closely with its salvific action. The limitless and perfect salvific efficacy that Buddha, understood as maximally great, must necessarily possess, requires that Buddha be present and active everywhere and at all times. Hence, Buddha must be permanent, without beginning or end in time.

The digests thus refuse to predicate any temporal properties of Buddha considered *in se*. Buddha is not earlier or later than anything, not temporally related to anything in any way. All Buddha's temporal properties are of the kind described in chapters four and five: *seems to S to be P at t*.

Correlated with this refusal is a denial to Buddha of any causal properties: Buddha is not caused to do anything, nor does Buddha cause any non-Buddha to do anything. Buddha is, metaphysically speaking, simply identical with all atemporal states of affairs.

Chapter 7

Doctrinal Criticism

In the first three chapters of this book I argued: (1) that the category 'doctrine-expressing sentences,' properly defined, denotes the products of an intellectual practice characteristically engaged in by religious communities, and characteristically judged by them to be of considerable value to their own continued existence and proper functioning; (2) that virtuoso Buddhist intellectuals in medieval India developed and used concepts that make it reasonable to regard their intellectual practices as instances of those productive of doctrine; and (3) that, for these same Buddhist intellectuals, the nature of Buddha was a topic of considerable importance, the object of many doctrine-expressing sentences. Chapters four, five, and six were largely exegetical. In them I attempted to show the essential points of the system of buddhalogical doctrine set forth in the doctrinal digests.

I suggested in chapter one that the application of the category 'doctrine' to these Buddhist materials would have some heuristic benefits. Some of these have already been realized; I have been able to treat buddhalogical doctrine as a system of ideas without relating it to the social or institutional setting within which it was developed (though also without denying either that it had such a setting, or that paying attention to it will be of use and value for some intellectual programs). That is, by treating buddhalogical doctrine seriously as doctrine, I have been able to take it with (descriptive) seriousness in its own terms. But I suggested in chapter one that another set of benefits might accrue as a result of taking buddhalogical doctrine seriously as doctrine: I mean the benefit of being able to subject the doctrinal system in question to properly doctrinal criticism, and so to take it with normative as well as descriptive seriousness. This concluding chapter is given over to that constructively critical enterprise.

Buddhalogical doctrine rests upon a single formal or procedural intuition: the intuition that Buddha is maximally great, that whatever great-making properties there are, Buddha has them maximally. It is arguably this intuition, more than any other single factor, that makes it useful to classify buddhalogical doctrine as an instance of religious doctrine (rather than, say, legal doctrine). It is because of this intuition that it is reasonable to think of buddhalogy as formally identical with Christian theology, since both enterprises are largely based upon and impelled by it. The maximal-greatness intuition entails its negative correlate: the intuition that whatever negative (non-great-making) properties there are, Buddha is maximally free of them. Flesh is put on the bones of these purely formal intuitions by decisions as to which the great-making properties are, and which the negative ones; and then by decisions as to what are the constraints upon maximality in given cases. Such constraints may be produced by the limits of logic or of conceivability: Buddha may have maximal power, but this cannot mean, for instance, that Buddha can produce a barren woman's son at will. Buddha may have maximal veridical awareness, but this cannot mean, for example, that the end of Samsara can be directly present to that awareness (for it is a contradiction in terms to predicate the property 'possessing an end' of Samsara).[1] Alternatively, constraints on maximality may be produced by conflicts among great-making properties, such that were Buddha to possess one such property maximally, another could not be so possessed. For example, the maximal possession of power might suggest that Buddha should be able to hinder the advancement toward Nirvana of some living being, but were this to be the case Buddha would not be maximally salvifically efficacious—and so what it means to possess maximal power is constrained by what it means to be maximally efficacious salvifically. Put differently: for Buddhist intellectuals, as for all those engaged in an intellectual practice grounded by the maximal-greatness intuition, there is a hierarchy operative among properties taken to be great-making. When there is a conflict of the kind just mentioned, it is resolved in favor of the property to which is given a more exalted position in the hierarchy.

This single and formally simple intuition is a powerful, perhaps a too-powerful, doctrine-producing engine. Those who take it seriously are required by so doing to sort out which properties are great-making, what the hierarchical order among those properties is, and what it means to possess any one of them maximally. Before attempting a restatement of this part of the buddhalogical enterprise, it is worth pausing for a moment to ask whether, given the rules of recognition and interpretation governing the doctrinal practices of those intellectual virtuosos who produced the digests, the maximal-greatness intuition should have been given doctrinal force for their communities. The first step in any doctrinal criticism must be to ask this kind of question: it amounts to asking whether the body of doctrine in question is a proper product of the procedural rules that are supposed to have governed its production. A negative answer, if given, would entail the conclusion that Buddhist intellectuals have misused their own rules of recognition and interpretation, and are therefore mistaken either about the fact that their doctrinal practice is constrained by those rules, or about the proper products of their practice.

The answer to this question is not immediately clear, mostly because, as I showed in chapter two, the rules of recognition and interpretation operative in the digests are (deliberately) largely parasitic upon prior and independent decisions as to what (metaphysically, epistemically, and ethically) is the case. It is certainly true that many of the epithets and titles given to Buddha either are or contain (grammatical) superlatives; it is true also that the natural-language sentences in which the predication of these superlatives of Buddha is made are properly doctrinal according to the rules of recognition operative in the digests. But it is less clear that the maximal-greatness intuition itself should be taken to have doctrinal force. It is not entailed by the sentences claiming that Buddha has some properties superlatively; that is, it would be perfectly possible to acknowledge the claim *Buddha possesses salvifically relevant awareness to a maximal degree* to be expressive of doctrine without thereby being forced to similarly acknowledge the claim *Buddha possesses awareness simpliciter to a maximal degree.* Neither is the maximal-greatness intuition itself stated explicitly in the digests (although, as I have shown, some approximations to it are found, and it can be shown to be operative in those works).

The most that can be said here is that the rules of recognition and interpretation operative in the digests do not require the judgment that the maximal-greatness intuition has doctrinal force, but do permit it. That there are other possibilities consonant with the doctrinal proclivities of the digests is evident from the fact that some among the earlier texts appear to share the maximal-greatness intuition, but make its object not Buddha but rather dharma. So, for example, among the three refuges, those three things that Buddhists understand to be of primary salvific benefit for them—Buddha, dharma (doctrine, what is preached), and sangha (monastic community)—some texts understand dharma to be the supreme refuge, while others so understand Buddha. This suggests that it would have been possible to accept the maximal-greatness intuition and to develop it not in connection with Buddha but with dharma. But the digests do not typically do this: rather, they take the complex of strictly metaphysical terms surrounding (and derived from) 'dharma' and make its members predicates of Buddha. Buddha thus swallows up dharma rather than the other way around. Perhaps it was unavoidable that the Buddhist intellectual tradition should come to employ the maximal-greatness intuition as its chief doctrine-producing engine; but it was not inevitable that it should take the possessor of maximal greatness to be Buddha. One way of understanding the buddhalogical enterprise, then, is as an attempt to delineate what is maximally great that is only incidentally concerned with the possessors of the title 'Buddha.' Looking at it like this goes a good way toward explaining why much of what is said about Buddha in the digests seems in fact to be about everything—about what all reals (dharma) have in common in virtue of being real—rather than about any particular salvifically efficacious real. Buddha swallows up dharma, it is true; but only by itself becoming assimilated to dharma, homologized to what there really is.

The maximal-greatness intuition may, then, be accepted as bearing doctrinal force for virtuoso Buddhist intellectuals, though it need not be. I suggest that when this intuition is so accepted the result, inevitable and quick, is doctrinal trouble; and this is true not only for Buddhists but for all who have made it, explicitly or implicitly, the principle upon which their doctrinal activity is based. By its nature it requires those who use it to push their thought to the limits of coherence; and this means that there is considerable likelihood of either passing beyond those limits, or of remaining within them and being forced to jettison other doctrines that are or have been of value to the community. I shall illustrate the presence of both these tendencies in the digests, and shall suggest that they lead to intellectual problems that in some cases appear to have no solutions.

But first I shall attempt an abstract restatement of what I take to be the main planks of the buddhalogical system of the digests. In so doing I shall be using terminology that is often distant from that found in the digests, and formulations not found there at all. But I intend the propositions that follow to be entirely consonant with what the digests do say, and to issue from the exegesis given in chapters four through six. What follows, then, is a list of propositions with interpretive glosses; these propositions will be the basis for the critical analysis to follow later in this chapter.

I begin with the axiom that

(1) Buddha is maximally salvifically efficacious

since the property 'being salvifically efficacious' is arguably, for the digests, the great-making property at the top of the hierarchical order of great-making properties.

To this should be added:

(2) Buddha is single,

which I take to mean that all plurality and multiplicity in Buddha are apparent, finally unreal, constituted exhaustively by apparently relational properties.

This is followed by an axiom based upon the intuition that veridical awareness is a great-making property, and which therefore claims that Buddha possesses it maximally:

> (3) Buddha is omniscient = (def.) the scope of Buddha's awareness is spatially and temporally coextensive with everything; and every possible object of awareness is directly present to that awareness.

In (3) "scope" denotes the reach or range of Buddha's awareness. To say that this is "spatially and temporally coextensive with everything" is to make the formal point that whatever account is given of the spatial and temporal extension of the cosmos (whether temporal relations among existents are said to be real or not, whether mind-independent spatially extended objects are thought to be real or not), Buddha's awareness must embrace all of it. To say that every possible object of awareness is "directly present" to Buddha's awareness I take to entail:

> (4) Buddha has no beliefs,

where "beliefs" are understood as propositional attitudes, whether dispositional or occurrent. This negation is required because, I take it, knowing something by way of having a belief about it is to have an object indirectly present to one's awareness, and (3) rules this out for Buddha by definition. So, for instance, the state of affairs described by the sentence *my mother-in-law's maiden name is Rudd* is known to me in virtue of the disposition I have to possess the occurrent belief that *my mother-in-law's maiden name is Rudd* in relevant circumstances (such as those constituted by my writing or reading or thinking this sentence). The state of affairs in question is not always present to my awareness; rather few states of affairs are because of the very limited scope of my awareness. But this is not true of Buddha: no state of affairs is present to its awareness through the mediation of a belief (or any other propositional attitude, such as doubt, hope, fear, and so forth) because the scope of its awareness is such that all states of affairs are necessarily directly present to it.

(3) also requires

> (5) Buddha has no nonveridical awareness,

because all the factors that might cause the presence of such awareness—all improper doxastic habits, inappropriate cognitive commitments, affective states of all kinds—are lacking for Buddha. Put differently, and taking (5) together with (3), we might say that all states of affairs not implicated with cognitive or affective error are directly present to Buddha's awareness.

(3) and (5) also require

> (6) Buddha's awareness entails no volition, effort, or attention on Buddha's part,

since this is part of what "directly present" in (3) means, and is required also by (5), since awareness that does entail volition and the rest necessarily involves both the possibility of error, and, given certain axioms about the implication of all concept-laden intentional acts of the mind with error, its actuality. All this is ruled out in principle for Buddha. Taking a slightly different route I would add:

> (7) Buddha's awareness does not have the phenomenal property of dualism,

where "dualism" means (ontologically) the state of affairs of there being at least two things such that one can be the object of another's awareness; and (phenomenologically) the separation between subject and object that may be a phenomenal property of an instance of awareness. This entails, given (5) and its gloss,

> (8) There are no dualistic states of affairs not implicated with conceptual or affective error,

for if there were Buddha's awareness would reflect them, and it does not.

Closely associated with (3) through (7)—which have to do with Buddha's awareness—is

> (9) Buddha's awareness has no temporal properties,

where the phrase "temporal properties" includes all relational temporal properties ('being earlier then,' 'being later than,' and 'being simultaneous with,' for example), and those temporal properties that indicate beginnings and endings ('having a beginning,' 'coming to an end,' and so forth). This is not to say that the object(s) of Buddha's awareness must also be without temporal properties. The notion of the 'specious present'[2] is useful in understanding how this can be: it is clear that human persons (and, presumably, also nonhumans of various kinds) are capable of being aware of temporally extended successions of states of affairs without their awareness also being characterized by temporal succession. That is, human persons often (perhaps always) perceive states of affairs extended briefly in time with an act of awareness that itself has no temporal parts among its phenomenal properties. So, for example, in listening to music it will often be the case that my auditory awareness of a short phrase (say, one one-eighth note in a piece written in six/eight time) is, speaking phenomenologically, temporally indivisible. I do not "first feel one end" of the note "and then feel the other after it, and from the perception of the succession infer an interval of time between"; rather, I "seem to feel the interval of time as a whole";[3] and so that particular instance of my awareness has no temporal properties internal to it. It is an example of my specious present, fully present to me as an indivisible temporal whole, and as such may serve to illustrate how Buddha's awareness of states of affairs with duration may itself be without temporal properties internal to it, even though its object(s) have such properties. My specious present is, naturally, extremely limited in duration; and as a result it necessarily has temporal properties that relate it to states of affairs external to itself. That is, it is related temporally (and causally) to other instances of my awareness (it comes before some and after others), and also bears temporal and causal relations with temporally extended states of affairs other than my awareness, such as material objects, causal processes, and the like.

But suppose my awareness were temporally coextensive with every state of affairs; suppose, that is to say, the extent of its specious present to be coeval with eternity. Then it would be free not only from internal temporal properties, but also from external or relational ones. There would be no states of affairs temporally extraneous to it, and so also none to which it could bear temporal relations. This, I suggest, is what the digests intend their users to understand about Buddha's awareness; it is free from both internal and external temporal properties, the former because of its phenomenology and the latter because of its eternality.

A similar line can be taken with Buddha's (apparently relational) salvifically efficacious acts, a line that yields

> (10) Buddha does not act in time.

If, from (9), Buddha has no temporally indexed volitions (for these would be instances of awareness with temporal properties)—and, indeed, if the exegesis in chapters four through six will stand, it must be said that Buddha has no volitions at all—and if temporally indexed volitions are among the necessary conditions of temporally indexed actions, then (10) is easy to derive. But it is important to see that (10) is compatible with

> (10') Buddha seems to non-Buddhas to act in time,

just as is (9) with

> (9') Buddha seems to non-Buddhas to have temporal properties.

Indeed, as I have emphasized throughout this study, the digests allow temporally and spatially indexed properties to Buddha only of the apparent kind mentioned in (9') and (10').

But just how are (9') and (10') to be held together with (9) and (10)? The most obvious way, familiar to western audiences from more than a thousand years of discussion in Christian philosophical theology, is to distinguish Buddha's action *ad intra* from Buddha's action *ad extra*,[4] a distinction that the conceptual machinery of the three-body system can be seen both to enshrine and require. *Ad intra* Buddha does not act, whether in time or in any other fashion, for Buddha is the *dharmadhātu*, the changeless ground of the real. But the effects of Buddha's changeless wisdom/compassion are necessarily (given [1], the axiom about Buddha's maximal salvific efficacy) apparently temporally indexed actions. The general point is that Buddha's action *ad intra* logically need not have all the temporal properties that Buddha's action *ad extra* has; the latter may (must) have temporal properties of the kind *seems to S to be P at t,* while the former does not (cannot) have these or any other temporal properties.

But there are several prices to be paid for affirming (1) through (10') as doctrinal, and it is not entirely clear that the digests are willing to pay them. The costs can be seen both in what must be affirmed about the epistemic and phenomenological condition of Buddha if (1) through (10') are affirmed, and in what must be affirmed metaphysically. I shall treat these different kinds of costs separately, as far as I can.

I shall consider first what can properly be said about the limitations on Buddha's awareness, and about the phenomenal properties of that awareness. The conclusions I draw here are not drawn by the digests for the very good reason that they are in tension, if not in outright contradiction, with other doctrines that both the digests and the Buddhist tradition as a whole consistently want to assert. If the arguments offered here are good, I will have isolated examples of doctrinal tensions: sets of incompatible claims about Buddha made or implied by the digests, and given doctrinal force by them.

The main problem here has to do with the phenomenal properties of Buddha's experience; it is an argument, in other words, about what it's like to Buddha to be Buddha, about the subjective character of Buddha's experience. The argument will try to show that the account of the subjective character of Buddha's experience most easily held together with the buddhalogical doctrine of the digests is one that claims Buddha's experience to have no phenomenal properties, no subjective character. My goal is to show, in other words, that the digests strongly suggest the conclusion that it is not like anything to Buddha to be Buddha. The argument is an instance of doctrinal criticism that remains internal to the doctrinal system being criticized: it introduces no criteria external to the system, and tries only to draw out some implications of the system that are not made explicit by the system itself.

Let me begin with Thomas Nagel who, more than twenty years ago, offered, in a famous essay called "What Is It Like to Be a Bat?" a powerful argument against physicalism. I am not interested here in the antiphysicalist implications of Nagel's argument (though I think he is correct that physicalism is false); I want rather to use Nagel's conceptual setup as a means of introduction to my argument.

The phrase 'what it's like to be a bat' is, as Nagel points out, systematically ambiguous in English. First, it can sometimes be used in a simple comparative sense, so that asking what it's like to be a bat comes out to be equivalent to the question 'what's a bat like?' An answer to this might be 'a bit like a mouse and a bit like a bird.' Second, it can be used to mean 'what does it seem like to a bat to be one?'; and, if so understood, it becomes a question about the phenomenal properties of the experience that a bat has, about how a bat's experiences seem to it. In the case of all sentient creatures, Nagel argues (and I would concur), there is an answer to this question, though it will usually be an exceedingly complex one, never capable of being given exhaustively even when the sentient being giving the answer is identical with the sentient being about whose experience the answer is being given.

In the case of bats, an account of the phenomenal properties of bat-experience would include such exotica as an account of how it seems to bats to assess the shape of physical objects by bouncing high-frequency sound waves off them; and an account of how it seems to hang upside down by one's feet for many hours at a time. A list of similarly complex phenomenal facts would have to be given in an attempt to answer the question 'what's it like to be a human person?'

The contrast here is with nonsentient objects. It seems natural to say, for instance, that the proper answer to the question 'what's it like to be a rock?' is just 'nothing,' which is precisely the same as to say that it doesn't seem, like anything to a rock to be one. There might well be marginal cases about which we have no clear intuitions as to whether it's like anything to be them or not. Is it, for instance, like anything to be a crab-apple tree? Or an Apple Macintosh computer? These are interesting questions about the boundaries of sentience, questions discussed extensively by both Buddhist and western theorists. I don't want, though, to pursue them here; for my purposes it will be enough to establish that the extreme cases are clear; it is like something to be a bat and it isn't like something to be a rock—which isn't at all the same thing as to say that a rock isn't like anything.

There is, then, an important and fundamental distinction between events that have phenomenal properties to their subject, on the one hand, and events that have no such properties, on the other. The former can be understood only to the extent that the viewpoint of the subject who has them is adopted, while the latter can be understood from many different viewpoints. So human persons can understand a great deal about the physical events that constitute bats, including the circulation of their blood, the aerodynamic properties of the membranes that cover their wings, the mechanisms by which they emit high-frequency sound waves, and the neuronal connections in their brains. And all this can be done without adopting the bat's viewpoint—indeed, it can be done better without adopting the bat's viewpoint. But this is not true for the understanding of what it's like to be a bat available to nonbats: since this is defined in terms of the phenomenal properties of bat-experience *to the bat,* it is available to nonbats only to the extent that they adopt the bat's viewpoint. And this leads to Nagel's second main application of his conclusion that it is like something to be a bat: nonbats can as a matter of fact know very little of what it is like to be a bat, even though they can know that it is like something.

Transposing Nagel's bat-discourse into a buddhalogical key, I want to argue that, according to classical Indian buddhalogy as summarized earlier in this chapter, we non-Buddhas are in much better epistemic condition in regard to what it's like to be Buddha than nonbats are in regard to what it's like to be a bat. We know all that there is to know about what it's like to be Buddha precisely because there is nothing to know, and we can know that formal fact.

Now, denying that it is like something to be Buddha is precisely the same as denying that Buddhas have conscious mental states, since having such states is just what it means for there to be something it is like to be a particular being. This denial is the same, in turn, as denying any subjective character to the indubitable behavioral and functional states in terms of which the digests characterize Buddha in its bodies of magical transformation and communal enjoyment.

Suppose we divide the kinds of experience that can possess subjective character for their experiencers into perceptual experience, conative experience, affective experience, judgmental experience, and memorial experience. This is a rough-and-ready division, but I think it covers the ground, and in addition is entirely consonant with categories employed by the digests. Then, based upon this division, we may say that the phenomenal properties of perceptual experience are constituted for some subject by the flavor of the way in which its physical context is made available to it through its perceptual equipment; those of its conative experience by the flavor of its decision- or choice-making procedures; those of its affective experience by the flavor of its emotional responses—pain, fear, hope, and the like; those of its judgmental experience by the flavor of its conceptual acts—constructing an argument, categorizing something as a member of some class-category, and the like; and those of its memorial experience by the flavor of its identifications with its past—and perhaps also by that of its projections into its future. These, I suggest, are among the more important components of what it is like for some subject to be the subject it is. The experience of bats comprises most, probably all, of these elements, as also does that of human persons; that of Buddha comprises none.

That is to say: first, the perceptual experience of Buddha has no phenomenal flavor; instead, it occurs in just the same way as does the representation of the objects that constitute a physical environment in a mirror or in the undisturbed smooth waters of a lake. Second, decision- or choice-making experience is denied to Buddha altogether by (1) and (6) above: choices are possible only when there are alternatives, and Buddha has no alternatives since Buddha always and spontaneously does exactly and only what is of maximal salvific effect in any specific situation. Third, Buddha has no affect, since the feeling of emotions is always and necessarily the product of desires of various kinds, and is thus ruled out by (5) and its entailments. Fourth, the deliberative decision-procedures involved in making conceptual judgments are also explicitly denied to Buddha, by both (4) and (6); this is because having beliefs, either dispositionally or occurrently, requires making judgments, which in turn requires making discriminations, which is taken to introduce the possibility of error. And finally, Buddha can have no memorial experience: it cannot identify with its own past nor project its own future, since such identifications and projections always involve both conceptual and affective error—inappropriate judgments, that is to say, about the nature of the relations between Buddha's (nonexistent) past and its (nonexistent) future (see [7] and [10])—as well as inappropriate affective responses to such judgments.

Memorial experience can be denied to Buddha straightforwardly by (10)—the denial of all temporal properties to Buddha's awareness—for memorial experience is by definition temporally indexed. But it will be useful here to give a rather more extended and precise argument as to why Buddha can have no memorial experience even if (10) is held in abeyance, for the argument will serve as a token of arguments of a similar type that could easily be constructed in support of some of the other claims made in the preceding paragraph.

The standard Buddhist account of memory employs two technical terms: *smṛti* and *pratyabhijñāna*. Here, for reasons that will become apparent, I shall translate the former as 're-presentation' (in the sense of presenting again what has been presented before), and the latter as 'recognition.' The former will denote the reappearance in a given mental continuum (*cittasantāna*) of the complete experiential content, including the phenomenal properties or subjective character, of a preceding moment or moments of experience. Examples: I hear again music I heard twenty years ago; I see again the buttons on a coat my mother used to wear when I was a child; I touch again my first lover's lips. In all cases the re-presentation (*smṛti*) is of the complete experiential content of the original experience. Recognition (*pratyabhijñāna*) denotes a conscious acknowledgment or judgment on the part of the subject that an experience she has just had was in fact an instance of re-presentation. So, for example, I acknowledge to myself that the music I just heard with my mind's ear was a re-presentation of the version of Beethoven's Seventh Symphony that I heard in the Royal Albert Hall when I was fifteen. And so forth.

It follows from (4)—the claim that Buddha has no beliefs—that judgments of the kind denoted by *pratyabhijñāna* are not available to it. This by itself is enough to show that Buddha cannot have memorial experience in the full sense. But suppose we limit our attention to *smṛti*, to memorial experience in a narrower sense; it is not difficult to show that Buddha cannot have this either.

The digests typically say that there are three severally necessary and jointly sufficient conditions that a given mental event must fulfil if it is to be classified as an instance of a re-presentation, a *smaraṇacitta*. First, it must have as its object something previously experienced (*pūrvānubhūtārtha*), and must re-present that object in the sense given. Second, it must be connected causally with that previously experienced object. And third, the mental event in which the original object was experienced and that in which it is re-presented must be part of the same mental continuum (*ekasantānika*).[5]

A re-presentation (*smṛti*) is meant, recall, to re-present the full content of a previous moment of experience. If we add the straightforward (and pan-Buddhist) premise that every instance of experience belonging to non-Buddhas is tainted with passions of various sorts—especially egocentricity (*asmimāna*) and its concomitants—and the premise, arrived at through the maximal-greatness intuition, that Buddha's experience can comprise no passions or other affective errors, then the conclusion follows directly that Buddha cannot experience a re-presentation of a moment of experience that putatively belongs to its past before it became Buddha.

This means that memorial experience is unavailable to Buddha, from whch it follows that none of the kinds of such experience attributed by the digests to Buddha—I think here especially of the memory of previous lives—are available to it either. Exactly analogous arguments can be constructed to show that Buddha lacks all other kinds of experience that are potential bearers of phenomenal properties.

Since all these kinds of experience are denied to Buddha by the buddhalogical doctrine of the digests, and since these appear to be the chief kinds of experience capable of possessing phenomenal properties—of seeming a certain way to those who have them—it follows that it cannot seem like anything to Buddha to be Buddha. An exhaustive account of what Buddha is can thus be given solely in terms of how Buddha seems to others. To put this more formally: all the properties that Buddha has are of the kind *seems to S to be P at t*. So, should I be fortunate enough to enter into Buddha's presence and have Buddha speak to me or touch me, a complete account of those events can be given in terms of how they seem to me: no appeal to the phenomenal properties of Buddha's experience is either necessary or possible.

There are infinitely many of these *seems to S to be P at t* properties, and they are infinitely varied. But both their number and their variety are due to variations in the conditions and needs of non-Buddhas, not to variations in the phenomenal properties of Buddha's experience. There are no variations of this latter kind. Would the digests be uneasy about this conclusion (which, recall, is not drawn explicitly by them)? Does it stand in tension with anything else that, doctrinally speaking, they are committed to? I do not think that it does, not, at least, if we take seriously the procedural principle that what is said about Buddha *in se* must act as an interpretive control upon what is said about Buddha *pro nobis*, even when what is said in this latter connection is said with doctrinal force. So, for instance, even though it is the case that Buddha is said, among many other things, to remember its previous lives and to be confident that it can say and do nothing inappropriate, these affirmations must be, strictly, false, for the kind of memorial experience affirmed by the one and the kind of affective experience affirmed by the other are ruled out in principle by the doctrinal positions taken here. This position can be maintained coherently as long as it is stated (as it generally is by the digests) with careful attention to the proper relations between the sentences claiming that Buddha has the properties that Buddha actually has ([1] through [10']), and those claiming that Buddha appears to have the properties that Buddha appears to have (such as those expounded in chapters four and five).

But while there is no formal incompatibility between the properties mentioned in (1) through (10') and the Buddha-properties predicated of Buddha when the digests come to talk about what it does in its bodies of magical transformation and communal enjoyment, there are certainly some deep tensions. Consider the titles and epithets of Buddha discussed in chapter three. These titles and epithets—the attribution of which to Buddha is paradigmatically doctrinal—emphasize that Buddha is both worthy and blessed, worthy to receive worship and homage, and blessed in the sense of being both ultimately auspicious and unsurpassably meritorious. The meditational exercises surrounding Buddha, especially that of recollecting the glories and beauties of the bodies of magical transformation, emphasize similar facts about Buddha. And the Buddha-legend in its entirety presents Buddha as a person, an identifiable center of compassionate activity with whom it is possible to have personal relations. This last point is true to an even greater extent of Buddhist devotional poetry, story, and ritual practice. All these things are called into question in a radical way by the doctrinal positions outlined in this study. They are bracketed, put under erasure, set forth only to be set aside as efficacious instruments for those who know no better. Even in the case of the digests themselves, unremittingly abstract and systematic as they are, the amount of attention given to Buddha as Buddha *appears* is much greater than the amount given to Buddha as Buddha *is*. This is reflected in the structure and proportions of this book: chapters three, four, and five, taken together, are substantially longer than chapter six; the former deal with Buddha as it appears, and the latter with Buddha as it is.

Given these matters of emphasis and structure, it is difficult not to conclude that the digests, while they do provide a defensible intellectual resolution of this tension, do not make a proper marriage between this resolution and the structure and emphasis of the systems they use to express and argue for their buddhalogy. This point may be put more strikingly, perhaps, by saying that even the traditional doctrinal claim that there are three refuges (Buddha, dharma, sangha) from suffering, and that each of the three has an important salvific function to fulfil, is judged by the digests to be false: not only the dharma, what is real as well as what is preached, but also the sangha, the community that preserves the doctrine to be preached, are absorbed into the omnipresent Buddha. *Sarvaṃ buddhatvam*—everything is Buddhahood; and this means that Buddha is no longer the possessor of the cognitive, active, and aesthetic excellences for which traditional buddhalogy exalted and praised it; it means that the dharma is no longer the structure of the cosmos, discovered and preached by Buddha to those in need of succor; and it means that the sangha is no longer the unexcelled field in which merit can be made. All these are, instead, spontaneous actions of the ever- and omnipresent Buddha; for in the end there can be nothing else, if the buddhalogy of the digests is indeed to be defended, than Buddha *in se*: no non-Buddhas, no dharma, and no sangha. This is a properly metaphysical claim. I take it to be entailed by the buddhalogy of the digests, and it is with it that we finally reach the point at which the thrust of the digests' buddhalogical discourse can be made clear. This is the final move in the metaphysical game whose strategy I have been mapping since chapter three.

The argument here is very simple indeed. Recall the characterization given of Buddha's omniscience in chapter six, and restated in (3) and (7) above. The point of these claims is to say that every possible object of awareness is directly present to Buddha; that Buddha's awareness is entirely veridical; and that it is entirely free from dualism. As I put it rather more Sanskritically in chapter six: all the phenomenal properties (*ākāra*) of Buddha's awareness (*jñāna*) are veridical (*aviparīta*); and all states of affairs (*dharma, tattva*) not implicated with conceptual or affective error (*prapañca, viparyāsa, kleśa,* or more generally *abhūtaparikalpa*) are directly present (*sākṣātkṛ-, saṃmukhībhū-*) to Buddha. It follows directly from these claims that there are no dualistic states of affairs not implicated with conceptual or affective error, for if there were they would be directly present to Buddha's awareness; and they are not. And if by a 'dualistic state of affairs' we mean, in accord with the digests, when speaking ontologically a state of affairs in which there are at least two things such that one can be the object of another's awareness; and when speaking phenomenologically, the separation between subject and object that may be a phenomenal property of an instance of awareness, then it follows that there are no subjects and no objects other than Buddha, which is itself strictly neither subject nor object. Monism of at least this kind is unavoidable, and the metaphysical game ends with the claim that Buddha is the only thing there is: not only is everything well-spoken spoken by Buddha, but every instance of veridical awareness is an instance of Buddha-awareness.

This conclusion could be arrived at in a number of other ways. One would be to construct an argument parallel and obverse to that offered above for the conclusion that Buddha cannot have memorial experience because memorial experience is always implicated with error. Such an argument would issue in the conclusion that whenever there is an instance of experience not implicated with error it must, by definition, be an instance of Buddha-awareness. Another would be to begin from what the digests say about error, about all defilements, passions, taints, and so forth: they are all, recall, adventitious, accidental, merely apparent; when removed, pure actuality (*tathatāviśuddhi*) becomes apparent, which is just the same thing as Buddha, and which is all there is.

There is an important difference between this argument and the account offered above of how it is possible for Buddha's awareness to be without temporal properties even if its objects have them. The 'specious present' account offered in that argument remains a coherent possibility for the digests just so long as temporal properties are not identified or defined as themselves being implicated with error. If they are so defined then it is no longer a possibility, since temporal properties would themselves become instances of adventitious or accidental defilements; whether temporal properties need to be defined in one way or the other is not a question I shall decide here since the digests offer different and mutually inconsistent accounts of time and change, and to survey and analyze them would take me further afield than I want to go. Suppose we assume, for the sake of this argument, that an account of them can be given that allows them not to be classified as adventitious defilements: in that case, they can be real, and yet still not properties of Buddha because Buddha is identified with the second-order property (or properties) that all temporal properties have in common (see the account in chapter six), second-order properties that are not themselves temporal properties (such as *pratītyasamutpannatva*). But this move cannot be made in the case of the property 'the fact of being other than Buddha' (*abuddhatvam*?), for this (obviously) cannot be among the set of properties that conjointly constitute Buddha. (The property 'the fact of seeming to be other than Buddha' [*abuddhapratibhāsatā*?] is quite another matter, as I hope to have demonstrated throughout this work.) So that way of avoiding the conclusion that nothing has the property of being other than Buddha is ruled out.

This monistic conclusion is most easily worked out metaphysically in terms of absolute idealism, in which the claim that Buddha is everything is taken to mean that there is nothing other than Buddha's awareness; only in this way can the claim that there are no entities other than Buddha be preserved without complex intellectual gymnastics. Not all the digests take this route, however, though even those that refuse to do so explicitly (as is the case for many Mādhyamika works) are equally clear in their refusal to assert realism about extramental objects. The digests therefore show evidence of only two possibilities: one that took the implications of its own buddhalogy seriously, and so argued, in a strictly metaphysical way, for an absolute idealism; and another that refused, rhetorically at least, the metaphysical route altogether, while still engaging in constructive buddhalogy.

This metaphysical conclusion is something that creates conceptual tensions even deeper than those already indicated. It leads directly toward, perhaps has already arrived at, a monism in which all beings are already Buddha; in which the gradualist salvific efficacy of the practice of the path is called into question in favor of a subitist and spontaneous removal of adventitious defilements and passions; and in which, finally, there are no beings other than Buddha to be awakened in any case. It ends, I think, by denying the most fundamental doctrinal commitment of the digests, which is not the assertion of the absence of self, nor that of impermanence, but rather that of radical unsatisfactoriness (*duḥkhatā*): the diagnostic and prescriptive soteriological commitments of the digests, on which they spend even more of their time than they do on their depiction of Buddha's action in the world and in heaven (though in the end the two cannot be readily separated), are left aside in favor of a quietist contemplation of what the contemplator already is.

Is there, then, another way out of this intellectual impasse? One possibility, mentioned several times already in the course of this study, is the abandonment of the maximal-greatness intuition as the major buddhalogical doctrine-producing engine: the digests could have (though they did not) come to think of Buddha simply as maximally soteriologically important, not as maximally metaphysically significant. But this possibility was, as I have shown, considered and rejected; and that there are great difficulties for religious thinkers in rejecting it is suggested by the grip the same intuition has had and continues to have upon Christian theological thinking. The only other possibility is radical change in one or more of the digests' intuitions as to what count as great-making properties. Most of the intellectual problems discussed in this chapter are related more or less closely to the intuition that the lexical item 'Buddha' must denote the collection of second-order properties held in common by all first-order existents; and that, as an entailment of this position, Buddha must necessarily be changeless, eternal, and so forth. This move could have been avoided (as its Christian counterpart, I believe, can also be avoided); had it been it would have been possible for the Buddhist intellectual tradition in India to avoid the subsumption of dharma into Buddha, and so to preserve a critically realist, nonmonistic metaphysic.

Notes

Preface

1. For this usage, see Snellgrove, *Indo-Tibetan Buddhism.*

Chapter 1. The Doctrinal Study of Doctrine

1. Among those working on Christianity I think of Pelikan, whose recently completed history of doctrine in five volumes (*Christian Tradition*) is self-conscious about treating doctrine as doctrine and not as an epiphenomenon of something else; and of McGrath who, in his 1990 Bampton Lectures (*Genesis of Doctrine*), called for the rehabilitation of doctrinal criticism as both an academic and a theological discipline. Among studies of Buddhist doctrine there are Ruegg's many works, especially his classic *La théorie*, and his 1987 Jordan Lectures, published as *Buddha-Nature.*

2. Lindbeck, *Nature of Doctrine.* This work is the most influential study of the nature and theological significance of doctrine to have been published in the 1980s. Important collections of responses to it are in *The Thomist* (1985) and *Modern Theology* (1988). See also Frei, "George Lindbeck."

3. Christian, *Doctrines.* There is a useful collection of discussions of this book in *The Thomist* 52 (1988).

4. Unger, *Critical Legal Studies,* 1.

5. It is, moreover, a thesis that no one would now seriously argue, even in the realm of jurisprudence. Dworkin's engagement with Hart has adequately demonstrated its weaknesses in that sphere, and there is no need to argue its merits for the study of religious doctrine. See Dworkin, *Philosophy of Law,*

38–65; *Taking Rights Seriously*, 14–80; *Law's Empire*, 33–52; Hart, *Concept of Law*.

6. Bourdieu, *Le sens pratique*, 112.

7. Dworkin, *Law's Empire*, 14.

8. Dworkin, *Law's Empire*, 12.

9. Frye, *Anatomy of Criticism*, 3–29.

10. Frede, *Essays*, ix–xxvii.

11. Christian, *Doctrines*, 1.

12. Christian, *Doctrines*, 12–86.

13. Griffiths, "Apology"; *Apology*.

14. See Hart, *Concept of Law*, 89–107; Dworkin, *Philosophy of Law*, 38–65; Peczenik et al., *Theory of Legal Science*.

15. Christian, *Doctrines*, 12–34.

16. Frei has made the strongest case for this. See especially *Eclipse*; " 'Narrative.' "

17. McGrath, *Genesis of Doctrine*, 63.

18. Christian, for example, gives an account of rules of recognition couched in terms of criteria of authenticity (*Doctrines*, 87–114).

19. Wainwright's most detailed presentation of this point is in his *Doxology*.

20. Lindbeck, *Nature of Doctrine*, 3–12 and passim.

21. For example, it seems to be constitutive of much that is important in Whitehead's scattered and unsystematic work on religion (*Adventures of Ideas*, 206–12). It is also operative in various ways in the work of such diverse theorists as James, Wach, Eliade, Tillich, Rahner, and Lonergan. The discussion of the historical roots of this position by Proudfoot (*Religious Experience*, 1–40), and Lindbeck (*Nature of Doctrine*, 30–45), provides some documentation for these broad claims.

22. There has been considerable debate on this issue. The collections edited by Katz are important (*Mysticism and Philosophical Analysis*; *Mysticism and Religious Traditions*; *Mysticism and Language*). The contributors to these volumes argue for a broadly constructivist position: that the phenomenal properties of religious experience are culturally determined. A collection edited by

Forman (*Problem*) provides counterarguments to the claims made by Katz and his contributors; many of its contributors think that there are, or might be, elements of religious or mystical experience that are invariant across cultures. My own essay in Forman's volume (71–97) discusses whether Indian Buddhists made such a claim.

23. Proudfoot, *Religious Experience*, 11.

24. These claims are strongly supported by recent work in cultural anthropology, to the theory informing which Geertz's methodological and theoretical works provide an engaging introduction. See especially *Interpretation of Cultures*; *Local Knowledge*. Lakoff's work on category-formation also supports these claims. See *Women*.

25. I borrow here from Smart's terminology in "Interpretation."

26. Forman, *Problem*, 3–49.

27. Mansini, *What Is a Dogma?* 322 n.3.

28. For my understanding of these Roman Catholic debates I have drawn principally upon the following works: Schrodt, "Continuing Discussion of Dogma"; Böhm, *Dogma und Geschichte*; König, *Dogma als Praxis*.

29. For this point, see Rahner, "What is a Dogmatic Statement?"; McGrath, *Genesis of Doctrine*, 72–80.

30. One theorist who appears to think this is Lindbeck. He claims, for instance (*Nature of Doctrine*, 19), that the only job doctrines can do is a regulative one; they cannot make first-order descriptive claims. This suggestion is not convincing, as I have tried to show elsewhere (*Apology*, 19–44), though I cannot reprise all the arguments here.

Chapter 2. Buddhist Doctrine

1. On the style and genre of scholastic Sanskrit works of the kind under consideration here, see Renou, *Histoire*; "Genre du sūtra."

2. Quine, "Epistemology Naturalized."

3. I have explored the idea of a denaturalized discourse elsewhere, mostly in "Denaturalizing Discourse."

4. The attentive and buddhalogically sophisticated reader will notice that, in citing and discussing matter from the digests, I make almost no distinctions

among successive layers of commentary within a particular corpus. That is, I do not signal whether material comes from a root-text, a primary commentary, or a subcommentary: a corpus is treated as an organic whole. I do this in part because of the doctrinal approach of this volume; but I do it also as an attempt to correct an excessively historicist approach to Buddhist thought.

5. See Pollock, "Theory of Practice"; "Idea of *Śāstra*"; "Playing by the Rules."

6. Pollock, "Theory of Practice," 515.

7. Shastri, *Abhidharmakośa*, 10.

8. Peking Tanjur, ngo-mtshar TO 21a6–8.

9. Yamaguchi, *Madhyāntavibhāgaṭīkā*, 4.

10. Krishnamacharya, *Tattvasaṅgraha*, 7.

11. Krishnamacharya, *Tattvasaṅgraha*, 8.

12. On *siddhānta*, see recently Cabezón, "Canonization."

13. Nagao, *Madhyāntavibhāga*, 17.

14. Yamaguchi, *Madhyāntavibhāgaṭīkā*, 1.

15. Yamaguchi, *Madhyāntavibhāgaṭīkā*, 4.

16. Yamaguchi, *Madhyāntavibhāgaṭīkā*, 4.

17. Yamaguchi, *Madhyāntavibhāgaṭīkā*, 4.

18. Yamaguchi, *Madhyāntavibhāgaṭīkā*, 4.

19. On this concentration, see Odani, *Daijō shōgon*, 235.

20. Yamaguchi, *Madhyāntavibhāgaṭīkā*, 2.

21. For the attribution of the *Mahāyānasūtrālaṅkāra* to Maitreya, see the colophon to the Tibetan version, Derge Tanjur, sems-tsam PHI 39a2–3. Bu-ston attributes the *bhāṣya* to Vasubandhu and the *ṭīkā* to Ngo bo nyid med pa (Asvabhāva or Niḥsvabhāva). See Nishioka, "Bu-ston bukkyōshi," part II, 56. Hakamaya has explored the historical problems surrounding the traditional Tibetan attribution of five treatises to Maitreya. See "Chibetto ni okeru."

22. Shastri, *Abhidharmakośa*, 3.

23. Shastri, *Abhidharmakośa*, 3.

24. Shastri, *Abhidharmakośa*, 1186–87.

25. Shastri, *Abhidharmakośa*, 1187.

26. Compare Krishnamacharya, *Tattvasaṅgraha*, 1–2.

27. Shastri, *Abhidharmakośa*, 3.

28. Krishnamacharya, *Tattvasaṅgraha*, 7.

29. Krishnamacharya, *Tattvasaṅgraha*, 7.

30. La Vallée Poussin, *Madhyamakāvatāra*, 406.

31. Shastri, *Abhidharmakośa*, 11–12; Derge Tanjur, ngo-mtshar THO 17a1–3.

32. Nagao, *Madhyāntavibhāga*, 17.

33. Renou, *Histoire*, 133.

34. Yamaguchi, *Madhyāntavibhāgaṭīkā*, 3; La Vallée Poussin, *Madhyamakavṛttiḥ*, 3.

35. Other translations and discussions of this important verse may be found in Friedmann, *Sthiramati*, 89 n.46; Stcherbatsky, *Madhyānta-Vibhanga*, 06 n.48; idem, *Conception of Buddhist Nirvāṇa*, 87–88; Sprung, *Lucid Exposition*, 32; Pollock, "Theory of Practice," 501 n.12.

36. Shastri, *Abhidharmakośa*, 12–15; Derge Tanjur, ngo-mtshar THO 17a6–20a6.

37. Funahashi, *Nepōru shahon*, 5; La Vallée Poussin, *Madhyamakavṛttiḥ*, 1–4; La Vallée Poussin, *Madhyamakāvatāra*, 408–409.

38. tathā hy abhyudayaniḥśreyasāvāptir jagaddhitam ucyate/ tasya cāviparyāso hetuḥ sarvasaṅkleśasya viparyāsamūlatvāt (Krishnamacharya, *Tattvasaṅgraha*, 9).

39. Shastri, *Abhidharmakośa*, 777; Lévi, *Vijñaptimātratāsiddhi*, 23; La Vallée Poussin, *Madhyamakavṛttiḥ*, 451–74.

40. This issue comes explicitly to the surface in Lévi, *Mahāyāna-Sūtrālaṃkāra*, 1–8; and in Hahn, *Nāgārjuna's Ratnāvalī*, 118–31. See also Cabezón, "Vasubandhu's Vyākhyāyukti."

41. I draw here upon discussions by Lamotte, "La critique d'authenticité"; Bareau, *Recherches*, volume 1, 229; Bond, *Word of the Buddha*, 22–33; Davidson, "Introduction."

42. Rhys Davids and Carpenter, *Dīgha-Nikāya*, volume 2, 123–36; Morris et al., *Anguttara-Nikāya*, volume 2, 167–70.

43. These questions are found, inter alia, in Lévi, *Mahāyāna-Sūtrālaṃkāra*, 4–5; Derge Tanjur, sems-tsam MI 22a4–23a7; La Vallée Poussin, *Bodhicaryāvatārapañjikā*, 431; Jaini, *Abhidharmadīpa*, 197.

44. Lévi, *Mahāyāna-Sūtrālaṃkāra*, 53–54.

45. Lévi, *Mahāyāna-Sūtrālaṃkāra*, 5; Derge Tanjur, sems-tsam MI 22a4–23a7; BI 46a7–47a2.

46. Derge Tanjur, sems-tsam MI 22a5–22b2; BI 46b4–5.

47. Derge Tanjur, sems-tsam MI 22a5–23a2; BI 46b4–5.

48. For example, the contradictory of the claim *persons exist as substances* (*pudgalasya dravyato 'stitvam*) is so designated at Lévi, *Mahāyāna-Sūtrālāṃkāra*, 156.

49. La Vallée Poussin, *Bodhicaryāvatārapañjikā*, 431–32; Vaidya, *Śikṣāsamuccaya*, 12. Both digests identify this formula as coming from the *Adhyāśayasañcodanasūtra*.

50. On *pratibhāna*, see Shastri, *Abhidharmakośa*, 1102–5; Lamotte, *La somme*, volume 2, 53*–54*; idem, *Le traité*, 1614–24; MacQueen, "Inspired Speech," 310–15; Griffiths, *Realm*, 140–43.

51. Shastri reads *pudgalaḥ* for *vyañjanam*.

52. Shastri, *Abhidharmakośa*, 1202. See also La Vallée Poussin, *Madhyamakavṛttiḥ*, 43–44; Lévi, *Mahāyāna-Sūtrālāṃkāra*, 138–39; Dutt, *Bodhisattvabhūmiḥ*, 175–76; Derge Tanjur, sems-tsam TSI 95b1–98b3; Derge Tanjur, sems-tsam BI 144a7–144b7. Discussions of this set of four points of refuge may be found in Lamotte, *Le traité*, 536–40; idem, "La critique d'interprétation"; Hakamaya, "Shie."

53. See, inter alia, La Vallée Poussin, *Madhyamakavṛttiḥ*, 43, citing the *Samādhirājasūtra* and the *Akṣayamatinirdeśasūtra*.

54. Lamotte, "La critique d'interpretation," n.40, cites and discusses older studies of these terms. Among newer studies, the following seem to me important: Wayman, "Concerning saṃdhā-bhāṣā"; Broido, "Abhiprāya and Implication"; idem, "Intention and Suggestion"; Lopez, *Buddhist Hermeneutics*; Ruegg, "Purport, Implicature and Presupposition"; idem, "An Indian Source"; idem, "Allusiveness and Obliqueness."

Chapter 3. Buddhalogical Doctrine

1. "Die menschliche Vernunft bedarf einer Idee der höchsten Vollkommenheit, die ihr zum Maaßtabe dienet, um darnach bestimmen zu können" (Kant, *Philosophische Religionslehre*, 993).

2. Kant, *Philosophische Religionslehre*, 994–95.

3. This tenfold list is found in many relatively early Sanskrit texts. See Dutt, *Bodhisattvabhūmiḥ*, 64; Samtani, *Arthaviniścaya-Sūtra*, 45, 242–48; Schlingloff, *Ein buddhistisches Yogalehrbuch*, 174. It is probably the most common list, though it is certainly not the only one. For a study of another, much longer list, see Waldschmidt, "Varṇaśatam." There are some difficulties with the tenfold list. First, and interestingly, a list almost the same as this one occurs frequently in the Pali texts that make up the *Suttapiṭaka*; a convenient list of text-places is given by Lamotte, *Le traité*, 115 n.1. In the Pali texts, canonical and postcanonical, the list is usually introduced with the formula *iti pi so bhagavā* . . . , meaning something like "For the following reasons, indeed, he [Buddha] is a blessed one . . . "; it then goes on to list only nine epithets, omitting *tathāgata*, the first item in the Sanskrit list. See, e.g., Warren and Kosambi, *Visuddhimagga*, 62–175. The reasons for this difference are not clear to me. The ninefold list (again without *tathāgata*) can also be found in the Pali materials introduced by the phrase *tathāgato loke uppanne* . . . , rather than by the *iti pi so* formula, e.g., at Trenckner and Chalmers, *Majjhima Nikāya*, volume 1, 179; volume 2, 38, 226. In such cases the term *tathāgata* is included as part of the introduction, but is still not part of the formulaic list and is best not taken as an epithet. Second, the numbering and division of the epithets in the list are conventional: it could be analyzed in different ways to yield different numbers of epithets, as Nattier has suggested (*Once upon a Future Time*, 88 n.80), but I shall take it, as do most of its expositions in the digests, to contain ten distinct honorifics, and shall make brief comments on each.

4. For glosses on *tathā* in the digests, see Dutt, *Bodhisattvabhūmiḥ*, 64; Samtani, *Arthaviniścaya-Sūtra*, 242; Vaidya, *Aṣṭasāhasrikā*, 351. Ruegg has made the point that words meaning 'thus,' 'in such a way' (*tathā*, *evam*, and so forth), often seem to mean 'precise,' 'exact,' 'certain,' or 'complete' in Buddhist texts, and that there is some etymological evidence from Vedic and Avestan to suggest that this meaning was not present only in Buddhist texts. See "Védique *addhā*"; *La théorie*, 499–501 n.1. The early Tibetan translation of *tathāgata* was *yang dag par gshegs pa*, 'gone with precision,' which carries just this meaning (it was later changed to *de bzhin gshegs pa*; see the comments by Schrader,

"Some Tibetan Names"). Hopkins, "Buddha as Tathāgata," has shown that in non-Buddhist texts the term sometimes means simply 'dead'; and Thomas, "Tathāgata and Tahāgaya," has argued that the term may be an improper sanskritization of a prakrit original.

5. See Lamotte, *Le traité*, 131–132; Dutt, *Bodhisattvabhūmiḥ*, 64; Samtani, *Arthaviniścaya-Sūtra*, 244. Norman has recently suggested that, in Pali texts at least, the motif of going apparently present in both *tathāgata* and *sugata* should not be understood to refer primarily to a change of location, but simply to a condition. He translates *sugata* as "[one who is] in a [particularly] good way," and *tathāgata* as "[one who is] in that sort of [= very good] way." See "Pāli Lexicographical Studies VIII." There is, I have no doubt, force in this as a historical and etymological suggestion, but the fact remains that indigenous commentators in India, China, and Tibet make great play with the motif of 'going' understood as salvifically efficacious change of location.

6. Kern and Nanjio, *Saddharmapuṇḍarīka*, 209–10.

7. Dutt, *Bodhisattvabhūmiḥ*, 64; La Vallée Poussin, *Madhyamakavṛttiḥ*, 486; Vaidya, *Aṣṭasāhasrikā*, 273.

8. Samtani, *Arthaviniścaya-Sūtra*, 242; Vaidya, *Aṣṭasāhasrikā*, 351.

9. Shastri, *Abhidharmakośa*, 15; Lévi, *Vijñaptimātratāsiddhi*, 9; Sørensen, *Candrakīrti*, 14–17.

10. It remains unclear just why the concept of *pratyekabuddha* was developed and used. Wilshire, in his *Ascetic Figures*, has recently made some new suggestions about this, but they have not met with much approval from others. See especially Collins' lengthy discussion of this book ("Problems"). The best studies on this difficult question remain Kloppenborg's *Paccekabuddha* and Norman's "Pratyeka-Buddha."

11. Dutt, *Bodhisattvabhūmiḥ*, 64; Samtani, *Arthaviniścaya-Sūtra*, 243.

12. Vaidya, *Aṣṭasāhasrikā*, 352.

13. Vaidya, *Aṣṭasāhasrikā*, 352; Samtani, *Arthaviniścaya-Sūtra*, 243.

14. Vaidya, *Aṣṭasāhasrikā*, 352; Samtani, *Arthaviniścaya-Sūtra*, 246.

15. Dutt, *Bodhisattvabhūmiḥ*, 64.

16. On which, see Rowell, "Background."

17. As at Shastri, *Abhidharmakośa*, 5–10.

18. Vaidya, *Aṣṭasāhasrikā*, 272; Shastri, *Abhidharmakośa*, 5; Samtani, *Arthaviniścaya-Sūtra*, 242.

19. Shastri, *Abhidharmakośa*, 4.

20. The standard list is found, inter alia, in: Lévi, *Mahāyāna-Sūtrālaṃkāra*, 184–88; Derge Tanjur, sems-tsam BI 169b5–174a7; Griffiths, *Realm*, 302–35 (on this, see also Hakamaya, "Chos kyi sku"; idem, "Mahāyānasūtrālaṃkāraṭīkā"); Gokhale, "Fragments," 37–38; Tatia, *Abhidharmasamuccayabhāṣyam*, 124–33; Dutt, *Bodhisattvabhūmiḥ*, 259–82. There are partial versions of the standard list in Shastri, *Abhidharmakośa*, 1083–1124; La Vallée Poussin, *Madhyamakāvatāra*, 369–96; Vaidya, *Aṣṭasāhasrikā*, 535–40; Jaini, *Sāratamā*, 174–82; Johnston, *Ratnagotravibhāga*, 91–95. There are also nonstandard lists. One such is given in Nagao, *Shōdaijōron*, volume 1, 99–100; and in Lamotte, *Saṃdhinirmocana*, 32–33. Lists also typically occur in texts concerned with describing how to visualize Buddha (see Waldschmidt, "Varṇaśatam"), and in those dealing with the making of Buddha-images (Bentor, "Redactions"). I shall not discuss these, interesting and revealing though they are, since my interests here are largely systematic rather than historical. It is in any case still too soon to attempt a historical account of the development of these lists, an account to which all these materials would be relevant.

21. Griffiths, *Realm*, 331.

22. Odani, *Daijō shōgon*, 273.

23. Lévi, *Mahāyāna-Sūtrālaṃkāra*, 96.

24. Tatia, *Abhidharmasamuccayabhāṣyam*, 132.

25. Tatia, *Abhidharmasamuccayabhāṣyam*, 129.

26. Two of the most important among these, the *Suvarṇaprabhāsa* and the *Saddharmapuṇḍarīka*, devoted a chapter to these questions, in which it is said that Gautama's life is really without limit, though without explaining the metaphysic required to give this assertion sense. See Nobel, *Suvarṇabhāsottamasūtra*, 16–19; Kern and Nanjio, *Saddharmapuṇḍarīka*, 315–26. For a more extended discussion see Vaidya, *Aṣṭasāhasrikā*, 336–39.

27. Among the more important occurrences are: (1) Johnston, *Ratnagotravibhāga*, 25–30, 79–88. The first of these uses the sixfold set to analyze *tathāgatagarbha* and the second to analyze *anāsravadhātu*. In both cases the six are used as part of a larger analytical set, but Takasaki (*Study*, 401–8) has convincingly shown that the set of six is older than these larger sets and constitutes their core. (2) Lévi, *Mahāyāna-Sūtrālaṃkāra*, 44; *Ankeizō daijō*,

108–17; Derge Tanjur, sems-tsam BI 72a4–73a7; Nishio, *Buddhabhūmi-Sūtra*, 22–23, 119–27. In these contexts the categories are used to analyze the purity (*viśuddhi*) of the realm of the real (*dharmadhātu*). (3) Griffiths, *Realm*, 335–36 = Lévi, *Mahāyāna-Sūtrālaṃkāra*, 188. Here, the six categories are used to analyze *dharmakāya*. But the six categories are also used to analyze more mundane concepts, as, for example, in Peking Tanjur, sems-tsam LI 117a7–117b5, and Tatia, *Abhidharmasamuccayabhāṣyam*, 141–42, where they are used as part of a discussion of hermeneutical method; or in Lévi, *Mahāyāna-Sūtrālaṃkāra*, 25–27, and Derge Tanjur, sems-tsam MI 82a7–89a3.

28. Lévi, *Mahāyāna-Sūtrālaṃkāra*, 44.

29. Griffiths, *Realm*, 336. For discussion, see Schmithausen, *Der Nirvāṇa-Abschnitt*, 105–13.

30. For *nitya*, see Nagao, *Madhyāntavibhāga*, 23; for *avikāra*, see Yamaguchi, *Madhyāntavibhāgaṭīkā*, 50; for mirroring terms, see Vaidya, *Mahāyānasūtrasaṃgraha*, 101.

31. Tatia, *Abhidharmasamuccayabhāṣyam*, 14; Nagao, *Madhyāntavibhāga-Bhāṣya*, 67; Yamaguchi, *Madhyāntavibhāgaṭīkā*, 221–22.

32. Schmithausen, *Der Nirvāṇa-Abschnitt*, 107.

33. Johnston, *Ratnagotravibhāga*, 80.

34. Johnston, *Ratnagotravibhāga*, 26–27.

35. Nishio, *Buddhabhūmi-Sūtra*, 118–19; *Ankeizō daijō*, 111–12; Derge Tanjur, sems-tsam BI 72b4.

36. The Tibetan translators vacillate on this, sometimes offering *de bzhin nyid kyi gnas* (Derge Tanjur, sems-tsam BI 72b4); and sometimes *de bzhin nyid gnas* (*Ankeizō daijō*, 111; Nishio, *Buddhabhūmi-Sūtra*, 118).

37. Hakamaya, "'Sanshu tenne' kō," and Schmithausen, *Der Nirvāṇa-Abschnitt*, 95–102, have both given extensive discussion to this matter, though not with any final conclusions.

38. Lévi, *Mahāyāna-Sūtrālaṃkāra*, 44; *Ankeizō daijō*, 111; Derge Tanjur, sems-tsam BI 72b6–73a1. Compare Nishio, *Buddhabhūmi-Sūtra*, 120.

39. Griffiths, *Realm*, 335–37; Lévi, *Mahāyāna-Sūtrālaṃkāra*, 44; *Ankeizō daijō*, 112–13; Derge Tanjur, sems-tsam BI 73a1–3; Nishio, *Buddhabhūmi-Sūtra*, 123.

40. Lévi, *Mahāyāna-Sūtrālaṃkāra*, 44.

41. That Buddha's salvific availability really is maximal is made explicit in Griffiths, *Realm*, 336–37, which identifies *phala* with preeminence (*āgratā*).

42. Johnston, *Ratnagotravibhāga*, 81.

43. *Ankeizō daijō*, 138–39; Nishio, *Buddhabhūmi-Sūtra*, 102–6; Keenan, "Study," 717–54.

44. Griffiths, *Realm*, 336; Johnston, *Ratnagotravibhāga*, 36–37; Lévi, *Mahāyāna-Sūtrālaṃkāra*, 44.

45. *Ankeizō daijō*, 114–15; Nishio, *Buddhabhūmi-Sūtra*, 123–24.

46. Lévi, *Mahāyāna-Sūtrālaṃkāra*, 47.

47. Griffiths, *Realm*, 336; Lévi, *Mahāyāna-Sūtrālaṃkāra*, 44; *Ankeizō daijō*, 116.

48. Griffiths, *Realm*, 336–37; Lévi, *Mahāyāna-Sūtrālaṃkāra*, 45, 188; *Ankeizō daijō*, 116; Derge Tanjur, sems-tsam BI 174a6–7; Nishio, *Buddhabhūmi-Sūtra*, 125–26.

49. Lévi, *Mahāyāna-Sūtrālaṃkāra*, 45.

50. See, e.g., La Vallée Poussin, *Madhyamakāvatāra*, 355–68; Lévi, *Mahāyāna-Sūtrālaṃkāra*, 184–89; Dutt, *Bodhisattvabhūmiḥ*, 264–82; Nishio, *Buddhabhūmi-Sūtra*, 22–23, 199–216.

51. See, e.g., Stcherbatsky and Obermiller, *Abhisamayālaṅkāra*, 33–39; Vaidya, *Aṣṭasāhasrikā*, 534–42; Jaini, *Sāratamā*, 172–94; Amano, "Sanskrit Manuscript," 3–14; Griffiths, *Realm* (in toto).

52. See, e.g., Shastri, *Abhidharmakośa*, 1083–1124; Peking Tanjur, sems-tsam LI 111b4–114b5; Tatia, *Abhidharmasamuccayabhāṣyam*, 124–33.

53. I have in mind here the *Ratnagotra*-corpus and the *Madhyānta-vibhāga*-corpus. In these works the melding of buddhalogy in the restricted sense with systematic metaphysics in a broader sense has gone so far that the two are indistinguishable. All of the former is both systematic metaphysics and systematic buddhalogy; and the same, though in a rather different way, is true of the latter.

Chapter 4. Buddha in the World

1. Classical versions of the Buddha-legend, representing what was known to and presupposed by the authors of the digests, are found in such texts as the *Mahāvastu*, the *Lalitavistara*, and the *Buddhacarita*. The versions found in these texts differ in many respects, but discussion of these points of detail is not relevant to this study. Among modern studies Thomas's *Life of Buddha* is important, even if many of the historical questions discussed in it no longer

seem as interesting as they did to those working in the intellectual shadow of those obsessed by the quest for the historical Jesus. Bareau's *Recherches* is indispensable for its detailed analyses of the textual sources, as also is Waldschmidt's *Die Überlieferung vom Lebensende* for the more limited question of the events surrounding Buddha's death. More recently still the following studies are of use: Lamotte, *Histoire*, 13–25; Pye, *Buddha*; Snellgrove, *Indo-Tibetan Buddhism*, 5–38; Nagao, "Life of Buddha"; Reynolds and Hallisey, "Buddha"; Khosla, *Buddha-Legend*.

2. Johnston, *Buddhacarita*, 2.

3. In the subsequent discussion I draw upon the following materials: Griffiths, *Realm*, 279–82; Stcherbatsky and Obermiller, *Abhisamayālaṅkāra*, 38; Vaidya, *Aṣṭasāhasrikā*, 541–542; Johnston, *Ratnagotravibhāga*, 85–86, 107; La Vallée Poussin, *Madhyamakāvatāra*, 363–68; Lévi, *Mahāyāna-Sūtrālaṃkāra*, 45; *Ankeizō daijō*, 126–28; Derge Tanjur, sems-tsam BI 73b7–74a2.

4. *Ankeizō daijō*, 122–23, 143–44.

5. Williams, *Mahāyāna Buddhism*, 179–84.

6. Griffiths, *Realm*, 281. Compare Johnston, *Ratnagotravibhāga*, 87–88.

7. Griffiths, *Realm*, 371.

8. Johnston, *Ratnagotravibhāga*, 101. Compare Griffiths, *Realm*, 282.

9. Susan Huntington, in her essay "Early Buddhist Art," has recently called into question the aniconic view. She claims that the bas-reliefs that have been taken as representations of events from Buddha's life, bas-reliefs wherein Buddha is typically represented by a wheel or a footprint, are in fact best understood as scenes of later Buddhist ritual activity. If they are so taken, then the apparent aniconism of the depictions is natural: Buddha is dead, and so can only be present as a focus for ritual activity. There are, argues Huntington, no profound philosophical or doctrinal reasons for the kind of aniconism evident in these early bas-reliefs. She may be right about all this (though the interpretation of the bas-reliefs and of the inscriptions that accompany them is still in dispute). But even if she is, whether the aniconism is located at the historical or the ritual level makes little difference for the philosophical point I want to make. Either way, the focus of interest is on the actions of a body of magical transformation as constituted by the needs of those with whom it apparently enters into relation, not upon such a body as an independent source of action and intention. Eckel's recent study, "Power of the Buddha's Absence," makes some broadly similar points about Mahāyāna Buddhist ritual.

10. Griffiths, *Realm,* 281; Lévi, *Mahāyāna-Sūtrālaṃkāra,* 46; *Ankeizō daijō,* 125–28.

11. Griffiths, *Realm,* 370–72.

12. Griffiths, *Realm,* 371.

13. Lévi, *Mahāyāna-Sūtrālaṃkāra,* 46; *Ankeizō daijō,* 125–26; Johnston, *Ratnagotravibhāga,* 97.

14. The list of the marks is given in many of the digests: Dutt, *Bodhisattvabhūmiḥ,* 259–60; Stcherbatsky and Obermiller, *Abhisamayālaṅkāra,* 35–36; Vaidya, *Aṣṭasāhasrikā,* 537–38; Johnston, *Ratnagotravibhāga,* 94–5. I base the exposition that follows mostly upon the *Bodhisattvabhūmiḥ.* Among secondary studies I have found Burnouf's classic analysis (*Lotus,* 553–83) still useful, and have profited also from: Thomas, *Life of Buddha,* 220ff.; Wayman, "Thirty-Two Characteristics"; Roth, "Physical Presence of Buddha."

15. This is true, for instance, of the *Bodhisattvabhūmiḥ* and the *Ratnagotra.* Compare Lévi, *Mahāyāna-Sūtrālaṃkāra,* 185; Griffiths, *Realm,* 316–17; Peking Tanjur, sems-tsam LI 113b2–3; Tatia, *Abhidharmasamuccayabhāṣyam,* 128–29.

16. This is especially true of the *Abhisamayālaṅkāra*-corpus: Stcherbatsky and Obermiller, *Abhisamayālaṃkāra,* 35; Vaidya, *Aṣṭasāhasrikā,* 537; Jaini, *Sāratamā,* 178–79. I think it likely that this corpus's attribution of the marks to the bodies of communal enjoyment in the heavenly realms was the result of its identification of the promulgator of the *Prajñāpāramitā Sūtras* (Gautama Śākyamuni on its view) as one such, an identification also made in, for example, *Ankeizō daijō,* 120. Makransky, "Controversy over Dharmakāya," 329–37, has provided some useful discussion of these matters.

17. Lévi, *Mahāyāna-Sūtrālaṃkāra,* 185.

18. Dutt, *Bodhisattvabhūmiḥ,* 259–60.

19. Lévi, *Mahāyāna-Sūtrālaṃkāra,* 47. Compare the definitions and analyses given in Nishio, *Buddhabhūmi-Sūtra,* 15–19, 106–12; Keenan, "Study," 754–81.

20. *Ankeizō daijō,* 144; Derge Tanjur, sems-tsam BI 74b6–7.

21. Griffiths, *Realm,* 293.

22. For more on this, see Griffiths, "Buddha and God," 518–20.

23. Nishio, *Buddhabhūmi-Sūtra,* 23, 123–25; La Vallée Poussin, *Madhyamakāvatāra,* 359–60.

24. Funahashi, *Nepōru shahon,* 36–37; *Ankeizō daijō,* 116.

25. Yamaguchi, *Madhyāntavibhāgaṭīkā*, 174.

26. On *ābhoga,* see La Vallée Poussin, "Notes Bouddhiques I–III," 40: "Ils [i.e., the practices of the path] dégagent l'activité du saint, tant interne qu'externe, tant «pour soi» (*svārtha*) que «pour autrui» (*parārtha*), de tous les caractères essentiels de l'activité «effort, acte d'attention, acte de volonté»: car tel est le sens du mot *ābhoga*." For the denial of effort, see Lévi, *Mahāyāna-Sūtrālaṃkāra*, 184–85; Derge Tanjur, sems-tsam BI 171a7–171b1; Griffiths, *Realm*, 311–12.

27. Funahashi, *Nepōru shahon*, 35.

28. *Ankeizō daijō*, 101.

29. *Ankeizō daijō*, 101–2; Johnston, *Ratnagotravibhāga*, 100–101.

30. Analogous points are made in the causal account offered of Buddha's appearance in Stcherbatsky and Obermiller, *Abhisamayālaṃkāra*, 35; Vaidya, *Aṣṭasāhasrikā*, 537; Jaini, *Sāratamā*, 177–78; Amano, "Sanskrit Manuscript," 6.

31. Johnston, *Ratnagotravibhāga*, 102–4; compare Funahashi, *Nepōru shahon*, 28; *Ankeizō daijō*, 46–47; Derge Tanjur, sems-tsam BI 68a1–3; Lamotte, *La somme*, volume 1, 78; Peking Tanjur, sems-tsam LI 216b8–217a2, 326a3–5.

32. Johnston, *Ratnagotravibhāga*, 102.

33. *Ankeizō daijō*, 47–48; Funahashi, *Nepōru shahon*, 28; Johnston, *Ratnagotravibhāga*, 109–10; Derge Tanjur, sems-tsam BI 68a3–5; Lamotte, *La somme*, volume 1, 78; Peking Tanjur, sems-tsam LI 217a2–4, 326a5–6.

34. Johnston, *Ratnagotravibhāga*, 110.

35. Johnston, *Ratnagotravibhāga*, 110.

36. Johnston, *Ratnagotravibhāga*, 110.

37. Johnston, *Ratnagotravibhāga*, 100–102.

38. Johnston, *Ratnagotravibhāga*, 101.

39. Johnston, *Ratnagotravibhāga*, 101.

40. Griffiths, *Realm*, 322–27.

41. Derge Tanjur, sems-tsam BI 172b6–173a2 = Griffiths, *Realm*, 325–26.

42. Stcherbatsky and Obermiller, *Abhisamayālaṃkāra*, 35; Vaidya, *Aṣṭasāhasrikā*, 537; Jaini, *Sāratamā*, 173–74; Funahashi, *Nepōru shahon*, 28–29;

Ankeizō daijō, 41–43, 48–51; Derge Tanjur, sems-tsam BI 67b6–68a1, 68a5–7. Compare La Vallée Poussin, *Madhyamakāvatāra*, 363–69.

43. *Ankeizō daijō*, 49–50.

44. Johnston, *Ratnagotravibhāga*, 104–5; Funahashi, *Nepōru shahon*, 26; *Ankeizō daijō*, 17–18; Derge Tanjur, sems-tsam BI 66b6–67a1.

45. Johnston, *Ratnagotravibhāga*, 107–9; Funahashi, *Nepōru shahon*, 31–32, 35; *Ankeizō daijō*, 62–69, 104–5; Derge Tanjur, sems-tsam BI 69b1–70a3.

46. Johnston, *Ratnagotravibhāga*, 110.

47. Funahashi, *Nepōru shahon*, 28, 31; *Ankeizō daijō*, 43, 62; La Vallée Poussin, *Madhyamakāvatāra*, 355–56.

48. Funahashi, *Nepōru shahon*, 28; Johnston, *Ratnagotravibhāga*, 71.

49. Funahashi, *Nepōru shahon*, 29; *Ankeizō daijō*, 41; Derge Tanjur, sems-tsam BI 67b6–68a1; Johnston, *Ratnagotravibhāga*, 70.

50. See Hakamaya, "Asvabhāva's Commentary"; "Sthiramati and Śīlabhadra"; "Realm of Enlightenment".

51. Johnston, *Ratnagotravibhāga*, 105.

52. Johnston, *Ratnagotravibhāga*, 108–9.

53. Johnston, *Ratnagotravibhāga*, 107–8.

54. La Vallée Poussin, *Madhyamakāvatāra*, 355–56.

55. Griffiths, *Realm*, 338.

56. Griffiths, *Realm*, 338.

57. Standard lists are found in Rhys Davids and Carpenter, *Dīgha-Nikāya*, volume 3, 228; Trenckner and Chalmers, *Majjhima Nikāya*, volume 1, 48, 261; Warren and Kosambi, *Visuddhimagga*, 285–90; Shastri, *Abhidharmakośa*, 492–501; Bhattacharya, *Yogācārabhūmi*, 99–100; Wayman, *Analysis*, 136–62; Gokhale, "Fragments," 28; Tatia, *Abhidharmasamuccayabhāṣyam*, 45. Useful background may be found in Collins, *Selfless Persons*, 208–10, which contains a good discussion of Theravāda views about *āhāra*; and in Dundas, "Food and Freedom," which has a discussion of Jaina debates as to whether the *kevalin* needs to eat.

58. Wayman, *Analysis*, 155.

59. Shastri, *Abhidharmakośa*, 496.

60. Shastri, *Abhidharmakośa*, 496.

61. Griffiths, *Realm*, 338.

62. Griffiths, *Realm*, 338–39.

63. Griffiths, *Realm*, 312–14; Lévi, *Mahāyāna-Sūtrālaṃkāra*, 185; Derge Tanjur, sems-tsam BI 171b1–2; RI 113a4; Tatia, *Abhidharmasamuccayabhāṣyam*, 128; Shastri, *Abhidharmakośa*, 1102–5; Samtani, *Arthaviniścaya-Sūtra*, 51–52, 257–58; Lamotte, *Saṃdhinirmocana*, 75–78; Dutt, *Bodhisattvabhūmiḥ*, 176.

64. Lévi, *Mahāyāna-Sūtrālaṃkāra*, 138–39.

65. Shastri, *Abhidharmakośa*, 1104–5. Compare Aung and Rhys Davids, *Points of Controversy*, 378–80.

66. On *pratibhāna*, see MacQueen, "Inspired Speech."

67. Acts ii.5–13.

68. I base my discussion of this *bala* principally upon: Shastri, *Abhidharmakośa*, 1085–89; Derge Tanjur, sems-tsam RI 113b6–114a1; Tatia, *Abhidharmasamuccayabhāṣyam*, 129; Dutt, *Bodhisattvabhūmiḥ*, 265–66; Griffiths, *Realm*, 319–20; Lévi, *Mahāyāna-Sūtrālaṃkāra*, 186; Derge Tanjur, sems-tsam BI 171b6–172b2; Samtani, *Arthaviniścaya-Sūtra*, 48, 260–62; Johnston, *Ratnagotravibhāga*, 91–92; La Vallée Poussin, *Madhyamakāvatāra*, 369–72.

69. Shastri, *Abhidharmakośa*, 1085. Compare La Vallée Poussin, *Madhyamakāvatāra*, 371.

70. Samtani, *Arthaviniścaya-Sūtra*, 261.

71. As in the examples from the practice of the path in La Vallée Poussin, *Madhyamakāvatāra*, 370–71.

72. Dutt, *Bodhisattvabhūmiḥ*, 265.

73. Griffiths, *Realm*, 319–20.

74. I draw here principally upon Dutt, *Bodhisattvabhūmiḥ*, 65–66; Griffiths, *Realm*, 287–88; Funahashi, *Nepōru shahon*, 40; *Ankeizō daijō*, 146–49; Derge Tanjur, sems-tsam BI 75a2–6; Samtani, *Arthaviniścaya-Sūtra*, 116–18.

75. Griffiths, *Realm*, 288.

76. The arguments are given most clearly in Shastri, *Abhidharmakośa*, 550–52, and in Dutt, *Bodhisattvabhūmiḥ*, 65–66.

77. Griffiths, *Realm*, 370–72; Yamaguchi, *Madhyāntavibhāgaṭīkā*, 152–53.

78. Shastri, *Abhidharmakośa*, 550; Rhys Davids and Carpenter, *Dīgha-Nikāya*, volume 3, 114; Trenckner and Chalmers, *Majjhima Nikāya*, volume 3, 65.

79. Shastri, *Abhidharmakośa*, 528–29.

80. Griffiths, *Realm*, 375–76.

Chapter 5. Buddha in Heaven

1. Much less attention has been paid by scholars to this body than to the other two. Rowell's work on *buddhakṣetra* ("Background"), though now almost sixty years old, is still in many ways the most useful. There are also useful brief discussions in Takasaki, *Introduction*, 61–64, and in Williams, *Mahāyāna Buddhism*, 224–27.

2. I am influenced here by Mus, *Barabuḍur*, *263-*265; Macdonald, "La notion du saṃbhogakāya"; and Makransky, "Controversy over Dharmakāya," 180–82.

3. For example, in Jaini, *Sāratamā*, 173–74.

4. Masson-Oursel, "Les trois corps," 588.

5. Dutt, *Bodhisattvabhūmiḥ*, 65.

6. Kern and Nanjio, *Saddharmapuṇḍarīka*, 315–26; Prāsādika and Joshi, *Vimalakīrtinirdeśasūtra*, 379–96, 475–76, 499–511. See also Lamotte, *Le traité*, 403–20.

7. Lamotte, *Saṃdhinirmocana*, 161–62.

8. Stcherbatsky and Obermiller, *Abhisamayālaṃkāra*, 10; Vaidya, *Aṣṭasāhasrikā*, 320; Jaini, *Sāratamā*, 8–9; Amano, "Sanskrit Manuscript," 23; Pensa, *Abhisamayālaṅkāravṛtti*, 105–6; Nagao, *Madhyānta-Vibhāga*, 16–17; Yamaguchi, *Madhyāntavibhāgaṭīkā*, 105–6; La Vallée Poussin, *Madhyamakāvatāra*, 347–48.

9. Nagao, *Madhyānta-Vibhāga*, 75; Yamaguchi, *Madhyāntavibhāgaṭīkā*, 256.

10. Tucci, *Minor Buddhist Texts*, volume 1, 63.

11. Notably in Stcherbatsky and Obermiller, *Abhisamayālaṃkāra*, 26; Vaidya, *Aṣṭasāhasrikā*, 494–95; Jaini, *Sāratamā*, 124–25; Griffiths, *Realm*, 208–22; Samtani, *Arthaviniścaya-Sūtra*, 1–2, 29–39; Lamotte, *Saṃdhinirmocana*, 31–32.

12. Cleary, *Flower Ornament Scripture*, volume 1, 497.

13. In the comments that follow I draw upon: Funahashi, *Nepōru shahon*, 37; *Ankeizō daijō*, 120–21; Griffiths, *Realm*, 281; Johnston, *Ratnagotravibhāga*, 87; Nagao, *Madhyāntavibhāga-Bhāṣya*, 56; Yamaguchi, *Madhyāntavibhāgaṭīkā*, 191; Stcherbatsky and Obermiller, *Abhisamayālaṃkāra*, 35; Vaidya, *Aṭṣasāhasrikā*, 537–38; Jaini, *Sāratamā*, 178–79; Amano, "Sanskrit Manuscript," 7. Secondary sources are again relatively few. Nagao, "Buddha-Body," 107–12, makes some useful comments; see also La Vallée Poussin, "Studies in Buddhist Dogma"; "Note sur les corps"; *Vijñaptimātratā*, 762ff.; Akanuma, "Triple Body." And see, again, Lamotte, *Le traité*, 403–20.

14. Funahashi, *Nepōru shahon*, 37.

15. In this I follow work done by Makransky, "Controversy over Dharmakāya," 84–86.

16. *Ankeizō daijō*, 120–21.

17. Vaidya, *Daśabhūmikasūtra*, 6–7.

18. Vaidya, *Mahāyānasūtrasaṃgraha*, 98–99.

19. Nanjio, *Laṅkāvatāra*, 1.

20. On these figures, see Mallmann, *Introduction*; Sponberg and Hardacre, *Maitreya*.

21. See, for example, Vaidya, *Daśabhūmikasūtra*, 93.

22. Griffiths, *Realm*, 368–70.

23. Griffiths, *Realm*, 369.

24. The theory is given classical formulation in the *Triṃśikā*-corpus and in the *Mahāyānasaṅgraha*-corpus. The fullest analysis is in La Vallée Poussin, *Vijñaptimātratāsiddhi*; and I have given the theory a brief analysis in *On Being Mindless*, 80–96.

25. Funahashi, *Nepōru shahon*, 27–29, 33–34; *Ankeizō daijō*, 32–46, 79–93; Derge Tanjur, sems-tsam BI 67b5–68a1, 70b6–71b7; Griffiths, *Realm*, 283, 289–90, 368–70; Lévi, *Vijñaptimātratāsiddhi*, 43–44; Jaini, "Sanskrit Fragments," 491. See also La Vallée Poussin, *Vijñaptimātratāsiddhi*, 607–12, 661–67; Schmithausen, *Nirvāṇa-Abschnitt*, 90–104; Lamotte, *La somme*, volume 2, *16–*17; Hakamaya, " 'Sanshu tenne' kō.' "

26. *Ankeizō daijō*, 80.

27. Funahashi, *Nepōru shahon*, 33.

28. *Ankeizō daijō*, 85.

29. Lévi, *Mahāyāna-Sūtrālaṃkāra*, 65; *Ankeizō daijō*, 85–86. See also Nguyen, *Sthiramati's Interpretation*, 405–6.

30. *Ankeizō daijō*, 85–86.

31. This is an issue that has received a great deal of attention from western scholars. See, classically, Demiéville, "Le miroir spirituel." More recent contributions include: Stein, "Illumination subite"; Galloway, "Sudden Enlightenment in Indian Buddhism"; idem, "Sudden Enlightenment in the Abhisamayālaṃkāra"; Gomez, "Indian Materials"; Gregory, *Sudden and Gradual*; Buswell and Gimello, *Paths to Liberation*.

Chapter 6. Buddha in Eternity

1. Yamaguchi, *Madhyāntavibhāgaṭīkā*, 191.

2. Connecting the *dharmakāya* with mastery (*vaś-* or *vibhū-*) is a standard move in the digests. See especially Lévi, *Vijñaptimātratā*, 44–45; Funahashi, *Nepōru shahon*, 32–33; *Ankeizō daijō*, 75–79; Derge Tanjur, sems-tsam BI 70b3–6; Griffiths, *Realm*, 283–85.

3. Johnston, *Ratnagotravibhāga*, 172; Nagao, *Madhyāntavibhāga*, 24; Schmithausen, *Der Nirvāṇa-Abschnitt*, 145–46.

4. Ryle, *Concept of Mind*, 133–34. Ryle is largely concerned here with an analysis of knowing-how rather than knowing-that.

5. For an excellent review of the history of these debates in the 1960s and 1970s, see Shope, *Analysis of Knowing*. This book focuses, as does so much of the literature, on the problems posed for the 'standard' analysis of knowledge (as justified true belief) by the kinds of counterexample first given by Gettier in his now-classic paper "Is Justified True Belief Knowledge?" For an extensive and lively review of the current state of play in epistemology, see Plantinga, *Warrant: The Current Debate*.

6. See, e.g., Matilal, *Perception*, 97–140.

7. Derge Tanjur, sems-tsam RI 93a1. The *bhāṣya*'s quotation of this phrase reads *samasamālambyālambanajñāna* (Tatia, *Abhidharmasamuccayabhāṣyam*, 76), but following Schmithausen's suggestion ("Darśanamārga Section," 262 n.25), the proper reading is *samasamālambyālambakajñāna*. The gloss reads *grāhyagrāhakābhavatathatāprativedha*.

8. See, e.g., the discussion that follows the text-place mentioned in Tatia, *Abhidharmasamuccayabhāṣyam*, as well as the extensive analysis of the kinds of awareness that result from the practice of the path in Shastri, *Abhidharmakośa*, 1033–1124.

9. *niścitaṃ ca jñānam iṣyate nāniścitam* (Shastri, *Abhidharmakośa*, 1034). Compare the definition of perception as an awareness (*jñāna*) that is "of a definite character" (*vyavasāyātmaka*) in *Nyāyasūtra* 1.1.4. For discussion of this and related matters see Wayman, "Notes"; Hattori, *Dignāga*, 39–40; Potter, "Indian Epistemology."

10. On *vikalpa*, see my "Pure Consciousness," 85–87; Matilal, *Perception*, 309–14; Potter, "Karmic A Priori."

11. The comments that follow are largely based upon the eightfold analysis given in Dutt, *Bodhisattvabhūmiḥ*, 34–36. For a translation of this interesting passage, see Willis, *On Knowing Reality*, 125–33. Compare Derge Tanjur, sems-tsam RI 116b6–117a2; Tatia, *Abhidharmasamuccayabhāṣyam*, 138–39; Nagao, *Shōdaijōron*, 179–83; Peking Tanjur, sems-tsam LI 176b8–180a2, 279a5–281b5; Stcherbatsky and Obermiller, *Abhisamayālaṃkāra*, 27–28; Vaidya, *Aṣṭasāhasrikā*, 511–512; Nagao, *Madhyāntavibhāga*, 70–72; Yamaguchi, *Madhyāntavibhāgaṭīkā*, 233–51.

12. Funahashi, *Nepōru shahon*, 41.

13. They most often do this by defining the essential nature (*svabhāva*) of *nirvikalpajñāna* through a fivefold negation. See Derge Tanjur, sems-tsam PHI 48a6–7; BI 35a1–35b1; RI 117a4–5; Tatia, *Abhidharmasamuccayabhāṣyam*, 139. See also Hakamaya, "Yuishiki bunken." I base my comments in the immediately following paragraphs largely upon these negations.

14. The digests usually make these points by denying that *nirvikalpajñāna* is *amanasikāra*. *Manasikāra* ('activity of thought' of an attentive kind) is left behind in the second *rūpadhyāna*.

15. I have discussed this extensively in *On Being Mindless*.

16. For example: *atha vyūpaśamatas tena saṃjñāveditanirodhasamāpattir nirvikalpatāṃ prāpnoti tatra cittacaittavikalpavyūpaśamāt tataś ca jñānābhāvaḥ prasajyate* (Tatia, *Abhidharmasamuccayabhāṣyam*, 139), following the emendation in Hakamaya, "Yuishiki bunken," 243.

17. For example: *de ltar na ye shes kyi yul de kho na nyid la rnam pa thams cad du de'i yul na sems dang sems las byung ba rnams mi 'jug pas sku kho nas mngon sum du mdzad par kun rdzob tu rnam par bzhag go* (La Vallée Poussin, *Madhyamakāvatāra*, 362.

18. I rely here especially upon the comments in Tatia, *Abhidharmasamuccayabhāṣyam*, 139: *api tv ālambane 'anabhisaṃskārato draṣṭavyā/ kathaṃ kṛtvā/ yadā hy asya bodhisattvasyānulomikaṃ avavdām āgamya prakṛtyā sarvadharma-nimittāny apariniṣpannānīti vicārayatas tadvicāraṇābhyāsabalādhānāt pratyātmam anabhisaṃskāreṇaiva yathāvan niṣprapañcadhātau sarvadharmatathatāyāṃ cittaṃ samādhīyate sāsāv ucyate niṣprapañcanirvikalpateti.*

19. *Anugam-* is one of the terms most often used by the digests in this connection.

20. Lamotte, *La somme*, volume 1, 75. The Sanskrit original probably included a negation of *tattvārthacitrīkāra* as a predicate of Buddha's *jñāna*. See Lamotte, *La somme*, volume 2, 243; Hakamaya, "Yuishiki bunken," 230 n.2; Peking Tanjur, sems-tsam LI 212b4–213a4, 322b4–8.

21. Yamaguchi, *Madhyāntavibhāgaṭīkā*, 222.

22. Lamotte, *La somme*, volume 1, 77–78; Peking Tanjur, sems-tsam LI 216a4–216b3, 325b1–8.

23. Ñāṇānanda, *Concept and Reality*, is the best introduction to the complex of ideas surrounding the term *prapañca*.

24. This is said in Lamotte, *La somme*, volume 1, 76; Peking Tanjur, sems-tsam LI 214a1–7, 324a1–7. Compare Nagao, *Shōdaijōron*, volume 1, 84–85; Derge Tanjur, sems-tsam RI 150a3–150b5, 230a4–230b4. The comments that follow are largely based upon these text-places. Also significant is La Vallée Poussin, *Madhyamakavṛttiḥ*, 372, 374, where *nirvikalpa* is given as one of the glosses on the "defining characteristic of the way things are" (*tattvasya lakṣaṇa*), and is glossed to mean the absence of speech or utterance. See also Peking Tanjur, sems-tsam LI 332b4, where it is claimed that *nirvikalpajñāna* is defined negatively just because it is *nirabhilāpya*. See Hakamaya, "Rigen," for a detailed study of *nirabhilāpyatā* in Yogācāra texts.

25. As Yandell makes abundantly clear in his "Some Varieties of Ineffability."

26. La Vallée Poussin, *Madhyamakavṛttiḥ*, 364.

27. See, for example, Funahashi, *Nepōru shahon*, 36; *Ankeizō daijō*, 110–11; Derge Tanjur, sems-tsam BI 72b3–73a1, 73b2–5; Samtani, *Arthaviniścaya-Sūtra*, 9, 119–20; Lamotte, *La somme*, volume 1, 77–79; Peking Tanjur, sems-tsam LI 215b1–220b1, 325a5–327b7. I have drawn upon all these text-places in the comments that follow.

28. Lamotte, *La somme*, volume 1, 78.

29. Funahashi, *Nepōru shahon,* 38. See also *Ankeizō daijō,* 130–33; Derge Tanjur, sems-tsam BI 74a–74b1; Samtani, *Arthaviniścaya-Sūtra,* 9, 89–90.

30. Funahashi, *Nepōru shahon,* 38.

31. For example, *sākāras tasyaivālambanasya prakāreṇākāraṇāt,* Shastri, *Abhidharmakośa,* 1062. Compare Funahashi, *Nepōru shahon,* 38.

32. Lipner, *Face of Truth,* 20.

33. Biardeau, *Théorie,* 75.

34. Shastri, *Abhidharmakośa,* 1062.

35. *sarve sālambanā dharmā ākārayanti* (Shastri, *Abhidharmakośa,* 1062).

36. One of the digests, discussing the sense in which three important words for the mental (*citta, manas, vijñāna*) all have the same meaning or referent (*eko 'rthaḥ*), explains that all mental events share the same basic characteristics: *ta eva hi cittcaittāḥ sāśrayā ucyante indriyāśritatvāt/ sālambanāḥ viṣayagrahaṇāt/ sākāras tasyaivālambanasya prakāreṇa ākāraṇāt/ samprayuktāḥ samaṃ samprayuktam* (Shastri, *Abhidharmakośa,* 208–9). This links the attribute 'having an object' with the attribute 'having an *ākāra,*' both essential to any member of the class-category 'mental event.' This necessary coexistence of *ākāra* and *ālambana* is also made clear thus: *dmigs pa dang bcas pa'i chos rnams ni rnam pa dang bcas pa'i phyir dmigs pa dang 'dzin par byed do,* (Peking Tanjur, sems-tsam LI 267b2). Compare also: *na hi nirālambanaṃ nirākāraṃ vā vijñānaṃ yujyate* (Lévi, *Vijñaptimātratāsiddhi,* 19).

37. Derge Tanjur, sems-tsam BI 74a5–6.

38. *Ankeizō daijō,* 130–31, citing Samtani, *Arthaviniścaya-Sūtra,* 9.

39. Though the digests do preserve a complex set of debates as to whether consciousness is inherently or necessarily *sākāra,* possessed of phenomenal properties, or constitutively *nirākāra,* pure, empty, not conformed to anything other than its naturally radiant self. The decision one comes to about this will naturally affect how one understands Buddha's awareness. But even though some of the digests deny modes of appearance to Buddha's awareness, the dominant position—certainly in those texts that predate Dharmakīrti—is as I have expounded it here. For more on the mirror-imagery in the digests see Demiéville, "Le miroir spirituel"; Wayman, "Mirror-Like Knowledge"; idem, "Mirror as a Pan-Buddhist Metaphor-Simile."

40. The digests sometimes go so far as to identify buddhahood with omniscience in just this sense. See Jaini, *Sāratamā,* 12; Derge Tanjur, sems-tsam TSI 193b3–4.

41. Bagchi, *Mahāyānasūtrālaṅkāra*, 167.

42. See my "Omniscience" for a detailed discussion of the differences in meaning among various terms used to denote Buddha's omniscience in the Sūtrāl-corpus.

43. See Vaidya, *Aṣṭasāhasrikā*, 436–37.

44. Shastri, *Abhidharmakośa*, 1205.

45. For discussion, see Jaini, "Sarvajñatva"; Naughton, "Buddhist Omniscience."

46. For example, Krishnamacharya, *Tattvasaṅgraha*, 862–63.

47. *Ankeizō daijō*, 7; compare 9–10; Shastri, *Abhidharmakośa*, 1088, 1097; Krishnamacharya, *Tattvasaṅgraha*, 847–50, 862–63, 912, 929–31, 933.

48. This point is explicitly made in Krishnamacharya, *Tattvasaṅgraha*, 821, 964; and in Vaidya, *Aṣṭasāhasrikā*, 436–37.

49. Krishnamacharya, *Tattvasaṅgraha*, 880.

50. Jaini, *Sāratamā*, 18.

51. Krishnamacharya, *Tattvasaṅgraha*, 929; Jaini, *Sāratamā*, 170–71; Vaidya, *Aṣṭasāhasrikā*, 533.

52. Vaidya, *Aṣṭasāhasrikā*, 532; Amano, "Sanskrit Manuscript," 137.

53. For a list of these terms and glosses upon them, see Nagao, *Madhyāntavibhāga*, 23–24; Yamaguchi, *Madhyāntavibhāgaṭīkā*, 50.

54. Yamaguchi, *Madhyāntavibhāgaṭīkā*, 49–50.

55. Johnston, *Ratnagotravibhāga*, 80. See also Nagao, *Madhyāntavibhāga*, 67; Jaini, *Sāratamā*, 18, 173; Nagao, *Shōdaijōron*, volume 1, 86–87; Peking Tanjur, sems-tsam LI 180a6–181a2, 282a8–282b5; Griffiths, *Realm*, 296, 350; Funahashi, *Nepōru shahon*, 29, 36; Bagchi, *Mahāyānasūtrālaṇkāra*, 24, 59; *Ankeizō daijō*, 51–52, 110–11; Derge Tanjur, sems-tsam BI 68a7–68b2. For some analysis of this theme, see Hakamaya, "Realm of Enlightenment."

56. Nagao, *Shōdaijōron*, volume 1, 86.

57. These are the *bodhipakṣadharma*, for an exhaustive study of which in Pali materials, see Gethin, *Buddhist Path*.

58. Lamotte, *Saṃdhinirmocana*, 52. There are discussions of the Sanskrit original that underlies this Tibetan version in Lamotte, *Saṃdhinirmocana*, 181 n.17;

Hakamaya, "Consideration." See also La Vallée Poussin, *Vijñaptimātratāsiddhi,* 743; idem, *Théorie des douze causes,* 109–13. For an earlier text with somewhat similar implications, see Feer, *Samyutta Nikāya,* volume 2, 25–26.

59. Translating *ther zug* (*dhruva*?), on which, see Griffiths, *Realm,* 288–89.

60. See the common gloss on *tathatā*: *nityaṃ tathaiveti kṛtvā* (Nagao, *Madhyāntavibhāga,* 23).

61. In translating *dharmadhātu* in this way I follow the standard gloss on *dhātu* in this compound, which is *hetu.* See, e.g., Johnston, *Ratnagotravibhāga,* 72; Nagao, *Madhyāntavibhāga,* 24; Schmithausen, *Der Nirvāṇa-Abschnitt,* 145–46.

62. Griffiths, *Realm,* 288–89.

63. E.g., Nagao, *Madhyāntavibhāga,* 24 (*tathatā* as *ananyathā*); Jaini, *Sāratamā,* 18 (*dharmadhātu* as beginningless and endless); Griffiths, *Realm,* 349, 373–74 (*dharmakāya* as *nitya*); Nagao, *Madhyāntavibhāga,* 41; Yamaguchi, *Madhyāntavibhāgaṭīkā,* 126–27 (*parinişpanna* as *avikāra*); Stcherbatsky and Obermiller, *Abhisamayālaṅkāra,* 16, 35; Vaidya, *Aṣṭasāhasrikā,* 411, 537; Jaini, *Sāratamā,* 80–82, 173–74; Amano, "Sanskrit Manuscript," 50, 6–7 (*prajñāpāramitā* as *avikāra* and Buddha as *nitya* because *akṣaya*); La Vallée Poussin, *Madhyamakāvatāra,* 356 (spatial and temporal division both denied of Buddha).

Chapter 7. Doctrinal Criticism

1. Lopez, "Paths Terminable," has provided some useful discussion of this question.

2. This is a notion given classical formulation by James in *Psychology: Briefer Course,* 266–67. For more recent applications of the idea in Christian philosophical theology, see Alston, *Divine Nature,* 136–38; Quinn, "On the Mereology."

3. James, *Psychology: Briefer Course,* 266.

4. See, classically, Aquinas, *Summa Contra Gentiles,* II.35–36. For recent discussion, see Stump and Kretzmann, "Eternity," where an account is offered of the peculiar kind of simultaneity that an eternal being must have with temporally indexed events. This account has been much discussed. See Lewis, "Eternity Again"; Fitzgerald, "Stump and Kretzmann." The recent literature on the associated topics of God's timelessness, the reality of tensed facts (or tempo-

rally indexed states of affairs), and the possibility of holding together claims as to the reality of both the former and the latter, is enormous. Good places to start are Pike, *God and Timelessness*; Swinburne, "Tensed Facts" Gale, "Omniscience-Immutability Arguments"; Wierenga, *Nature of God*, 166–201.

5. This is the burden of the account in Shastri, *Abhidharmakośa*, 1215–17.

Glossary

I list here, in English alphabetical order, the more important Sanskrit technical terms that occur in the buddhalogical discourse of the digests. My preferred translation is given first, and is usually followed by a brief gloss.

abhidharma	'metaphysics'; often left untranslated
abhijñā	'supernatural awareness'—of which there are six kinds, all possessed maximally by Buddha
abhilāpyatā	'expressibility'—negated of Buddha's awareness
abhisaṃskāra	'volitional mental activity'—negated of Buddha's awareness
ābhoga	'effort'—negated of Buddha's awareness
ādarśajñāna	'mirror-awareness'—the fourth of the four kinds of awareness possessed by Buddha
āgantuka	'adventitious'—a predicate of the taints, defilements, and afflictions that appear to affect reality
ākāra	'mode of appearance'—phenomenal property of awareness. See *nimitta, vijñapti*

ālambana	'mental object'
ālayavijñāna	'store-consciousness'
arhat	'worthy one'—epithet of Buddha, usually left untranslated
artha	'object'; or, sometimes, 'meaning'
āsrava	'defilement'
āśraya	'basis'; or, adjectivally, 'radical'—sometimes used to mean 'body'; sometimes to mean *ālayavijñāna* (q.v.)
āśrayaparivṛtti	'radical reorientation'—a technical term for the moment at which awakening occurs
āvaraṇa	'obstacle'—of two kinds, *kleśa-* (q.v.), and *jñeya-* (q.v.)
āveṇika	'exclusive'—Buddha has eighteen properties called this
bhagavat	'blessed one'—epithet of Buddha
buddhakṣetra	'Buddha-field'
buddhavacana	'Buddha's word'
caitta	'mental concomitant'—usually compounded with *citta* (q.v.)
citta	'mind'
dharma	'real'—in the singular, 'a real' in the sense of 'an existent'; or, sometimes, as a collective singular, 'doctrine'
dharmadhātu	'ground of the real'
dharmadhātuviśuddhi	'purity of the ground of the real'
dharmakāya	'real body'
dharmatā	'reality'
dharmatākāya	'body of reality'
dhruva/dhruvatva	'everlasting/everlastingness'—attribute of Buddha
gaurava	'significance'—a property of Buddha's word and of the texts that contain it
gocara	'scope,' 'sphere of influence'—usually of a sense-organ. See *viṣaya*
jñāna	'awareness'

jñeya	'object of awareness'
karuṇā	'compassion'
kleśa	'affliction'
kliṣṭamanas	'afflicted organ of thought'
kṛtyānuṣṭhānajñāna	'awareness that does what has to be done'—the fourth of Buddha's four kinds of awareness, correlated with its activity (*karman*)
mala	'taint'
manas	'organ of thought'
manasikāra	'activity of thought'
manovijñāna	'thinking consciousness'
nimitta	'mental image'—with specifiable properties. See *vijñapti, ākāra.*
nirmāṇa (nairmāṇika) kāya	'body of (in its) magical transformation'
nirvikalpajñāna	'construction-free awareness'
nitya/nityatva	'permanent/permanence'—attribute of Buddha
pāramitā	'perfection'—of which there are six, all possessed maximally by Buddha
prajñā	'discernment'
pramāṇikatva	'authority' or 'authoritativeness'—a property of Buddha's word and of the texts that contain it
prapañca	'conceptual proliferation'—denied of Buddha's awareness
pratibhāna	'eloquence'; 'eloquent discourse'—a property of Buddha's speech
pratisamvit	'specific understanding'—of which there are four kinds, all possessed maximally by Buddha
pratyavekṣaṇa [ka] jñāna	'differentiated observational awareness'—the third of Buddha's four kinds of awareness, correlated with its result (*phala*)
pṛṣṭhalabdhajñāna	'subsequently attained awareness'

sāmānyalakṣaṇa	'defining characteristic possessed in common'—that which all reals possess in virtue of being reals; paired with and opposed to svalakṣaṇa
samatājñāna	'awareness of equality'—the second of Buddha's four kinds of awareness, correlated with its cause (*hetu*)
sambhoga (sāmbhogika) kāya	'body of (in its) communal enjoyment'
samyaksambuddha	'fully and completely awakened'—an epithet of Buddha
sarvākārajñāna	'awareness of all modes of appearance'
śāstra	'treatise'
śūnyatā	'emptiness'
sūtra	'sacred text'—often left untranslated; a work usually said to have been spoken by Buddha
svabhāva (svābhāvika) kāya	'essence body'; 'body in its essence'
svalakṣaṇa	'specific defining characteristic'—that which makes a particular real what it is and not something else; paired with and opposed to *sāmānyalakṣaṇa*
tathāgata	'thus-gone'—epithet of Buddha, usually left untranslated
tathatā	'actuality'
vāsanā	'propensity'; 'tendency'
vijñāna	'consciousness'
vijñapti	'representation'—mental image with phenomenal properties. See *ākāra, nimitta*
vikalpa	'construction'; 'constructive mental activity'. See *nirvikalpajñāna*
viparyāsa	'cognitive error'
viṣaya	'sphere'—as in sphere of operation of a sense-organ. See *gocara*

Bibliography

Akanuma Chizen. "The Triple Body of Buddha." *Eastern Buddhist* 2 (1922), 1–29.

Alston, William P. *Divine Nature and Human Language: Essays in Philosophical Theology*. Ithaca, N.Y.: Cornell University Press, 1989.

Amano Hirofusa. (ed.) "Sanskrit Manuscript of the Abhisamayālaṃkāra-vṛtti." In six parts. *Bulletin of the Hijiyama Women's Junior College* 17 (1983), 1–15; *Bulletin of the Faculty of Education of Shimane University* 19 (1985), 124–38; 20 (1986), 67–86; 21 (1987), 39–51; 22 (1988), 10–25; 23 (1989), 1–7.

Ankeizō daijō shōgon kyōron shakuso: bodaihon. [Sthiramati's Commentary on the Mahāyānasūtrālaṅkāra: The Chapter on Awakening]. Edited by the Chibetto Bunten Kenkyūkai. Chibetto bunken ni yoru bukkyō shisō, volume 1. Tokyo: Chibetto Bunten Kenkyūkai, 1979–81.

Aung, Shwe Zan, and C. A. F. Rhys Davids. (transl.) *Points of Controversy, or Subjects of Discourse, Being a Translation of the Kathāvatthu from the Abhidhammapiṭaka*. London: Pali Text Society, 1979. First published 1915.

Bagchi, Sitansusekhar. (ed.) *Mahāyānasūtrālaṅkāra of Asaṅga*. Buddhist Sanskrit Texts, volume 13. Darbhanga: Mithila Institute, 1970.

Bareau, André. *Recherches sur la biographie du Bouddha dans les Sūtrapiṭaka et les Vinayapiṭaka anciens*. Two volumes. Publications de l'École Française d'Extrême-Orient, volumes 53, 77. Paris: École Française d'Extrême-Orient, 1963, 1977.

Bentor, Yael. "The Redactions of the Adbhutadharmaparyāya from Gilgit." *Journal of the International Association of Buddhist Studies* 11 (1988), 21–52.

Bhattacharya, V. (ed.) *The Yogācārabhūmi of Ācārya Asaṅga.* Calcutta: University of Calcutta Press, 1957.

Biardeau, Madeleine. *Théorie de la connaissance et philosophie de la parole dans le brahmanisme classique.* Paris: École Française des HautesÉtudes, 1964.

Böhm, Irmingard. *Dogma und Geschichte: Systematische Überlegungen zum Problem der Dogmenentwicklung in der Auseinandersetzung zwischen Alfred Loisy und dem Lehramt der Katholischen Kirche.* Bad Honnef: Bock und Herchen, 1987.

Bond, George D. *The Word of the Buddha: The Tipiṭaka and its Interpretation in Theravāda Buddhism.* Colombo: Gunasena, 1982.

Bourdieu, Pierre. *Le sens pratique.* Paris: Éditions de Minuit, 1980. English translation by Richard Nice, *The Logic of Practice.* Stanford: Stanford University Press, 1990.

Broido, Michael M. "Abhiprāya and Implication in Tibetan Linguistics." *Journal of Indian Philosophy* 12 (1984), 1–33.

Broido, Michael M. "Intention and Suggestion in the Abhidharmakośa: Sandhabhāṣā Revisited." *Journal of Indian Philosophy* 13 (1985), 327–81.

Burnouf, Eugène. *Le Lotus de la Bonne Loi.* Paris, 1852.

Buswell, Robert E., Jr., and Robert M. Gimello. (eds.) *Paths to Liberation: The Mārga and its Transformations in Buddhist Thought.* Studies in East Asian Buddhism, volume 7. Honolulu: University of Hawaii Press, 1992.

Cabezón, José Ignacio. "The Canonization of Philosophy and the Rhetoric of Siddhānta in Tibetan Buddhism." In *Buddha Nature,* 7–26. Edited by Paul J. Griffiths and John P. Keenan. Reno, Nev.: Buddhist Books International, 1990.

Cabezón, José Ignacio. "Vasubandhu's Vyākhyāyukti on the Authenticity of the Mahāyāna Sūtras." In *Texts in Context:*

Traditional Hermeneutics in South Asia, 221–43. Edited by Jeffrey R. Timm. Albany, N.Y.: SUNY Press, 1992.

Christian, William A., Sr. *Doctrines of Religious Communities: A Philosophical Study.* New Haven: Yale University Press, 1987.

Cleary, Thomas F. (transl.) *The Flower Ornament Scripture: A Translation of the Avataṃsaka Sūtra.* Three volumes. Boulder and London: Shambhala, 1984–87.

Collins, Steven. *Selfless Persons: Imagery and Thought in Theravāda Buddhism.* Cambridge: Cambridge University Press, 1982.

Collins, Steven. "Problems with Pacceka-Buddhas." *Religion* 22 (1992), 271–78.

Davidson, Ronald M. "An Introduction to the Standards of Scriptural Authenticity in Indian Buddhism." In *Chinese Buddhist Apocrypha,* 291–325. Edited by Robert E. Buswell, Jr. Honolulu: University of Hawaii Press, 1990.

Demiéville, Paul. "Le miroir spirituel." *Sinologica* 1/2 (1947), 112–37. Reprinted in Demiéville, *Choix d'études bouddhiques (1929–70),* 131–56. Leiden: Brill, 1973. English translation by Neal Donner, "The Mirror of the Mind." In *Sudden and Gradual: Approaches to Enlightenment in Chinese Thought,* 13–40. Edited by Peter N. Gregory. Studies in East Asian Buddhism, volume 5. Honolulu: University of Hawaii Press, 1987.

Dundas, Paul. "Food and Freedom." *Religion* 15 (1985), 161–98.

Dutt, Nalinaksha. (ed.) *Bodhisattvabhūmiḥ: Being the XVth Section of Asaṅgapāda's Yogācārabhūmiḥ.* Tibetan-Sanskrit Works Series, volume 7. Patna: Kashi Prasad Jayaswal Research Institute, 1978.

Dworkin, Ronald. (ed.) *The Philosophy of Law.* Oxford: Oxford University Press, 1977.

Dworkin, Ronald. *Taking Rights Seriously.* Cambridge, Mass: Harvard University Press, 1977.

Dworkin, Ronald. *Law's Empire.* Cambridge, Mass: Harvard University Press, 1986.

Eckel, Malcolm David. "The Power of the Buddha's Absence: On the Foundations of Mahāyāna Buddhist Ritual." *Journal of Ritual Studies* 4/2 (1990), 61–95.

Feer, Léon. (ed.) *Samyutta-Nikāya.* Six volumes (including index volume). London: Pali Text Society, 1884–1904.

Fitzgerald, Paul. "Stump and Kretzmann on Time and Eternity." *Journal of Philosophy* 82 (1985), 260–69.

Forman, Robert K. C. (ed.) *The Problem of Pure Consciousness: Mysticism and Philosophy.* New York: Oxford University Press, 1990.

Frede, Michael. *Essays in Ancient Philosophy.* Minneapolis: University of Minnesota Press, 1987.

Frei, Hans W. *The Eclipse of Biblical Narrative: A Study in Eighteenth and Nineteenth Century Hermeneutics.* New Haven: Yale University Press, 1974.

Frei, Hans W. " 'Narrative' in Christian and Modern Theology." In *Theology and Dialogue: Essays in Conversation with George Lindbeck,* 149–63. Edited by Bruce D. Marshall. Notre Dame, Ind.: University of Notre Dame Press, 1990.

Frei, Hans W. "George Lindbeck and the Nature of Doctrine." In *Theology and Dialogue: Essays in Conversation with George Lindbeck,* 275–82. Edited by Bruce D. Marshall. Notre Dame, Indiana: University of Notre Dame Press, 1990.

Friedmann, David L. (transl.) *Sthiramati: Madhyāntavibhāgaṭīkā.* Utrecht: Utrecht Typ. Ass., 1937.

Frye, Northrop. *Anatomy of Criticism: Four Essays.* Princeton: Princeton University Press, 1957.

Funahashi Naoya. *Nepōru shahon taishō ni yoru daijō shōgon kyōron no kenkyū* [A Study of the Mahāyānasūtrālaṅkāra Based upon Nepalese Manuscripts]. Tokyo: Kokushokankōkai, 1985.

Gale, Richard. "Omniscience-Immutability Arguments." *American Philosophical Quarterly* 23 (1986), 319–55.

Galloway, Brian. "Sudden Enlightenment in Indian Buddhism." *Wiener Zeitschrift für die Kunde Südasiens* 25 (1981), 205–11.

Galloway, Brian. "Sudden Enlightenment in the Abhisamayālaṃkāra, the Lalitavistara, and the Śikṣāsamuccaya." *Wiener Zeitschrift für die Kunde Südasiens* 32 (1988), 141–47.

Geertz, Clifford. *The Interpretation of Cultures*. New York: Basic Books, 1973.

Geertz, Clifford. *Local Knowledge*. New York: Basic Books, 1983.

Gethin, Rupert M. L. *The Buddhist Path to Awakening: A Study of the Bodhi-Pakkhiyā Dhammā*. Brill's Indological Library, volume 7. Leiden: Brill, 1992.

Gettier, Edmund. "Is Justified True Belief Knowledge?" *Analysis* 23 (1963), 121–23.

Gokhale, V. V. "Fragments from the Abhidharmasamuccaya of Asaṃga." *Journal of the Bombay Branch of the Royal Asiatic Society* 23 (1947), 13–38.

Gomez, Luis O. "Indian Materials on the Doctrine of Sudden Enlightenment." In *Early Ch'an in China and Tibet*, 393–434. Edited by Whalen Lai and Lewis R. Lancaster. Berkeley Buddhist Studies Series, volume 5. Berkeley, Calif.: Asian Humanities Press, 1983.

Gregory, Peter N. (ed.) *Sudden and Gradual: Approaches to Enlightenment in Chinese Thought*. Honolulu: University of Hawaii Press, 1987.

Griffiths, Paul J. *On Being Mindless: Buddhist Meditation and the Mind-Body Problem*. La Salle, Ill.: Open Court, 1986.

Griffiths, Paul J. "An Apology for Apologetics." *Faith and Philosophy* 5 (1988), 399–420.

Griffiths, Paul J. "Buddha and God: A Contrastive Study in Ideas about Maximal Greatness." *Journal of Religion* 69/4 (1989), 502–529.

Griffiths, Paul J. "Pure Consciousness and Indian Buddhism." In *The Problem of Pure Consciousness: Mysticism and Philosophy*, 71–97. Edited by Robert K. C. Forman. New York: Oxford University Press, 1990.

Griffiths, Paul J. "Denaturalizing Discourse: Ābhidhārmikas, Propositionalists, and the Comparative Philosophy of Religion." In *Myth and Philosophy*, 57–91. Edited by Frank

E. Reynolds and David Tracy. Albany, N.Y.: SUNY Press, 1990.

Griffiths, Paul J. "Omniscience in the Mahāyānasūtrālaṅkāra and Its Commentaries." *Indo-Iranian Journal* 33 (1990), 85–120.

Griffiths, Paul J. *An Apology for Apologetics: A Study in the Logic of Interreligious Dialogue.* Maryknoll, N.Y.: Orbis, 1991.

Griffiths, Paul J., Hakamaya Noriaki, John P. Keenan, and Paul L. Swanson. *The Realm of Awakening: A Translation and Study of the Tenth Chapter of Asaṅga's Mahāyānasaṅgraha.* New York: Oxford University Press, 1989.

Hahn, Michael. (ed.) *Nāgārjuna's Ratnāvalī. Vol.1: The Basic Texts (Sanskrit, Tibetan, Chinese).* Indica et Tibetica, volume 1. Bonn: Indica et Tibetica, 1982.

Hakamaya Noriaki. "Asvabhāva's Commentary on the Mahāyāsūtrālaṃkāra IX.56–76." *Indogaku bukkyōgaku kenkyū* 20/1 (1971), (23)–(31).

Hakamaya Noriaki. "A Consideration of the Byams sus kyi le'u from the Historical Point of View." *Indogaku bukkyōgaku kenkyū* 24/1 (1975), (20)–(30).

Hakamaya Noriaki. "'Sanshu tenne' kō" [On the Threefold Āśrayaparivṛtti/parāvṛtti]. *Bukkyōgaku* 2 (1976), 46–76.

Hakamaya Noriaki. "Sthiramati and Śīlabahadra." *Indogaku bukkyōgaku kenkyū* 25 (1977), 35–37.

Hakamaya Noriaki. "The Realm of Enlightenment in Vijñaptimātratā: The Formulation of the 'Four Kinds of Pure Dharmas.'" Transl. John P. Keenan. *Journal of the International Association of Buddhist Studies* 3 (1980), 21–41. Originally published (in Japanese) in *Komazawa daigaku bukkyōgaku kenkyūkiyō* 34 (1976), 1–46.

Hakamaya Noriaki. "Chos kyi sku la gnas pa'i yon tan la bstod pa to sono kanren bunken" [Texts Associated with a Hymn of Praise to the Good Qualities of the Dharmakāya]. *Komazawa daigaku bukkyōgakubu ronshū* 14 (1983), 342–24.

Hakamaya Noriaki. "Mahāyānasūtrālaṃkāraṭīkā saishūshō wayaku." [A Japanese Translation of the Final Chapter of the Mahāyānasūtrālaṃkāraṭīkā]. *Komazawa daigaku bukkyōgakubu kenkyū kiyō* 41 (1983), 452–17.

Hakamaya Noriaki. "Yuishiki bunken ni okeru mufunbetsushi" [Nirvikalpajñāna in Vijñaptimātra Literature]. *Komazawa daigaku bukkyōkakubu kenkyūkiyō* 43 (1985), 252–15.

Hakamaya Noriaki. "Chibetto ni okeru Maitreya no gohō no kiseki" [The Tibetan Tradition of the Five Treatises Attributed to Maitreya]. In *Chibetto no bukkyō to shakai,* 235–68. Edited by Yamaguchi Zuiho. Tokyo: Shunjūsha, 1986.

Hakamaya Noriaki. "Shie (catuṣ-pratisaraṇa) hihankō josetsu" [Introductory Notes towards a Critique of the Catuṣpratisaraṇa Theory]. In *Takasaki Jikidō hakushi kanreki kinenronshu: indogaku bukkyōgaku ronshū,* 269–91. Tokyo: Shunjūsha, 1987.

Hakamaya Noriaki. "Rigen (nirabhilāpya) no shisō haikei" [The Background to the Idea of Inexpressibility]. *Komazawa daigaku bukkyōgakubu kenkyūkiyō* 49 (1991), 169–225.

Hart, H. L. A. *The Concept of Law.* Oxford: Clarendon Press, 1961.

Hattori Masaaki. (transl.) *Dignāga, On Perception, being the Pratyakṣapariccheda of Dignāga's Pramāṇasamuccaya from the Sanskrit Fragments and the Tibetan Versions.* Harvard Oriental Series, volume 47. Cambridge, Mass.: Harvard University Press, 1968.

Hopkins, E. Washburn. "Buddha as Tathāgata." *American Journal of Philology* 32 (1911), 205–9.

Huntington, Susan L. "Early Buddhist Art and the Theory of Aniconism." *Art Journal* 49 (1990), 401–8.

Jaini, Padmanabh S. "On the Sarvajñatva (Omniscience) of Mahāvīra and the Buddha." In *Buddhist Studies in Honour of I. B. Horner,* 71–90. Edited by Lance S. Cousins et al. Dordrecht: Reidel, 1974.

Jaini, Padmanabh S. (ed.) *Abhidharmadīpa with Vibhāṣāprabhāvṛtti.* Second edition. Tibetan-Sanskrit Works

Series, volume 4. Patna: Kashi Prasad Jayaswal Research Institute, 1977.

Jaini, Padmanabh S. (ed.) *Sāratamā: A Pañjikā on the Aṣṭasāhasrikā Prajñāpāramitā Sūtra*. Tibetan-Sanskrit Works Series, vol. 18. Patna: K. P. Jayaswal Research Institute, 1979.

Jaini, Padmanabh S. (ed.) "The Sanskrit Fragments of Vinītadeva's Triṃśikāṭīkā." *Bulletin of the School of Oriental & African Studies* [University of London] 48 (1985), 470–92.

James, William. *Psychology: Briefer Course*. In *William James: Writings 1878–1899*, 1–443. Library of America. New York: Literary Classics of the United States, 1992. First published 1892.

Johnston, E. H. (ed.) *The Ratnagotravibhāga Mahāyānottaratantraśāstra*. Patna: Bihar Research Society, 1950.

Johnston, E. H. (ed. and transl.) *The Buddhacarita: Or, Acts of the Buddha*. Delhi: Banarsidass, 1972. First published Lahore, 1936.

Kant, Immanuel. *Vorlesungen über die philosophische Religionslehre*. In Kant, *Gesammelte Schriften*, volume 28.2.2, 989–1126. Berlin: de Gruyter, 1972. English translation by Allen W. Wood and Gertrude M. Clark, *Lectures on Philosophical Theology*. Ithaca and London: Cornell University Press, 1978.

Katz, Steven T. (ed.) *Mysticism and Philosophical Analysis*. New York: Oxford University Press, 1978.

Katz, Steven T. (ed.) *Mysticism and Religious Traditions*. New York: Oxford University Press, 1983.

Katz, Steven T. (ed.) *Mysticism and Language*. New York: Oxford University Press, 1992.

Keenan, John P. "A Study of the Buddhabhūmyupadeśa: The Doctrinal Development of the Notion of Wisdom in Yogācāra Thought." Ph.D dissertation, University of Wisconsin-Madison, 1980.

Kern, Hendrik, and Bunyiu Nanjio. (eds.) *Saddharmapuṇḍarīka*. Bibliotheca Buddhica, volume 10. St. Petersburg: Académie Impériale des Sciences, 1908–12.

Khosla, Sarla. *The Historical Evolution of the Buddha-Legend.* Delhi: Banarsidass, 1989.

Kloppenborg, Ria. *The Paccekabuddha, A Buddhist Ascetic: A Study of the Concept of the Paccekabuddha in Pāli Canonical and Commentarial Literature.* Orientali Rheno-traiectiana, volume 20. Leiden: Brill, 1974.

König, Otto. *Dogma als Praxis und Theorie: Studien zum Begriff des Dogmas in der Religionsphilosophie Maurice Blondels, vor und während der modernistischen Krise (1888–1908).* Graz: Institut für Ökumenische Theologie und Patrologie, 1983.

Krishnamacharya, Embar. (ed.) *Tattvasaṅgraha of Śāntarakṣita, With the Commentary of Kamalaśīla.* Two volumes. Baroda: Oriental Institute, 1984. A reprint of Gaekwad's Oriental Series, volume 30. Baroda: Oriental Institute, 1926.

Lakoff, George. *Women, Fire, and Dangerous Things: What Categories Reveal about the Mind.* Chicago and London: University of Chicago Press, 1987.

Lamotte, Étienne. *Saṃdhinirmocana Sūtra: l'explication des mystères.* Paris: Maisonneuve, 1935.

Lamotte, Étienne. *La somme du grand véhicule d'Asaṅga (Mahāyāna-Saṃgraha).* Two volumes. Publications de l'Institut Orientaliste de Louvain, volume 8. Louvain-la-neuve: Institut Orientaliste, 1973. First published 1938.

Lamotte, Étienne. "La critique d'authenticité dans le bouddhisme." In *India Antiqua: A Volume of Oriental Studies Presented by His Friends and Pupils to Jean Philippe Vogel, C.I.E.,* 213–22. Leiden: Brill, 1947.

Lamotte, Étienne. "La critique d'interprétation dans le bouddhisme." *Annuaire de l'Institut de Philologie et d'Histoire Orientales et Slaves* 9 (1949), 341–61. English translation by Sara Boin-Webb, "The Assessment of Textual Interpretation in Buddhism," in Donald S. Lopez, Jr., ed., *Buddhist Hermeneutics,* 11–27. Studies in East Asian Buddhism, volume 6. Honolulu: University of Hawaii Press.

Lamotte, Étienne. *Le traité de la grande vertu de sagesse de Nāgārjuna (Mahāprajñāpāramitāśāstra).* Five volumes, paginated consecutively. Publications de l'Institut Orientaliste de Louvain, volumes 2, 12, 24–26. Louvain-la-neuve: Institut Orientaliste, 1944–81.

Lamotte, Étienne. *Histoire du bouddhisme indien, des origines à l'ère Śaka*. Bibliothèque du Muséon, volume 43. Louvain: Institut Orientaliste, 1958. English translation by Sara Webb-Boin, *History of Indian Buddhism from the Origins to the Śaka Era*. Publications de l'Institut Orientaliste de Louvain, volume 36. Louvain-la-Neuve: Institut Orientaliste, 1988.

La Vallée Poussin, Louis de. (ed.) *Bodhicaryāvatārapañjikā: Prajñākaramati's Commentary to the Bodhicaryāvatāra of Çāntideva*. Bibliotheca Indica, New Series, numbers 983, 1031, 1090, 1126, 1139, 1305, 1399. Calcutta: Asiatic Society of Bengal, 1901–14.

La Vallée Poussin, Louis de. "Studies in Buddhist Dogma: The Three Bodies of a Buddha." *Journal of the Royal Asiatic Society* (1906), 943–77.

La Vallée Poussin, Louis de. (ed.) *Madhyamakāvatāra par Candrakīrti*. Bibliotheca Buddhica, volume 9. Tokyo: Meichofukyūkai, 1977. First published St. Petersburg: Académie Impériale des Sciences, 1907–12.

La Vallée Poussin, Louis de. "Note sur les corps du Bouddha." *Le Muséon* 14 (1913), 257–90.

La Vallée Poussin, Louis de. *Théorie des douze causes*. London: Luzac, 1913.

La Vallée Poussin, Louis de. (ed.) *Madhyamakavṛttiḥ: Mūlamadhyamakakārikās (Mādhyamika-sūtras) de Nāgārjuna avec la Prasannapadā, commentaire de Candrakīrti*. Bibliotheca Buddhica, volume 4. St. Petersburg: Académie Impériale des Sciences, 1913.

La Vallée Poussin, Louis de. "Notes Bouddhiques I–III." *Le Muséon* 15 (1914), 33–48.

La Vallée Poussin, Louis de. (transl.) *Vijñaptimātratāsiddhi: La Siddhi de Hiuan-Tsang*. Eight fascicles and index volume. Paris: Librairie Orientaliste Paul Geuthner, 1928–48.

La Vallée Poussin, Louis de. "Buddhica." *Harvard Journal of Asiatic Studies* 3 (1938), 137–60.

Lévi, Sylvain. *Mahāyāna-Sūtrālaṃkāra: exposé de la doctrine du grand véhicule selon le système Yogācāra.* Bibliothèque de l'École des Hautes Études, Sciences Historiques et Philologiques, volumes 159, 190. Paris: Librairie Ancienne Honoré Champion, 1907, 1911.

Lévi, Sylvain. (ed.) *Vijñaptimātratāsiddhi: deux traités de Vasubandhu: Viṃśatikā (La Vingtaine) accompagnée d'une explication en prose, et Triṃśikā (La Trentaine), avec le commentaire de Sthiramati.* Paris: Librairie Ancienne Honoré Champion, 1925.

Lévi, Sylvain. *Une système de philosophie bouddhique: matériaux pour l'étude du système Vijñaptimātra.* Paris: Librairie Ancienne Honoré Champion.

Lewis, Delmas. "Eternity Again: A Reply to Stump and Kretzmann." *International Journal for the Philosophy of Religion* 15 (1984), 73–79.

Lindbeck, George A. *The Nature of Doctrine: Religion and Theology in a Postliberal Age.* Philadelphia: Westminster Press, 1984.

Lipner, Julius. *The Face of Truth: A Study of Meaning and Metaphysics in the Vedāntic Theology of Rāmānuja.* Albany, N.Y.: SUNY Press, 1986.

Lopez, Donald S., Jr. (ed.) *Buddhist Hermeneutics.* Honolulu: University of Hawaii Press, 1988.

Lopez, Donald S., Jr. "Paths Terminable and Interminable." In *Paths to Liberation: The Mārga and Its Transformations in Buddhist Thought,* 147–92. Edited by Robert E. Buswell, Jr. and Robert M. Gimello. Studies in East Asian Buddhism, volume 7. Honolulu: University of Hawaii Press, 1992.

Macdonald, A. W. "La notion du saṃbhogakāya à la lumière de quelques faits ethnographiques." *Journal Asiatique* 243 (1955), 229–39.

McGrath, Alister E. *The Genesis of Doctrine: A Study in the Foundations of Doctrinal Criticism.* 1990 Bampton Lectures. Oxford: Blackwell, 1990.

MacQueen, Graeme. "Inspired Speech in Early Mahāyāna Buddhism." *Religion* 11 (1981), 303–319; 12 (1982), 49–65.

Makransky, John. "Controversy over Dharmakāya in Indo-Tibetan Buddhism: An Historical-Critical Analysis of Abhisamayālaṃkāra Chapter 8 and Its Commentaries in Relation to the Large Prajñāpāramitā Sūtra and the Yogācāra Tradition." Ph.D dissertation, University of Wisconsin-Madison, 1990.

Mallmann, Marie-Thérèse de. *Introduction à l'étude d'Avalokiteçvara*. Paris: Presses Universitaires de France, 1967.

Mansini, Guy, OSB. *What Is a Dogma? The Meaning and Truth of Dogma in Edouard Le Roy and His Scholastic Opponents*. Analecta Gregoriana, Cura Pontificiae Universitatis Gregorianae edita, volume 239, Series Facultatis Theologiae: sectio B, n.80. Rome: Editrice Pontificia Universita Gregoriana, 1985.

Masson-Oursel, Paul. "Les trois corps du bouddha." *Journal Asiatique* ser.11, 1 (1913), 581–618.

Matilal, Bimal Krishna. *Perception: An Essay on Classical Indian Theories of Knowledge*. Oxford: Clarendon Press, 1986.

Morris, R., et al. (eds.) *Anguttara-Nikāya*. Six volumes. London: Pali Text Society, 1885–1910.

Mus, Paul. *Barabuḍur: Esquisse d'une histoire du bouddhisme fondée sur la critique archéologique des textes*. Two volumes. Hanoi: Imprimerie d'Extrême-Orient, 1935.

Nagao Gadjin. (ed.) *Index to the Mahāyāna-Sūtrālaṃkāra (Sylvain Lévi Edition)*. Two volumes. Volume one, Sanskrit-Tibetan-Chinese; volume two, Tibetan-Sanskrit and Chinese-Sanskrit. Tokyo: Nippon Gakujutsu Shinkōkai, 1958–60.

Nagao Gadjin. (ed.) *Madhyāntavibhāga-Bhāṣya*. Tokyo: Suzuki Research Foundation, 1964.

Nagao Gadjin. (ed. and transl.) *Shōdaijōron: wayaku to chūkai* [Mahāyānasaṅgraha: A Japanese Translation and Commentary]. Two volumes. Tokyo: Kodansha, 1982, 1987.

Nagao Gadjin. "The Life of the Buddha: An Interpretation." *Eastern Buddhist* 20/2 (1987), 1–31.

Nagao Gadjin. "On the Theory of Buddha-Body (Buddha-kāya)." Translated by U Hirano; revised by Leslie S. Kawamura. In Nagao, *Mādhyamika and Yogācāra: A Study of Mahāyāna Philosophies,* 103–22. Albany, N.Y.: SUNY Press, 1991. First published in English in *Eastern Buddhist* 6/1 (1973), 25–53.

Nagel, Thomas. "What Is It Like to Be a Bat?" In Nagel, *Mortal Questions,* 165–80. Cambridge: Cambridge University Press, 1979. First published in *Philosophical Review* 83 (1974).

Ñāṇananda <Bhikkhu>. *Concept and Reality in Early Buddhist Thought.* Second edition. Kandy:Buddhist Publication Society, 1976. First edition 1971.

Nanjio, Bunyiu. (ed.) *The Laṅkāvatāra Sūtra.* Kyoto: Otani University Press, 1923.

Nattier, Jan. *Once upon a Future Time: Studies in a Buddhist Prophecy of Decline.* Nanzan Studies in Asian Religions, volume 1. Berkeley: Asian Humanities Press, 1991.

Naughton, Alex. "Buddhist Omniscience." *Eastern Buddhist* 24/1 (1991), 28–51.

Nguyen, Cuong Tu. (transl.) "Sthiramati's Interpretation of Buddhology and Soteriology." Ph.D thesis, Harvard University, 1989.

Nishio Kyoo. (ed. and transl.) *The Buddhabhūmi-Sūtra and the Buddhabhūmi-vyākhyāna of Çīlabhadra.* Tokyo: Kokushokankōkai, 1982.

Nishioka Soshū. (ed.) "Bu-ston bukkyōshi mokurokubu sakuin." [Index to the Catalogue Section of Bu-ston's "History of Buddhism"]. *Annual Report of the Institute for the Study of Cultural Exchange* [University of Tokyo], 4 (1980), 61–92; 5 (1981), 43–94; 6 (1983), 47–201.

Nobel, Johannes. (ed.) *Suvarṇabhāsottamasūtra, Das Goldglanz-Sūtra, ein Sanskrittext des Mahāyāna-Buddhismus.* Leipzig: Harrassowitz, 1937.

Norman, K. R. "The Pratyeka-Buddha in Buddhism and Jainism." In *Buddhist Studies Ancient and Modern,* 92–106. Edited by Philip Denwood and Alexander Piatigorsky. Collected Papers on South Asia, volume 4. London: Curzon Press, 1983.

Norman, K. R. "Pāli Lexicographical Studies VIII: Seven Pāli Etymologies." *Journal of the Pali Text Society* 15 (1990), 145–54.

Odani Nobuchiyo. *Daijō shōgon kyōron kenkyū* [Research into the Mahāyānasūtrālaṅkāra]. Kyoto: Bunei Jōshoten, 1984.

Peczenik, Aleksandr, Lars Lindahl, and Bert Van Roermund. (eds.) *Theory of Legal Science.* Proceedings of the Conference on Legal Theory and Philosophy of Science, Lund, Sweden, December 11–14, 1983. Synthese Library, volume 176. Dordrecht: Reidel, 1984.

Pelikan, Jaroslav. *The Christian Tradition: A History of the Development of Doctrine.* Five volumes. Chicago: University of Chicago Press, 1971–89.

Pensa, Corrado. (ed.) *L'Abhisamayālaṅkāravṛtti di Ārya Vimuktisena.* Serie Orientale Roma, volume 37. Rome: Istituto Italiano per il Medio ed Estremo Oriente, 1967.

Pike, Nelson. *God and Timelessness.* New York: Schocken, 1970.

Plantinga, Alvin. *Warrant: The Current Debate.* New York: Oxford University Press, 1993.

Pollock, Sheldon. "The Theory of Practice and the Practice of Theory in Indian Intellectual History." *Journal of the American Oriental Society* 105 (1985), 499–519.

Pollock, Sheldon. "The Idea of *Śāstra* in Traditional India." In *Shastric Traditions in Indian Arts,* 17–26. Edited by Anna Libera Dallapiccola. Stuttgart: Steiner, 1989.

Pollock, Sheldon. "Playing by the Rules: *Śāstra* and Sanskrit Literature." In *Shastric Traditions in Indian Arts,* 301–12. Edited by Anna Libera Dallapiccola. Stuttgart: Steiner, 1989.

Potter, Karl H. "Does Indian Epistemology Concern Justified True Belief?" *Journal of Indian Philosophy* 12 (1984), 307–27.

Potter, Karl H. "The Karmic a Priori in Indian Philosophy." *Philosophy East and West* 42 (1992), 407–19.

Prāsādika <Bhikṣu>, and Lal Mani Joshi. *Vimalakīrtinirdeśasūtra: Tibetan Version, Sanskrit Restoration and Hindi Translation.* Bibliotheca Indo-Tibetica, volume 5. Sarnath: Central Institute of Higher Tibetan Studies, 1981.

Proudfoot, Wayne. *Religious Experience.* Berkeley: University of California Press, 1985.

Pye, Michael. *The Buddha.* London: Duckworth, 1979.

Quine, W[illard] V[an] O[rman]. "Epistemology Naturalized." In *Empirical Knowledge,* 59–74. Edited by Roderick M. Chisholm and Robert J. Swartz. Englewood Cliffs, N.J.: Prentice-Hall, 1973.

Quinn, Philip L. "On the Mereology of Boethian Eternity." *International Journal for the Philosophy of Religion* 32 (1992), 51–60.

Rahner, Karl. "What Is a Dogmatic Statement?" In Rahner, *Theological Investigations,* volume 5, 42–66. English translation Karl-H Kruger. Baltimore: Helicon Press, 1966.

Renou, Louis. *Histoire de la langue Sanskrite.* Lyon: IAC, 1956.

Renou, Louis. "Sur le genre du sūtra dans la littérature Sanskrite." *Journal Asiatique* 251 (1963), 165–216.

Reynolds, Frank E., and Charles Hallisey. "The Buddha." In *Buddhism and Asian History,* 29–49. Edited by Joseph M. Kitagawa and Mark D. Cummings. London and New York: Macmillan, 1989.

Rhys Davids, T. W., and J. E. Carpenter. (eds.) *Dīgha-Nikāya.* Three volumes. London: Pali Text Society, 1889, 1903, 1910.

Roth, Gustav. "The Physical Presence of the Buddha and Its Representation in Buddhist Literature." In *Investigating Indian Art,* 291–312. Edited by Marianne Yaldiz and Wibke Lobo. Veröffentlichungen des Museums für indische Kunst (Berlin). Berlin: Staatliche Museen Preußischer Kulturbesitz, 1987.

Rowell, Teresina. "The Background and Early Use of the Buddha-Kṣetra Concept." *Eastern Buddhist* 6 (1932–35), 199–246; 7 (1936–39), 131–45.

Ruegg, David Seyfort. "Védique *addhā* et quelques expressions parallèles à Tathāgata." *Journal Asiatique* 243 (1955), 163–70.

Ruegg, David Seyfort. *La théorie du tathāgatagarbha et du gotra: études sur la sotériologie et la gnoséologie du bouddhisme.* Publications de l'École Française d'Extrême-

Orient, volume 70. Paris: École Française d'Extrême-Orient, 1969.

Ruegg, David Seyfort. "Purport, Implicature and Presupposition: Sanskrit Abhiprāya and Tibetan dgoṅs pa/dgoṅs gži as Hermeneutical Concepts." *Journal of Indian Philosophy* 13 (1985), 309–25.

Ruegg, David Seyfort. "An Indian Source for the Tibetan Hermeneutical Term Dgoṅs Gži." *Journal of Indian Philosophy* 16 (1988), 1–4.

Ruegg, David Seyfort. "Allusiveness and Obliqueness in Buddhist Texts: Saṃdhā Saṃdhi, Sadhyā and Abhisaṃdhi." In *Dialectes dans les littératures Indo-Aryennes*, 295–328. Edited by Colette Caillat. Publications de l'Institut de Civilisation Indienne, fascicle 55. Paris: Institut de Civilisation Indienne, 1989.

Ruegg, David Seyfort. *Buddha-Nature, Mind and the Problem of Gradualism in a Comparative Perspective: On the Transmission and Reception of Buddhism in India and Tibet.* London: School of Oriental Studies [University of London], 1989.

Ryle, Gilbert. *The Concept of Mind.* London: Hutchinson, 1949.

Samtani, N. H. (ed.) *The Arthaviniścaya-Sūtra and Its Commentary (Nibandhana).* Tibetan-Sanskrit Works Series, volume 13. Patna: Kashi Prasad Jayaswal Research Institute, 1971.

Schlingloff, Dieter. (ed.) *Ein buddhistisches Yogalehrbuch.* Sanskrittexte aus den Turfanfunden, volume 7. Berlin: Akademie-Verlag, 1964.

Schmithausen, Lambert. *Der Nirvāṇa-Abschnitt in der Viniścayasaṅgrahaṇī der Yogācārabhūmiḥ.* Vienna: Böhlaus, 1969.

Schmithausen, Lambert. "The Darśanamārga Section of the Abhidharmasamuccaya and Its Interpretation by Tibetan Commentators with Special Reference to Bu Ston Rin Chen Grub." In *Contributions on Tibetan Religion and Philosophy*, 259–74. Edited by Ernst Steinkellner and Helmut Tauscher. Vienna: Arbeitskreis för tibetische und buddhistische Studien, 1983.

Schrader, F. O. "On Some Tibetan Names of the Buddha." *Indian Historical Quarterly* 9 (1933), 46–48.

Schrodt, Paul E. "The Continuing Discussion of Dogma in Germany." *Heythrop Journal* 14 (1973), 65–71.

Shastri, Dwarikadas. (ed.) *Abhidharmakośa and Bhāṣya of Ācārya Vasubandhu with Sphuṭārthā Commentary of Ācārya Yaśomitra.* Two volumes, continuous pagination. Bauddha Bharati Series, volumes 5–6. Varanasi: Bauddha Bharati, 1981.

Shope, Robert K. *The Analysis of Knowing: A Decade of Research.* Princeton: Princeton University Press, 1983.

Smart, Ninian. "Interpretation and Mystical Experience." *Religious Studies* 1 (1965), 75–87.

Snellgrove, David. *Indo-Tibetan Buddhism: Indian Buddhists and Their Tibetan Successors.* Two volumes. Boston: Shambhala, 1987.

Sørensen, Per K. (ed.) *Candrakīrti: Triśaraṇasaptati. The Septuagint on the Three Refuges.* Wiener Studien zur Tibetologie und Buddhismuskunde, vol. 16. Vienna: Arbeitskreis für tibetische und buddhistische Studien, 1986.

Sponberg, Alan, and Helen Hardacre. (eds.) *Maitreya, the Future Buddha.* Cambridge: Cambridge University Press, 1988.

Sprung, Mervyn. (transl.) *Lucid Exposition of the Middle Way: The Essential Chapters from the Prasannapadā of Candrakīrti.* London and Henley: Routledge and Kegan Paul, 1979.

Stcherbatsky, Th. *The Conception of Buddhist Nirvāṅa.* Leningrad: Academy of Sciences of the USSR, 1927.

Stcherbatsky, Th. (transl.) *Madhyānta-Vibhanga: Discourse on Discrimination between Middle and Extremes, Ascribed to Bodhisattva Maitreya and Commented on by Vasubandhu and Sthiramati.* Bibliotheca Buddhica, volume 30. Tokyo: Meichofukyūkai, 1977. First published 1936.

Stcherbatsky, Th., and Ernst Obermiller. (eds.) *Abhisamayālaṅkāra-Prajñāpāramitā-Upadeśa-Śāstra.* Bibliotheca Buddhica, vol. 23. Tokyo: Meichofukyūkai, 1977. First published 1929.

Stein, R. A. "Illumination subite ou saisie simultanée: note sur la terminologie chinoise et tibétaine." *Revue de l'histoire des religions* 179/1 (1971), 3–30. English translation by Neal Donner, "Sudden Illumination or Simultaneous Comprehension: Remarks on Chinese and Tibetan Terminology." In *Sudden and Gradual: Approaches to Enlightenment in Chinese Thought*, 41–65. Edited by Peter N. Gregory. Studies in East Asian Buddhism, volume 5. Honolulu: University of Hawaii Press, 1987.

Stump, Eleonore, and Norman Kretzmann. "Eternity." *Journal of Philosophy* 78 (1981), 429–58.

Swinburne, Richard. "Tensed Facts." *American Philosophical Quarterly* 27 (1990), 117–30.

Takasaki Jikidō. (transl.) *A Study on the Ratnagotravibhāga (Uttaratantra), Being a Treatise on the Tathāgatagarbha Theory of Mahāyāna Buddhism.* Serie Orientale Roma, volume 33. Rome: Istituto Italiano per il Medio ed Estremo Oriente, 1966.

Takasaki Jikidō. *An Introduction to Buddhism.* Translated by Rolf W. Giebel. Tokyo: Tōhō Gakkai, 1987.

Tatia, Nathmal. (ed.) *Abhidharmasamuccayabhāṣyam.* Tibetan-Sanskrit Works Series, volume 17. Patna: Kashi Prasad Jayaswal Research Institute, 1976.

Thomas, E. J. *The Life of Buddha as Legend and History.* London: Routledge and Kegan Paul, 1975. First published 1927.

Thomas, E. J. "Tathāgata and Tahāgaya." *Bulletin of the School of Oriental and African Studies* [University of London] 8 (1936), 781–88.

Trenckner, V. and Robert Chalmers. (eds.) *Majjhima Nikāya.* Three volumes. London: Pali Text Society, 1888, 1896, 1899.

Tucci, Giuseppe. (ed.) *Minor Buddhist Texts.* Three volumes. Serie Orientale Roma, volumes 9.1, 9.2, 9.3. Rome: Istituto Italiano per il Medio ed Estremo Oriente, 1956, 1958, 1971.

Unger, Roberto Mangabeira. *The Critical Legal Studies Movement.* Cambridge, Mass.: Harvard University Press, 1986.

Vaidya, P. L. (ed.) *Aṣṭasāhasrikā Prajñāpāramitā with Haribhadra's Commentary Called Āloka.* Buddhist Sanskrit Texts, vol. 4. Darbhanga: Mithila Institute, 1960.

Vaidya, P. L. (ed.) *Śikṣāsamuccaya of Śāntideva.* Buddhist Sanskrit texts, volume 11. Darbhanga: Mithila Institute, 1961.

Vaidya, P. L. (ed.) *Mahāyānasūtrasaṃgraha.* Part one. Buddhist Sanskrit Texts, volume 17. Darbhanga: Mithila Institute, 1961.

Vaidya, P. L. (ed.) *Daśabhūmikasūtra.* Buddhist Sanskrit Texts, volume 7. Darbhanga: Mithila Institute, 1967.

Wainwright, Geoffrey. *Doxology: The Praise of God in Worship, Doctrine and Life.* New York: Oxford University Press, 1980.

Waldschmidt, Ernst. *Die Überlieferung vom Lebensende des Buddha.* Two volumes. Abhandlungen der Akademie der Wissenschaften in Göttingen, Philologisch-Historische Klasse, third series, volumes 29–30. Göttingen: Vandenhoeck & Ruprecht, 1944, 1948.

Waldschmidt, Ernst. "The Varṇaśatam: An Eulogy of One Hundred Epitheta of Lord Buddha Spoken by the Gṛhapati Upāli(n)." *Nachrichten der Akademie der Wissenschaften, Philologisch-historische Klasse* [Göttingen] (1979), 3–19.

Warren, Henry Clarke, and Dharmananda Kosambi. (eds.) *Visuddhimagga of Buddhaghosâcariya.* Harvard Oriental Series, volume 41. Cambridge, Mass.: Harvard University Press, 1950.

Wayman, Alex. "Notes on the Sanskrit Term Jñāna." *Journal of the American Oriental Society* 75 (1955), 253–268.

Wayman, Alex. "Contributions Regarding the Thirty-Two Characteristics of the Great Person." In *Liebenthal Festschrift,* 243–60. Edited by Kshitis Roy. Sino-Indian Studies, volume 5, parts 3 and 4. Santiniketan: Visvabharati, 1957.

Wayman, Alex. *Analysis of the Śrāvakabhūmi Manuscript.* University of California Publications in Classical Philology, volume 17. Berkeley and Los Angeles: University of California Press, 1961.

Wayman, Alex. "Concerning saṃdhā-bhāṣā/saṃdhi-bhāṣā/saṃdhyā-bhāṣā." In *Mélanges d'indianisme à la mémoire de Louis Renou*, 789–96. Publications de l'Institut de Civilisation Indienne, fascicule 28. Paris: de Boccard, 1968.

Wayman, Alex. "The Mirror-Like Knowledge in Mahāyāna Buddhist Literature." *Asiatische Studien* 25 (1971), 353–63.

Wayman, Alex. "The Mirror as Pan-Buddhist Metaphor-Simile." *History of Religions* 13 (1974), 251–69.

Whitehead, Alfred North. *Adventures of Ideas*. New York: Macmillan, 1933.

Wierenga, Edward. *The Nature of God: An Inquiry into Divine Attributes*. Ithaca, N.Y.: Cornell University Press, 1989.

Williams, Paul M. *Mahāyāna Buddhism: The Doctrinal Foundations*. London and New York: Routledge, 1989.

Willis, Janice Dean. (transl.) *On Knowing Reality: The Tattvārtha Chapter of Asaṅga's Bodhisattvabhūmi*. New York: Columbia University Press, 1979.

Wilshire, Martin G. *Ascetic Figures before and in Early Buddhism: The Emergence of Gautama as the Buddha*. Religion and Reason, volume 30. Berlin and New York: Mouton de Gruyter, 1990.

Yamaguchi Susumu. (ed.) *Madhyāntavibhāgaṭīkā: exposition systématique du Yogācāravijñaptivāda*. Three volumes. Nagoya: Librairie Hajinkaku, 1934–37.

Yandell, Keith E. "Some Varieties of Ineffability." *International Journal for the Philosophy of Religion* 10 (1979), 167–79.

Index

pratyavekeṣaṇa[ka]jñāna, 79–80
pratyekabuddha. See individual Buddha
primary doctrines, 6, 12, 15, 21, 23, 24
  criteria for acceptability, 7–9
  criteria for authority, 10, 11
  criteria for religious significance, 10
  descriptive use of, 21, 22, 205n30
  embeddedness, 11
  properties of, 6, 7
  recommendation function of, 22, 23
properties of Buddha, 60, 66, 72, 126, 130, 145, 146, 160, 179, 190, 196, 200, 211n20
  as five kinds of perfections, 70
  as of 18 kinds, 69
  equanimity, 67, 98
  four immeasurable states, 67
  four kinds of fearlessness, 68
  endurance, 70, 158
  eight liberations, 74
  eight spheres of mastery, 74
  five kinds of perfections, 75
  four kinds of purification, 74
  four kinds of specific understanding, 67
  friendliness, 67
  giving, 3, 35, 60, 70, 191
  great compassion, 69–71
  guardlessness, 69
  indigenous analysis of, 75
  joy, 67, 114, 132
  mastery, 75, 78
  mindfulness, 11, 69
  morality, 70
  noncontentiousness, 67
  nonvolitional spontaneity, 71, 74
  omniscience, 72
  perfections of action, 70–72
  perfections of appearance, 70
  perfections of attitude, 73
  perfections of cognition, 72–73
  perfections of control, 74
  purity, 75, 76
  six kinds of supernatural awareness, 68
  six perfections, 70
  standard list of, 67–70
  ten powers, 68, 118
  ten spheres of totality, 67, 74
  three guardlessnesses, 106
Proudfoot, Wayne, 18, 19

Quine, W. V. O., 28
Qur'ān, 14, 40

Radical reorientation, 143
  and mastery over all sense objects, 143
  and mastery over six sense consciousnesses, 144–145
  of actuality, 77
  of the sixth sensory consciousness, 144
Re–presentation, 194, 195
real body, 81, 82, 94–97, 108, 109, 115, 119, 126, 140, 141, 145, 147–150, 179
  and maximal veridical awareness, 153
  as body of reality, 149, 150
  as identical with everything there is as it really is, 150
  as identical with the stage of attainment, 148
  as omniscience, 150
  as the ground of the real, 150
  definitions of, 149
  epistemic predicates of, 148, 151
  metaphysical predicates of, 148
  nonrelational properties of, 126
  See also Buddha *in se*
reality, 47, 49, 60, 108, 149, 150, 154, 159–162, 173, 176–178, 189
recognition, 194–195
rules of interpretation
  four points of refuge, 52, 53, 55
  See also secondary doctrines